T0345047

Preventing Harmful Behaviour in Online Communities

Preventing Harmful Behaviour in Online Communities explores the ethics and logistics of censoring problematic communications online that might encourage a person to engage in harmful behaviour.

Using an approach based on theories of digital rhetoric and close primary source analysis, Zoe Alderton draws on group dynamics research in relation to the way in which some online communities foster negative and destructive ideas, encouraging community members to engage in practices including self-harm, disordered eating, and suicide. This book offers insight into the dangerous gap between the clinical community and caregivers versus the pro-anorexia and pro-self-harm communities – allowing caregivers or medical professionals to understand hidden online communities young people in their care may be part of. It delves into the often-unanticipated needs of those who band together to resist the healthcare community, suggesting practical ways to address their concerns and encourage healing. Chapters investigate the alarming ease with which ideas of self-harm can infect people through personal contact, community unease, or even fiction and song and the potential of the internet to transmit self-harmful ideas across countries and even periods of time. The book also outlines the real nature of harm-based communities online, examining both their appeal and dangers, while also examining self-censorship and intervention methods for dealing with harmful content online.

Rather than pointing to punishment or censorship as best practice, the book offers constructive guidelines that outline a more holistic approach based on the validity of expressing negative mood and the creation of safe peer support networks, making it ideal reading for professionals protecting vulnerable people, as well as students and academics in psychology, mental health, and social care.

Zoe Alderton is a lecturer in the School of Economics at the University of Sydney where she teaches rhetoric and argumentation across disciplines. Her research spans across digital communications, religion, and museum studies.

Preventing Harmful Behaviour in Online Communities

Censorship and Interventions

Zoe Alderton

 Routledge
Taylor & Francis Group

LONDON AND NEW YORK

Cover image: Getty images

First published 2022
by Routledge
4 Park Square, Milton Park, Abingdon, Oxon OX14 4RN

and by Routledge
605 Third Avenue, New York, NY 10158

Routledge is an imprint of the Taylor & Francis Group, an informa business

British Library Cataloguing-in-Publication Data
A catalogue record for this book is available from the British Library

Library of Congress Cataloguing-in-Publication Data
A catalog record has been requested for this book

ISBN: 978-0-367-64748-3 (hbk)
ISBN: 978-0-367-64740-7 (pbk)
ISBN: 978-1-003-12606-5 (ebk)

DOI: 10.4324/9781003126065

Typeset in Bembo
by MPS Limited, Dehradun

Dedicated with love to Alana Louise Bowden (1986–2021) who should still be with us in person and who will always be present in spirit. To those of you reading this book from a place of pain, I dedicate her words:

I can assure you that your own moment of catharsis will come – I can only imagine the ways you have been existing, surviving but not living. I don't know when, but it will come – when life will return to you, when things feel good again.

– ALB, *Honi Soit* (2021)

Contents

Acknowledgements

Thank you to my generous proofreaders who donated their time to review portions of this manuscript: Alana Bowden, Helen Flett, Sally James, Lynne Mullaney, Tara Smith, Suvarna Variyar, and Dr Andrew Wearring. My most profound thanks to my partner Dr Christopher Hartney for reading the entire volume. I could not have dedicated time to this project without your help and support.

Preface

Introduction

> May the starving commence...
> May I lay up in my bed and waste away
> May I break my own bones trying to see them.
>
> (☆Benji☆ 2019)

The internet is a space for the expression of a multitude of perspectives, lifestyles, and dreams. Since its inception, this has been viewed as a utopic dimension of this supra-national, supra-bodily realm. At the same time, it has become increasingly evident that online spaces can form dystopic spaces where people discuss their desires to partake in harmful behaviours like suicide, self-harm, and starvation. There are many online resources that aide in bodily destruction and communities that advocate for destructive behaviour as a valid alternative lifestyle choice. This leads to two primary questions: do dangerous behaviours like suicide, self-harm, and disordered eating spread online in an infectious manner? If so, should we censor any online community or resource that is connected to this spread? This book addresses and answers both questions. In short, self-harmful behaviour does seem to cluster and has significant potential to be infectious. The rise of the internet has allowed for clusters and contagions to spread further than ever before. While censorship might seem to be the logical reaction to any dangerous online spaces that could lead to contagion, this action has proven unfeasible and often counter-productive. Censorship also fails to address the underlying issues that lead people to express their pain through self-harmful behaviours. The most effective interventions are those that seek to address this pain rather than to delete all mention of it.

Contagions and Clusters: Untangling Dangerous, Infectious Behaviour

Is it possible that a vulnerable teenager will stumble across a blog containing pictures of emaciated women and respond by developing an eating disorder?

Or will seeing images of self-harm wounds on Tumblr cause a person to reach for a knife? Is it even safe to discuss self-harm, or can the mere mention of this behaviour spread dangerous tendencies throughout a community? In order to answer these questions, we should turn to the process of suicide contagion – the emulation of harmful behaviours that are known to a community or broadcast through various forms of media. This can also include material that is ostensibly preventative. For example, one participant in the pro-ana[1] sphere shares the common experience of learning about anorexia via daytime television panic pieces. 'Welsh Rose' was battling with disordered eating when she saw an episode of *The Sally Jessy Raphaël Show*. While the host, Sally, was adamant about raising awareness of the growing epidemic of anorexia amidst young American women, and thus preventing its spread, Welsh Rose was intrigued by this illness and communities built around it (Welsh Rose 2007). There are many stories of this nature, showcasing the rather dramatic consequences of discussing harmful behaviours in any form. Of particular relevance is what I dub 'echoing self-harmful behaviours': acts of violence against one's own body that occur in similar ways across time due to the impact of intense community groups like pro-harm forums found online. It is increasingly important to examine internet groups when tracing contagions, and to be aware that the social modelling within now has an international scope.

Emotional distress is an unavoidable part of the human experience. Exposure to pro-self-harm material is not responsible for the negative life events that a person may be faced with at some point. What it does seem to shape, however, is the kind of a reaction a person may opt for during times of negative affect. A lens for understanding this is offered in Kral's study of perturbation and lethality within suicide choices. He argues that a person becomes perturbed once their threshold of tolerance is crossed. This significant mental unease can then precipitate a suicide attempt if a person's coping mechanisms are maladaptive. This can happen to any person regardless of the culture they have consumed. The variable factor in such a scenario is the relative lethality of their suicidal behaviour. Ideas as to how suicide urges should be expressed are learned from our immediate social and broader cultural environments (2019, pp. 7, 75). Kulp agrees that "suicidal acts do not happen in a vacuum". They are planned, enacted, and responded to in keeping with cultural and communal perceptions (2013, p. viii). Media framing is a part of this process as the media can influence how the public perceive suicide or what they believe may prevent it (Canetto *et al.* 2017, p. 30). In this way, certain media environments can lead people to think that self-harmful behaviour is inevitable for certain people, a good solution for difficult circumstances, or the most effective way to express negative emotional states. Some online environments can also introduce them to new, and often more extreme, methods of harm. As such, it is important to look more closely at the specifics of echoing self-harmful behaviour and give consideration to ways this danger can be addressed.

Harmful Ideas Online: An Overview of Echoing Self-Harmful Behaviours and the Internet

A major venue for the dissemination of echoing self-harmful behaviour is the internet. Online, people discuss topics, including the positive dimensions of self-harm, and provide information that can be instructional in terms of restricting food intake, hiding wounds, or even effectively killing oneself. Extreme ideas such as these can be expressed with relative freedom, allowing for communities to form around shared support for countercultural behaviours and philosophies. This occurs in groups that, for example, see eating disorders as a lifestyle choice rather than as a medical problem (Bell 2007, p. 449). To provide an appropriate intervention or to plan for lasting recovery, healthcare professionals need to be aware of the mechanics of these spaces. One of the most dangerous aspects of this kind of community is behavioural scripting. It is common for participants to see self-harmful behaviour as an effective way to communicate their pain or to connect with others on a meaningful level.

To unpack these complex relations, I provide a discussion of the main elements seen in pro-ana communities including: tagging to share the philosophy across platforms, thinspiration to encourage greater degrees of emaciation, explicit instructions for the worsening of starvation behaviour, highly competitive environments, religious behaviour with thinness as an ultimate concern, strong boundary policing against outsiders and 'wannabes', and an abiding mood of loneliness and negative affect. While I focus on pro-ana specifically, many of these same themes are echoed in pro-self-harm and pro-suicide spaces – both of which have significant overlap with the pro-ana sphere. While these behaviours can certainly be dangerous, the actual way in which they manifest can be quote subtle and unpredictable. In sum, we need to focus far less on the idea that self-harmful behaviour is wrong, taboo, or foolish and look instead at what factors cause the pain subjects are responding to. As echoed in the final chapter of this work, we need to develop other outlets for people to express their grief, loneliness, or acute bodily dissatisfaction. We must direct new energy and enthusiasm into solutions rather than continue to focus on blame or play out unjustified obsessions with preventing so-called deviant behaviours from being amplified online.

Exploring Censorship: The Ethics and Logistics of Censorship to Address Echoing Self-Harmful Behaviour

The final section of this book thus turns to the question of censorship and its effectiveness. For the past twenty years, internet communities exploring or advocating self-harmful content have been the focus of international censorship efforts. They have been received with a sense of stigma and alarm, which has often led to a misunderstanding of how possible it actually is to control this material, or the many ways in which such communities self-censor and control entry to their online forums. A thorough examination of the history of censorship shows that the process has been unsatisfactory, with creators of this material simply changing servers or language use to evade detection and continue with their behaviour – more aware of public reaction but more likely to be radicalised than dissuaded by it. Censorship also ignores how hard these spaces are to abandon when they provide a rare source of genuine social support and allow people space to communicate ideas that they may be uncomfortable or unwilling to share with their family and friends or with medical professionals (Dias 2003, p. 32). Overall, this makes censorship a poor choice for managing self-harmful discussions. Instead, there are many opportunities for outreach to these communities to safely promote processes of healing.

An often-misunderstood source of help are peers who have also taken part in self-harmful behaviours or ideations. In a study of a forum run by an eating disorder charity, Kendal *et al.* noted several clear benefits, including peers taking on a mentoring role, discussion boards used as a safe space, friendship between users, flexible help, and peer support through journeys of recovery and relapse prevention (2017, p. 98). Peers can often be found supporting recovery in others, even if they do not choose this path for themselves. Their advice can feel compelling due to its authenticity. For example, on edtwt,[2] user 'rory' has compiled a list as to "why recovery is the best choice". She shows empathy towards common concerns held by other sufferers that may not be as meaningful to medical professionals, providing reassurance like "you wont automatically turn overweight when you go into recovery" [sic] (rory ✿ 2021). It is also important to appreciate the way in which pro-self-harmful spaces allow for the expression of 'difficult' emotions like feelings of rejection, enduring low mood, and discussions of interpersonal trauma. These expressions can be cathartic, and there is significant value in sharing them with an audience who tend to provide empathy or genuine support. Finally, supportive community spaces can potentially be used to introduce new meaningful identities that can supersede more destructive ones. There is real potential for health and healing if a focus on censorship is phased out in preference of creating genuine and empathetic sources of help for people in need.

Further Notes

Notes on Terminology

> You are the holder of my razorblade. You are the maker of my perfection. You are my slow suicide. Bulimia is your name (Chelsea 2005).

As with my previous book (see Alderton 2018, p. ixff), some conflation of normative medical terms is used to reflect popular discussion in pro-ana and pro-self-harm spaces. While authoritative texts like the *Diagnostic and Statistical Manual of Mental Disorders* clearly separate psychiatric disorders, this division is not as readily accepted by those who suffer from them. For example, it is easy to find claims like "A Eating disorder is a self injury [*sic*]" along with cutting or burning oneself (Ash and Heather 2002). Since the early days of their online existence, members of pro-ana communities have often included self-harm as one of their typical list of medical diagnoses – displayed prominently on websites along other diagnoses like EDNOS or COE³ (Polak 2007, p. 87). Statistically, there is significant crossovers between these different behaviours. When users of a pro-ana sites were polled on other self-harmful behaviours, 46.1% said they had attempted suicide, 83.2% had cut themselves, and 77.4% had injured themselves in some other manner (Yom-Tov *et al.* 2016, p. 111). Analysis of social media posts dealing with disordered eating showed that 40.6% also mentioned major depression (Pater *et al.* 2016, p. 1193). Another study found that major themes of Lusophone pro-ana blogs include cutting, self-punishment, and wishes for death when starvation goals are not met (Castro and Osório 2012, p. 180).

The boundaries between different eating disorder diagnoses are also regularly called into question. For example, one community member explains how she coined the term 'MiAna' to reflect her behaviours drawn from both anorexia and bulimia nervosa (Faux 2008). Even the more popular term 'pro-ana' refers to any or all eating disorders, not anorexia nervosa alone (Branley and Covey 2017, p. 1356).⁴ While medical professionals are concerned with giving a specific diagnosis that matches with a proven treatment program, those with these conditions have far more fluid definitions. For this reason, when engaging with their content, it is more relevant to mirror their blurred boundaries with the use of terms like 'self-harmful behaviour' rather than 'NSSI' or 'bulimia nervosa'.

Indeed, similar somatic experiences are often noted by those who feel they are a part of an argument that considers all self-harmful actions are essentially the same or can be used interchangeably for the same ultimate effect. For example, "I consider my eating disorder to be another manifestation of my self injury … there is a definite sensation thing happening, the sensation of a burning empty stomach and a burning wound" (SarahDarkBlue 2003) or "You wouldn't believe how much purging is like screaming and clawing your eyes out" (Joe 2005). For some, self-injury is used as punishment when they inevitably eat. For example, one young woman confesses that she skips meals, throws away foods, and will "cut myself when i do eat" as punishment for failing (Lucy 2008). Lavis noted similar behaviours when conducting fieldwork in an eating disorders inpatient unit. Here, patients were required to eat and often felt guilty as a result. To assuage these feelings, they would dig cutlery into their arms, hold ice cubes, or have self-harming episodes after the meal (2016, p. 35). Arndt has observed a strong correlation between these actions, especially cutting paired with anorexia, in her own work. She suspects they overlap because both behaviours "use the body as a way to express feelings that seem too big (and too intense) to express verbally" (Arndt 2000).

Also included in this umbrella terminology is passive suicidal ideation enacted through extreme personal neglect or hopes for accidental trauma. For example, "I desperately wanna just lay in the snow and freeze to death. To be found blue and frozen sounds so nice" (mike 2021). It is also relatively common for people to wish for a tragic accident like 'SarahDarkBlue' who felt that "maybe if I cross the street at just the right time that speeding car wont see me and it will kill me [*sic*]" or to believe "everything would be so much simpler if I just died while skiing". If severely injured or unconscious, she felt her condition would "make everyone leave me alone, make my mom nice to me" (SarahDarkBlue 2002). In this same way, Malson and Ussher see the anorexic body as one that engages in both the themes of physical death and of "symbolic self-destruction" leading towards a passive fatalism rather than a single suicidal gesture (1997, p. 51). Undue focus on specific medical terms and categories can easily distract from the fact that people within self-harmful communities identify with broader understandings of their behaviour and prefer to see commonalities rather than differences across these activities.

Notes on Disciplinary Focus

Another note on this book is that it diverts somewhat from traditional mental health literature and is instead a multidisciplinary study of psychology, psychiatry, sociology, and media. Issues such as eating disorders have been addressed by these fields, leading to an acknowledgement that the complexity of the topic requires it. Nevertheless, as Casilli *et al.* note, dialogue between fields has tended to be critical – an example being Gender Studies academics questioning normative clinical approaches. Each field brings with it an assumed modus operandi, with psychiatry and clinical psychology dominating (2012, p. 122). The physical and psychological clinical features of anorexia have been a primary academic focus with alternative readings such as anorexia as an online resistance and rebellion movement only emerging in more recent times (Watts and Crowe 2014). For such reasons, Gailey believes that explaining disordered eating through a single disciplinary lens is oversimplifies the matter and assumes similar motivations and experiences across diverse subjects. Instead, she recommends that a researcher should "immerse oneself in the culture and allow the women's stories to paint the picture" (Gailey 2009, p. 95). This is the approach I have taken here. It seeks to avoid this project being shaped by a single discipline and instead allow the findings to be shaped by the expression and experiences of anyone impacted by self-harmful behaviour.

The way that the internet itself has been approached also brings with it potential problems. Many commentators view the internet as something 'bad' or inherently negative for mental health or offline community bonds. However, as Bell explains, the internet is not a set of activities that can have a moral value. It is merely a medium through which these activities occur (2007, p. 445). It is the ideas shared through online mass communication and socialisation that are able to influence and educate users in either positive or negative ways (Boniel-Nissim and Latzer 2016, p. 156). There is no inherent psychological impact that the internet has on its users. Rather, specific outcomes derive from the kind of activities made available to a person and their own psychological attributes (Bell 2007, p. 445). For this reason, it is important that the internet is not merely dismissed as a bad or misleading space that creates only disease. As Pater *et al.* advocate, it can also be a rich space for developing recovery tools that can reduce recidivism and allow for a more wholistic approach to diagnosis and treatment. Conversely, new tools and innovative engagements with this space are undercut by actions like censorship that change the way behaviours are expressed online and create a conceptual divide between practitioners and participants (Pater *et al.* 2016, p. 1195). As such, this book is devoted not to censoring online discussions but rather to understanding how these discussions can be incorporated into a multidisciplinary pattern of healing.

Notes

1 Pro-ana, in broad terms, is a community where eating disorders are viewed as a valid lifestyle choice as opposed to a mental disorder. This community is defined more comprehensively later in this volume.

2 edtwt is a portmanteau of 'eating disorder' and the social media site 'Twitter'. This community functions as a safe space for discussing disordered eating behaviours in short form posts. It is also defined in more detail later in this volume.

3 EDNOS: Eating Disorder Not Otherwise Specified; COE: Compulsive Over-Eating.

4 There is a degree of professional debate surrounding these terms. Some feel that anorexia nervosa and bulimia nervosa share the same core symptoms ("body dissatisfaction; preoccupation with food, weight, and shape; certain ego deficits") even though diagnostic criteria vary. The primary difference is arguably the weight level around which a person fluctuates while symptomatic (Polivy and Herman 2002, pp. 188–189).

References

Alderton, Z., 2018. *The Aesthetics of Self-Harm: The Visual Rhetoric of Online Communities.* Abingdon: Routledge.

Arndt, L., 2000. Available from: https://web.archive.org/web/20001205052900fw_/ http://www.anorexicweb.com:80/InsidetheFridge/razorthin.html [Accessed 29 Mar 2018]. Razor Thin [online] Anorexic Web

Ash and Heather, 2002. Self Injury [online]. *Nothing Tastes As Good As Thin Feels.* Available from: https://web.archive.org/web/20030621230253fw_/http://myweb.ecomplanet. com/FUMB1613/mycustompage0013.htm [Accessed 12 Aug 2020].

Bell, V., 2007. Online information, extreme communities and internet therapy: Is the internet good for our mental health? *Journal of Mental Health,* 16 (4), 445–457.

☆Benji☆, 2019. I've starved myself for days [online]. *@taehyungsqueer.* Available from: https://twitter.com/taehyungsqueer/status/1149478356678635521 [Accessed 8 Sep 2021].

Boniel-Nissim, M., and Latzer, Y., 2016. The characteristics of pro-Ana community. *In*: Y. Latzer and D. Stein, eds. *Bio-Psycho-Social Contributions to Understanding Eating Disorders.* Cham: Springer International Publishing, 155–167.

Branley, D.B., and Covey, J., 2017. Pro-ana versus pro-recovery: A content analytic comparison of social media users' communication about eating disorders on Twitter and Tumblr. *Frontiers in Psychology*, 8, 1356.

Canetto, S.S., Tatum, P.T., and Slater, M.D., 2017. Suicide stories in the US media: Rare and focused on the young. *In:* T. Niederkrotenthaler and S. Stack, eds. *Media and Suicide: International Perspectives on Research, Theory, and Policy.* New Brunswick (U.S.A.): Transaction Publishers, 27–40.

Casilli, A.A., Tubaro, P., and Araya, P., 2012. Ten years of Ana: Lessons from a trans-disciplinary body of literature on online pro-eating disorder websites. *Social Science Information*, 51 (1), 120–139.

Castro, T.S., and Osório, A.J., 2012. Online violence: Not beautiful enough... not thin enough. Anorectic testimonials in the web. *PsychNology Journal*, 10 (3), 169–186.

Chelsea, 2005. Bulimia is Your Name [online]. *Fragile Innocence.* Available from: https://web.archive.org/web/20041214175152if_/http://winkin.phpwebhosting.com:80/~joeic/privet/thin/art/story005.html [Accessed 15 Nov 2018].

Connor, G., and Coombes, L., 2014. Gynetic organisms: Pro-anorexic techno bodies. *Ethnicity and Inequalities in Health and Social Care*, 7 (2), 62–71.

Dias, K., 2003. The Ana sanctuary: Women's pro-anorexia narratives in cyberspace. *Journal of International Women's Studies*, 4 (2), 31–45.

Faux, M., 2008. Pro-Ana acronyms, ect. [online]. *Fading Obsession:: Pro Ana Mia Website plus Forum.* Available from: https://web.archive.org/web/20080724115101/http://www.fading-obsession.com/information/acronyms.php [Accessed 23 Apr 2021].

Gailey, J.A., 2009. "Starving is the most fun a girl can have": The Pro-Ana subculture as edgework. *Critical Criminology*, 17 (2), 93–108. ·

Joe, 2005. [m]y story [online]. *Fragile Innocence.* Available from: https://web.archive.org/web/20041212013218if_/http://winkin.phpwebhosting.com:80/~joeic/privet/thin/me/mystory.html [Accessed 15 Nov 2018].

Kendal, S., Kirk, S., Elvey, R., Catchpole, R., and Pryjmachuk, S., 2017. How a moderated online discussion forum facilitates support for young people with eating disorders. *Health Expectations*, 20 (1), 98–111.

Kral, M.J., 2019. *The Idea of Suicide: Contagion, Imitation, and Cultural Diffusion.* Abingdon: Routledge.

Kulp, M., Williams Korteling, N., and McKay, K., 2013. *Searching for Words: How Can We Tell Our Stories of Suicide.* BRILL.

Lavis, A., 2016. The substance of absence: Exploring eating and anorexia. *In:* E.-J. Abbots and A. Lavis, eds. *Why We Eat, How We Eat: Contemporary Encounters between Foods and Bodies.* London: Routledge, 35–52.

Lucy, 2008. welcome [online]. *i just want to be beautiful.* Available from: https://web.archive.org/web/20080102035020/http://www.freewebs.com/ijustwanttobebeautiful/ [Accessed 3 Jun 2021].

Malson, H.M., and Ussher, J.M., 1997. Beyond this mortal coil: Femininity, death and discursive constructions of the anorexic body. *Mortality*, 2 (1), 43–61.

mike, 2021. Tw i guess? Suicide?? [online]. *@bunny_are_cool.* Available from: https://twitter.com/bunny_are_cool/status/1356525828683812864 [Accessed 5 May 2021].

Pater, J.A., Haimson, O.L., Andalibi, N., and Mynatt, E.D., 2016. "Hunger Hurts but Starving Works": Characterizing the Presentation of Eating Disorders Online. *In: Proceedings of the 19th ACM Conference on Computer-Supported Cooperative Work & Social Computing.* Presented at the CSCW '16: Computer Supported Cooperative Work and Social Computing, San Francisco California USA: ACM, 1185–1200.

Polak, M., 2007. 'I think we must be normal... There are too many of us for this to be abnormal!!!': Girls creating identity and forming community in pro-Ana/Mia websites. *In*: S. Weber and S. Dixon, eds. *Growing Up Online: Young People and Digital Technologies.* New York, NY: Palgrave Macmillan, 83–96.

Polivy, J., and Herman, C.P., 2002. Causes of eating disorders. *Annual Review of Psychology*, 53 (1), 187–213.

rory ✱, 2021. why recovery is the best choice [online]. *@findroryagain*. Available from: https://twitter.com/findroryagain/status/1424547002717810688 [Accessed 8 Sep 2021].

SarahDarkBlue, 2002. The beginning: My journey of self discovery about self injury and depression [online]. *Bleeding on the Couch.* Available from: https://web.archive.org/web/20021209063057/http://www.geocities.com/sarahdarkblue/begin.html [Accessed 12 Apr 2021].

SarahDarkBlue, 2003. Eating disorders and self injury [online]. *Bleeding on the Couch.* Available from: https://web.archive.org/web/20031213211226/http://www.geocities.com/sarahdarkblue/eating.htm [Accessed 12 Apr 2021].

Watts, M. and Crowe, N., 2014. Anorexia advocates turn medical condition into self-expression [online]. *The Conversation.* Available from: http://theconversation.com/anorexia-advocates-turn-medical-condition-into-self-expression-23955 [Accessed 20 May 2021].

Welsh Rose, 2007. About Me [online]. *Welsh Rose.* Available from: https://web.archive.org/web/20070113065007/http://welshrose.bravehost.com/aboutme.html [Accessed 24 May 2021].

Yom-Tov, E., Brunstein-Klomek, A., Hadas, A., Tamir, O., and Fennig, S., 2016. Differences in physical status, mental state and online behavior of people in pro-anorexia web communities. *Eating Behaviors*, 22, 109–112.

Section I

Contagions and Clusters

1 Untangling Dangerous, Infectious Behaviour

Introduction

Suicide at Bridgend

In February 2008, a headline in the UK's *Daily Express* read: "Another girl hangs herself in death town". *The Telegraph* led with "'Suicide cult' may have claimed new victim". This was in reference to Angie Fuller, described as "a pretty teenager" who became the latest in a series of deaths by suicide in the South Wales town of Bridgend. At the time of her death, she was the fourteenth young person to hang herself in the so-called suicide capital of Britain. Her death was immediately linked with her online activity as she was a member of the social networking sites Bebo[1] and Facebook. Angie had checked on her profile hours before she died and had recently posted status updates, including "I don't like myself". Friends explained that she was stressed by the responsibility of working and caring for her home and had a volatile relationship with her unemployed fiancé. She had also attempted suicide in the past (Bonnici and Dixon 2008). Media outlets noted that she and her partner "were goths" (Smith 2008). As a result of her sad death, Angie became one of 26 young people lost to suicide in Bridgend from 2007 to 2009.[2]

In the wake of such dramatic and sensationalist reporting, police had to insist that there was "no evidence of a suicide pact or an internet cult" causing the Bridgend cluster (Hughes 2008). The *Daily Express*, along with other publications, ignored several recommendations for the safe reporting of suicide in their discussion of Angie's death and the situation in her hometown. Even in regions where there are media guidelines about ethical and safe suicide reporting, such as in the United Kingdom, journalists and publishers do not always adhere to best practice. Reports of the Bridgend suicide cluster tended to be sensationalist with many engaging in dangerous practices such as noting the suicide method (including in headlines), referring explicitly to earlier suicides in the cluster, and using phrases deemed to be unsafe or unhelpful by professionals working in suicide prevention. Only a minority of reports included content known to be helpful, such as information and advice for

DOI: 10.4324/9781003126065-2

anyone negatively impacted by the story (John *et al.* 2017, p. 17). Sensationalist media coverage of suicides is known to increase suicide rates (Niederkrotenthaler *et al.* 2010, p. 241), and it is quite possible that this happened in Bridgend due to the numerous bad practices deployed by the national press.

As noted, the method of suicide was repeatedly detailed in newspaper reports. The *Daily Express* provided explicit details as to how Angie hanged herself on the bannister of a staircase and how another young man used a dressing gown cord to hang himself in a wardrobe (Bonnici and Dixon 2008). Both these hanging methods could easily be replicated in a standard home. The press also created a sense of the inevitability of suicide in 'Death Town'. Even when experts were contacted, their advice made suicide seem something impossible to understand or prevent. Tegwyn Williams, Bridgend's Suicide Prevention Strategy chief, told the *Daily Express* that "it is almost impossible to stop individuals from committing suicide" and said she did not understand why a cluster was persisting in the region (Bonnici and Dixon 2008).

The kind of victim we can expect from a harmful contagion is also outlined in the Bridgend reports. Angie was called "pretty" (as was Natasha Randall) in various press reports and described as a "bride-to-be... with everything to live for" (Smith 2008). Fellow youngster Jenna Parry was "very girly", "so bubbly and carefree", and a fan of butterflies and pop music (Hughes 2008). The victims also tend to be described as a bit silly and near-sighted. During a gap in suicides, *Vanity Fair* reported that locals hoped "the kids had come to their senses and gotten a grip". The generation at risk were criticised by locals for having "lost their tough-mindedness" (Shoumatoff 2009). While this is a radical (and dangerous) simplification of whose death by suicide we should fear, it does solidify the idea that pretty and happy girls are at risk of hanging – primarily due to their own immaturity and foolish ideas.

All of these comments go against UK press guidelines by Samaritans who ask that journalists do not explain methods of suicide, avoid dramatic headlines and front page placement of suicide stories, avoid sensationalist language like 'suicide epidemic', do not label areas as suicide hotspots, avoid excessive imagery that may lead readers to 'over-identify with the deceased', do not speculate about why a person may have committed suicide, and be especially cautious when dealing with suicide deaths of young people. This age group contains members who are more likely to imitate the methods used or see suicide as a valid solution to their problems. Samaritans also ask that suicide be referred to as preventable (not inevitable) and useful resources be signposted (Samaritans 2020, p. 6). Press coverage of Bridgend was highly irresponsible. It was done for the sake of engaging readers with shocking headlines and sensationalising sad stories of youths taking a woeful path. These irresponsible reporting decisions led parents to blame the media for "glamorised" takes on suicide that made the experience "more unbearable" for grieving families and gave their vulnerable teenagers an idea that suicide was a solution to feeling low or needing attention (Parents Attack Suicides Coverage 2008).

Despite these significant problems in reporting styles, it is interesting that articles about this cluster tended to focus instead on the dangers of the internet. Angie's death occurred in the wake of Natasha Randall's funeral – another Bridgend teenager who hanged herself. Natasha's friends set up a memorial page where mourners could place a virtual brick in a remembrance wall, sparking fears that "suicide had become 'cool' among the town's youngsters" (Bonnici and Dixon 2008). This kind of memorial page was popular for victims in Bridgend, with many receiving thousands of loving tributes – including from others who later killed themselves – leading to rumours of an internet suicide cult. In response to these fears, the memorial pages were removed by Bebo (Shoumatoff 2009). Before her death, Natasha was one of the many who had paid tribute to another young man who hanged himself in the local park (Bonnici and Dixon 2008). What is left out of this comment in the *Daily Express* is that Natasha was the first female to hang herself in the Bridgend cluster, which brought significant press attention to the region and resulted in front cover spreads in the tabloids. When interviewed, friends of the deceased claimed that the internet had nothing to do with their choices and was merely a mainstream channel for communication. Instead, they blamed a pervasive low mood amongst their friends and the lack of opportunities and mobility in the region (Shoumatoff 2009). Research into the antecedents for suicide would support this perspective, yet it is the idea of an insidious suicide cult that persists.

The death of Angie Fuller, and subsequent press treatment, is representative of many of the themes discussed within this chapter and this book as a whole. Firstly, it introduces the idea of a suicide cluster and the notion that suicide may be a contagious idea – both areas that have been heavily researched and debated in recent scholarship. The idea of the internet as a new, hidden venue for the dissemination of harmful ideas is also noted. To unpack these ideas, this chapter correlates some major proofs of the manner in which people really do copy each other in suicidal behaviour. In addition, there is also strong evidence for social modelling effects in a broader scope of activities that I dub echoing self-harmful behaviours. Nevertheless, this modelling and social learning comes from a variety of sources, including interpersonal relationships, institutions, news media, and fiction. It is not limited to sinister online 'suicide cults'. In this chapter, I look into evidence for contagion and clustering effects in harmful behaviours. This leads into subsequent chapters dealing with the specifics of echoing self-harmful behaviour online and the question of what we can, or should, do to address such dangers.

Suicide as Social Learning

The need to copy one another, even if actions may be perceived by some as dangerous or counterproductive, seems to stem from universal human behavioural patterns. Kral argues that copycat behaviour is inherent in the production and dissemination of culture, with processes of contagion and imitation present in most human activity. Imitation is the backbone of culture (2019, pp. xiii, 2). Social learning theory seems to be the backbone of such a process. This theory suggests that we develop new behaviours by watching other people and imitating their actions. These behaviours can be further encouraged or mitigated by observation of reward and punishment. We tend to be motivated when we see other people being rewarded for good behaviour or when they suffer the consequences of bad choices. We also tend to avoid actions that result in punishment or other social sanctions (Bandura 1977, pp. 3–4). While it may seem that social learning would naturally prevent something harmful like suicide from happening, society is not monolithic, and interpretation is inherently subjective. This means that a person may choose to observe a niche subculture and learn from peers in this space – even if subcultural norms are counter to cultural hegemony. It also means that a person may interpret suicide as a good way of achieving their personal goals such as a cessation of negative affect or making a profound statement on their social place or needs.

As such, recent scholarship has analysed suicide through a lens of social learning, finding that a copycat effect of this kind does seem to be at play in at least some suicidal behaviour (Mesoudi 2009, p. e7252). Social learning can account for mass and point clusters of suicide (discussed later) and should thus be kept in mind when reporting on suicide in the press or memorialising someone who has died in this way (Pirkis and Robinson 2014, p. 6). Imitation is most likely when vulnerable people feel "close temporal, geographic, interpersonal proximity" with a person who has died by suicide (Hanssens 2011, p. 14). Social learning should also be considered in fictional accounts of suicide, as it seems that we also internalise what mental illness looks like and how we should respond to it through media like television (Stout *et al.* 2004, p. 544). Overall, this social learning theory espouses suicide as something that occurs due to a person's ecological niche, their habitus, and the social stories that surround them as opposed to simply a malady that strikes those in specific structural circumstances or due to their own independent choices and responses to stress (Staples 2012, p. 142). In sum, suicide can be read as what Kral dubs "cultural mimesis … an idea that is internalized from culture and imitated" (2019, p. 2). Rather than viewing suicide as a symptom of individual mental or spiritual deficit, it is important to appreciate broader cultural forces at play.

Most of the work on clusters of harmful behaviour, and contagions that may cause clustering, relate directly to suicide. Far less examination has been done into the potential infectiousness of self-harm and even less into disordered eating. One scholar who has examined this possibility is Vandereycken who posits that eating disorders and other self-harming behaviours are developed through social learning processes of imitation, identification, and competition (2011, p. 289). That is, people with disordered eating may see others with similar conditions (e.g., in a treatment program) and identify deeply with them. If these people are part of a radical subculture, such as an anti-medial or anti-therapeutic philosophy, an individual might copy their behaviours or even escalate them in a process of competition. Significant evidence for such pro-harm subcultures and processes of social learning within is provided in the second chapter of this volume and is introduced later in this chapter. But, first, we shall turn to more traditional conceptual definitions developed in suicidology.

The Impact of Clusters and Contagions on Harmful Behaviour

Processes of imitation underlying suicide have been suspected and discussed for more than two centuries, resulting in many anecdotal reports of people hearing about real or fictional suicides then copying these actions. In the past 60 years, a more rigorous scientific method has been applied to work out more precisely how these processes manifest and at what rate (Pirkis and Blood 2010, pp. 1, 6).[3] Next, I summarise the key findings of this research and suggest ways in which these notions could be expanded to include a broader scope of self-harming behaviours and focus more attention on changes to social learning facilitated by the internet.

Introduction to Key Terminology

Cluster: In its traditional sense, a cluster refers to a grouping of suicide attempts or completions that are "nonrandomly 'bunched' in space or time" (Joiner 1999, p. 89). This means that suicide events happen "closer together in time and space than would generally be expected" (O'Carroll *et al.* 1988). The number of cases that make up a cluster has been proposed as two (Joiner 1999, p. 89) or three or more (Johansson *et al.* 2006, 3).

Some groups appear to be more vulnerable to clustering. This includes younger people/adolescents (Haw *et al.* 2013, p. 97; Robinson *et al.* 2016, p. 4), people in rural areas with poor service provision (Cheung *et al.* 2014, p. 139), males, those with a history of drug and alcohol abuse, those with a history of self-harm (Haw *et al.* 2013, p. 97), and people living in low socioeconomic areas (Too *et al.* 2017, p. 691).

Although clusters are relatively rare, their occurrence should be of significant concern as it tends to result in ongoing community trauma and complicated grief (Haw *et al.* 2013, p. 97; Robinson *et al.* 2016, p. 2).

A cluster refers to an accumulation of suicide cases, but not the reasons for their occurrence (Blasco-Fontecilla 2013, p. 49). Clusters are further divided into 'point' and 'mass', explored further.

Point Cluster: A point cluster traditionally refers to the spatio-temporal clustering of suicides. For example, a group of suicides that happens in a secondary school over the period of a year after a well-known student takes their life.

This form of cluster has the strongest ongoing evidence for its occurrence (Joiner 1999, 89). Because these clusters are based in specific localities, it seems that they are generated and supported by social learning amongst peers (Mesoudi 2009, p. e7252). When one's peers die by suicide, it is common to be overwhelmed by grief and believe that suicide is unpreventable (Abbott and Zakriski 2014, p. 668).

Point clusters seem to emerge from knowing *anyone* who has attempted or completed suicide – not just a family member or close friend. Any kind of social associate seems to be enough to start this trend (Kleiman 2015, p. 20). It also seems as though at-risk youth tend to overestimate the degree of suicidal behaviour in their friends, which exacerbates their own chance of engaging in such acts (Zimmerman *et al.* 2016, p. 31).

Point clusters can occur in educational institutions such as a residential hall at a university (Cheung *et al.* 2013, p. 6) or a secondary school. Instances of completed suicide in a school cohort tend to result in subsequent attempts and high levels of ideation amongst these peers. At particular risk are those close to the deceased or those with a history of affective disorders (Brent *et al.* 1989, p. 918).

Unsurprisingly, psychiatric units are a common locus for point clusters. For example, Haw studied one such cluster in London from 1987 to 1988. While she found no direct evidence of contagion, patients seemed to be reacting to shared negative feelings about the future of the treatment centre and changes in senior treatment staff (1994, pp. 264–265).

Point contagions can also stem from funerals. In some point clusters, suicides occur immediately before or after the funeral of other suicide victims (Hanssens 2008, 26). While this can obviously be a response to acute grief, there is also evidence that funerals can exacerbate point clusters by inadvertently glorifying death by suicide. Robertson *et al.* noted this effect in a New Zealand suicide cluster where several victims were Māori and were buried with a traditional *tangihanga* (funeral and rites for the dead). This ritual is impressive and deeply moving, and this may have accidentally inspired some of the vulnerable young people in attendance or inadvertently glorified death by suicide. Some were impressed by the *tangi* of their peers and hoped to receive the same commemoration when they died (Robertson *et al.* 2012, p. 242). It is understandable why people who generally receive negative feedback from their community might see their own memorial services as the easiest way to be esteemed by others.[4]

While they are not included in traditional definitions of point clusters, which are reserved for suicide only, self-harm and self-starvation point clusters can also be seen. Common locations are secondary schools, hospitals, and secure facilities (Vandereycken 2011, p. 289).

Mass Cluster: A mass cluster is one that occurs between more disparate people who have been influenced by the same fictional or non-fiction media. For example, a group of people who attempt suicide after reading about a celebrity who died in a similar way (Haw *et al.* 2013, 97ff). This cluster is grouped in time as opposed to specific space (Joiner 1999, p. 90).

The evidence for this form of cluster was initially equivocal (Joiner 1999, p. 89), but in more recent studies, it has been determined that there is a strong causal association between news media stimulus and suicide, and a probable causal relationship between television and suicide (Pirkis and Blood 2010, p. 3). More copycat suicides occur in the wake of press saturation with suicide stories or when suicide is discussed in the rich visual medium of television (Pirkis *et al.* 2006, pp. 2874, 2883). Conversely, media blackouts and strikes have led to lower suicide rates (Pirkis and Blood 2001a, p. 147).

Mass clusters are strongly influenced by the media – especially in the case of young people (Niederkrotenthaler and Stack 2017, p. 1). Media content can also confuse and distort the facts of suicide very easily. For example, it seems that people tend to incorrectly estimate the risk of suicide for themselves and others. This has led vulnerable people to the impression that suicidal actions are a common and socially acceptable way of reacting to suicide in the media (Scherr and Reinemann 2013, pp. 74–75). The media also tends to focus on sensational and highly lethal suicide methods, which suggests they are far more common than statistics prove (Sisask and Värnik 2012, p. 123).[5]

Some suicides are more infectious than others, and this seems to be due to the personality and notoriety of the person involved. Glamourised or sensationalised suicides (including those of celebrities) elevate the chance of copycat activities, and people are more at risk of copying the suicides of people in the same demographic as themselves (Pirkis *et al.* 2006, p. 2875; Niederkrotenthaler *et al.* 2009, p. 1086).

The most dangerous reporting styles seem to be articles about young people committing suicide, prominent positioning of a suicide story on a front page, or the inclusion of images. Broad and abstract discussions of suicide in the media are far less likely to cause clustering than specific stories about individuals, their personal details, suicide notes, or method (Gould *et al.* 2014).

As such, it is generally believed that controlling language and content in media articles can limit the formation of a cluster. Vienna was one of the first regions to attempt press guidelines of this kind after a spate of subway suicides. As a result, subway suicides dropped by 75% and the cluster ended (Sonneck *et al.* 1994; Etzersdorfer and Sonneck 1998). This has been carried through on a global level with most regions having recommendations for, or restrictions on, the reporting of suicide in order to protect readers.

While the media landscape has undergone significant changes in the modern era, this does not mean that mass clusters are necessarily new. For example, in the medieval Buddhist world, the trend of self-immolation was contextualised and distributed in a range of hagiographical texts celebrating monks who had died by this act. As Benn argues, self-immolation was not necessarily performed for identical reasons, but came to be seen as such after the homogenisation of different occurrences into a disseminated tradition. The more such texts were produced, the greater the legitimacy and popularity of the act (2012, pp. 206–207).

Echo Cluster: Clusters can also subsequently 'echo'. An echo cluster happens when distinct clusters persist in the same location but over long periods of time – longer than those typically expected for a point cluster (Hanssens 2010, p. 22).[6] Echo clusters are most likely to manifest in cases where suicide has become normalised and expected in a community group (Hanssens 2010, p. 20).

An example of an echo contagion continues to place in the Tiwi Islands. In the 1980s, four suicide attempts and two suicide completions occurred using the same specific method of hanging. Collective mourning rituals meant that significant numbers of people were aware of these deaths. Over the next two decades, forty-four people completed suicide with the same method and many also made life-threatening attempts (Hanssens 2011, p. 15).[7]

Echo clusters such as this can manifest over decades with occasional peaks of activity at the height of the contagion (Hanssens 2010, p. 17). While clusters are generally examined with a primary focus on their existence in geographical space, some echoes like this mean the phenomenon "resembles a slowly developing epidemic" and thus also needs to be examined for its temporal manifestations (Cheung *et al.* 2013, p. 1).

Factors associated with echo clusters are contagions within families and imitative behaviours amongst small community groups. They can also occur when suicide rates are so high within a community that it is no longer able to contain the threat or respond adequately to those in need (Hanssens 2010, p. 17). Even the most robust community members can start to suffer from "vicarious trauma and burnout" (Hanssens 2010, p. 23).

Contagion: Suicide contagion has been proposed as an overarching reason *why* clusters form. The underlying assumption of a contagion effect is that suicidal behaviour begets subsequent suicidal behaviour via direct contact (point clusters) or indirect contact (mass clusters) (Haw *et al.* 2013, p. 101).

The actual existence of contagions is heavily debated with many seminal researchers agreeing in general with the fact of clusters but debating whether contagion is a verifiable cause. While the clustering of suicide is generally taken as fact, "clustering does not contagion make" (Joiner 1999, p. 92). The strongest evidence is for contagion via news media, although there are also studies that demonstrate how this contagion is transferred through fiction (Gould *et al.* 2003, p. 1269).

The terminology of 'contagion' is taken from that of infectious diseases. Metaphorically speaking, suicidal ideas can be seen as a germ. When susceptible people (especially youths) are exposed to this germ, they can become infected, and infect each other, leading to a cluster (Johansson *et al.* 2006, pp. 3–4). Stanganelli *et al.* call youth suicide "a disaster zone" arguing that it spreads like a bushfire or bacteria (2012, p. S58). Even the *perception* of a cluster can become a risk factor for further suicide regardless of whether the perception is initially correct (Rezaeian 2012, p. 125).

Contagion also alludes to the unconscious processes behind suicide. Kral argues that, while suicide is a conscious act, "the ideas behind it may be outside of awareness". The idea of suicide spreads through a process of cultural diffusion and is imitated in a contagious fashion by vulnerable people (2019, p. 80).

Werther and Papageno Effects: There is a further possibility that contagion effects can be negative or positive, not merely the former. This is epitomised in the dichotomy of the Werther versus Papageno effect.

The Werther effect is named after Goethe's popular novel *The Sorrows of Young Werther* (1774). This story details the tragic suicide of the eponymous protagonist who kills himself after his beloved marries another man. After the book was published, young men who identified with Werther started to dress like him and copy his notable mannerisms. The popularity of the text across Europe coincided with a rise in suicide rates. The idea of a Werther effect appears in the developing corpus of academic literature on suicide contagion in the 19th century. For example, in 1838, Esquirol opined, "*la lecture des livres qui vantent le suicide est si funeste*" [reading books that extol suicide is quite disastrous] and "*la lecture du* Werther *de Goëthe a produit plus de suicides en Allemagne que toutes les femmes de ce pays*" [reading Goethe's *Werther* has produced more suicides in Germany than all the women in this country] (Esquirol 1976, p. 589). Although the connection between members of the public reading *The Sorrows of Young Werther* and then committing suicide in significant number is primarily anecdotal, Goethe's text was banned in many jurisdictions (Pirkis and Blood 2001b, p. 155).

The phrase 'Werther effect' was developed by Phillips (1974) to describe copycat suicidal behaviour in the wake of media articles discussing this theme – especially when those who subsequently show suicidal ideation emulated or idolised the initial casualty.

More recently, evidence has also emerged of a 'presumed Werther Effect'. This describes a tendency to overestimate the risk of copycat suicide for *other people* when they are exposed to media with a suicide theme. While there is strong evidence for a behavioural Werther effect, this indicates the existence of a perceptual level of the Werther effect. That is, the general public is aware enough of copycat suicide tendencies that they fear their existence and can overestimate real suicide risk (Scherr and Reinemann 2013, p. 79). The behavioural consequence of this overestimation can be the kind of kneejerk censorship discussed later in this volume.

Several decades after Phillips' theory, Niederkrotenthaler *et al.* introduced an alternative term – the 'Papageno effect' – referring to fictional suicide narratives that may have a positive impact on survival and healing. Papageno is a character in Mozart's opera *The Magic Flute* (1791) who undergoes a suicidal crisis. Three child spirits help him through his pain and show him other ways to cope. Papageno survives and lives happily with his true love Papagena as the opera draws to a close. Thus, a Papageno effect occurs when suicide is framed in a way that leads to a decrease in this behaviour – making it opposite to the Werther effect (Niederkrotenthaler *et al.* 2010, p. 234). Niederkrotenthaler *et al.* found persuasive evidence for a protective Papageno effect at play in the Austrian press. Of note are articles that report on suicidal ideation felt by an individual, which does not result in an attempted or completed suicide. A clear example of this is an article in which the singer Tom Jones was feeling suicidal before his first hit single and contemplated stepping in front of a train. He decided not to, and soon after became a superstar with his single "It's Not Unusual" (2010, pp. 235, 241). Research has also suggested that while fiction may influence harmful behaviours, we should also pay attention to the positive impacts such stories can have on prevention (Scalvini 2020, p. 1569).

While articles of this kind mention suicide, often in detail, readers seem to respond in a positive manner and learn that difficult times end and can be followed by periods of happiness, personal achievement, and satisfaction. As such, it is recommended that journalists prioritise suicide stories where a person models overcoming difficulty and seeks support so that vulnerable readers can imitate this kind of action instead (Samaritans 2020, p. 5).[8]

Assortative Relating: There is ongoing debate as to whether the occurrence of a cluster means there has been a contagion. Another possibility is 'assortative relating'. This is a phenomenon in which individuals with high suicide risk actively seek each other out and form social bonds.

This means that clusters of suicidal activity amongst such a friendship group would be more to do with shared risk factors rather than an external cause like a contagion (Randall *et al.* 2015, p. 219). The cluster would develop *before* a hypothetical suicide stimulus because members of such a group are already at risk of suicidality when faced with severe negative events (Joiner 1999, p. 91).

Homophily of this type has been proposed as something that might mimic point clusters (Mesoudi 2009, p. e7252).

However, Randall *et al.* found that assortative relating is not wholly responsible for clusters, as their data shows that exposure to a friend's suicidal behaviour significantly increases the likelihood that an individual will also attempt suicide. Suicide contagion does indeed seem to be a lead cause of suicide clusters (2015, pp. 222–223).

Methodological Debates and Conflicting Results

In trying to understand something as complex as infectious harmful behaviour, studies seem to bring up just as many flaws and limitations as they do conclusions. The majority have been described as lacking in "methodological rigour" and empirical evidence (Haw *et al.* 2013, p. 97), with theoretical underpinnings and assumptions often unchanged since investigations in the 1970s (Scherr and Reinemann 2013, pp. 73–74). Experimental design is often atheoretical and lacks in testable hypotheses (Pirkis and Robinson 2014, p. 5). Joiner calls the definition of "suicide contagion" "so vague as to defy analysis" (1999, pp. 90–91). Models are often used to correlate suicide data and predict future events, but modelling can lead to "extreme simplifications of a complex real-life phenomenon" (Mesoudi 2009, p. e7252). It is also very difficult to prove causation in cases such as individuals being motivated by the suicide of a celebrity (Manson *et al.* 2013, p. 394), with studies of this kind often falling prey to ecological fallacies (Pirkis and Blood 2010, p. 15). Data gathering is often limited in the wake of a suicide crisis (Brent *et al.* 1989, p. 922), and there is far more research on completed suicides as opposed to clusters of suicide attempts (Too *et al.* 2017, p. 491). Preventative effects of media content are also under-investigated (Niederkrotenthaler *et al.* 2010, p. 234). Conversely, there is the possibility that the over-investigation of youth clusters makes this occurrence seem more statistically significant than it really is (Rezaeian 2012, p. 129). Different kinds of clustering also have more evidence in their favour. Point clusters have been easier to prove and quantify than mass clusters thus far (Kleiman 2015, p. 17). But, while point clusters are smaller and tend to allow researchers to note the features of individuals within them, the sample size of such clusters tends to lack statistical significance (Rezaeian 2012, p. 128).

Studies in this area have thrown up a variety of results that are hard to reconcile with each other. Harris and Bettiol dub the findings in this field as ultimately "unclear and inconsistent" (2017, p. 71). Some studies have found no, or very limited, evidence of the existence of clustering or contagion (Scherr and Reinemann 2013, p. 77). For example, Manson *et al.* claim that the temporal clustering of suicide may just be random events that are perceived of as a cluster. In their analysis of possible point and mass suicide events, they found no proof of clustering (2013, p. 394). Other scholars have found different explanations for pockets of suicide such as concentration of deprivation in the area (Exeter and Boyle 2007, p. 731) or excessive exposure to negative life events (Harris and Bettiol 2017, p. 74). The Mercy study found that exposure to accounts of suicide in the media or in peer groups is a protective factor against nearly lethal suicidal behaviour. The researchers in this study are concerned that research proving suicide clusters is too entrenched in methodological weakness such as a lack of control groups or small sample sizes (2001, p. 120). Harris and Bettiol's comprehensive survey of people who were exposed to suicidal behaviours (by means of family or friends attempting or completing suicide) found that this exposure *could not* be seen as a risk factor for either suicidality or other psychopathologies. Rather, individuals viewed their exposure as a negative life event that they interpreted in individual ways. The young adults surveyed in this research were no more likely to become suicidal due to exposure than older participants despite other research indicating that they are the most susceptible (2017, p. 70). Indeed, the fear that vulnerable people might be negatively affected by a discussion of suicide has meant they have generally not been engaged in discussions about online interventions or educational programmes (Robinson *et al.* 2017).[9] This can create even more errors or misunderstanding in underlying research assumptions.

Nevertheless, over time, studies have responded to these issues in experimental design and methodological structure in order to develop a more sophisticated lens for viewing a very complex research challenge (Pirkis and Blood 2010, p. 14). For example, research into this topic relied primarily on anecdotal accounts of clustered suicide, based on case histories and narrative evidence. While this material certainly pointed towards a cluster effect, it was weakened by a lack of control data and modern statistical analysis. After it became apparent that clusters were a likely factor in the spread of suicide, researchers began to apply more rigorous methodologies to chart the spatio-temporal clustering of suicide. Many anecdotally identified suicide clusters have since been processed using in-depth statistical analysis, which has often shown clear space-time clustering of suicides. These clusters occur both in closed communities like prisons and in the general population (Gould *et al.* 2014). Overall, most studies with these more modern tweaks to research methods and problems show some evidence of clustering and contagion. For example, the majority do show that suicide rates increase after widely-publicised stories about people dying this way (Niederkrotenthaler and Stack 2017, p. 2). The existence of clustering and contagion effects is not universal and should not be assumed, but it is evident that these patterns do indeed exist and often manifest in cases where suicide is publicised or becomes endemic in a community.

Another important development in the understanding of suicide and clustering is a move towards the integration of other disciplines beyond psychology and psychiatry, and more attention given to the value of qualitative studies. In 2010, Pirkis and Blood noted in their review of the field that most consideration was given to media influence studies dominated by medicine, sociology, and psychology. These tend to be set apart from other theoretical lenses such as cultural or communication studies (2010, p. 6). Expansion into broader lenses has only recently become popular with the development of 'critical suicidology' from 2016 onwards. This field, into which the present book fits, prioritises new methodological processes and allows attention to shift towards more qualitative and subjective accounts of suicide such as an examination of experiences shared by those who have been suicidal (Kral 2019, pp. 11–12). Critical suicidology looks to the specific experiences and perspectives of those who are especially vulnerable, such as indigenous people and youths, examining texts as diverse as poetry and community-driven intervention. This helps to probe the vital cultural dimensions of suicide (Kral 2019, p. 18). As Boyce notes, quantitative, statistical methods are an excellent way of examining deaths in a set area and time period. Nevertheless, they cannot measure subjective data such as community experience or mood as a result of a suicide cluster, or predict what kind of social or cultural factors might cause suicidal ideation to spread (2011, p. 1452). Critical suicidology is an excellent way of expanding to include these important dimensions in an understanding of how harmful ideas spread through social mimesis.

Towards New Definitions to Reflect Contemporary Online Spaces

What is notable about the definitions shared above is their development during a pre-web 2.0 age. Joiner's foundational 1999 study was published at a time where households were only beginning to have internet connections – often used on a shared family computer. It took until 2012 for more engaging, personal internet tools like smartphones to have a notable impact on the psychological well-being of users (Twenge *et al.* 2018, p. 765). Since the late 2000s, there has been increasing evidence that online discussions about suicide have a direct relationship with actual suicidal behaviour and may be causal (Pirkis and Blood 2010, p. 4), even though it is challenging to measure the internet and its impact in a spatio-temporal manner (Sisask and Värnik 2012, p. 123). Geographical delineations of clusters have become less clear as stories like the suicide death of a celebrity can be spread around the globe in minutes – as can copycat reactions (Johansson *et al.* 2006, p. 3). Some of the most pertinent critiques of cluster and contagion definitions are those that consider these dramatic shifts that have occurred in communication and connectivity. This is the new area we need to probe in order to develop a relevant, cotemporary lens for understanding how harmful ideas may take flight through online social learning.

As noted, there are difficulties in providing clear quantitative research based on something as ephemeral and broad as an online pro-harm space. The internet is a volatile zone with almost boundless scope, making it far more difficult to identify suicide stimuli – in contrast to the relative ease of analysing reactions to something more contained in space and time like a printed newspaper article (Pirkis and Blood 2010, p. 25). This is a little easier when examining contagious harmful actions in the form of self-harm or self-starvation. Because people who favour these actions remain alive, they are able (and sometimes willing) to note sources of their dangerous ideas and triggers. Sisask and Värnik also make the valuable recommendation of analysing the kind of spontaneous comments left on online media portrayals of suicide to see how agents interact in this sphere (2012, p. 133). Nevertheless, this kind of data still lends itself more to a qualitative analysis and descriptive case studies in contrast to the scientifically rigorous quantitative studies favoured in the psychological study of suicide clustering.

In addition to a change in scholarly approaches, we also need a change in media guidelines and censorship efforts in order to be more realistic about this radically different communication medium. Media guidelines for suicide reporting have not been, and should not be, static. Leonard (2001) provides a history of this field, noting that academic literature hypothesising the connection between the way the press discusses suicide and suicide attempts started to appear in the 19th century. One of the first connections made between media reporting and suicide imitation occurred in 1837 after a young woman killed herself through arsenic ingestion. At that time, a similar case was being featured in the press. She was also exposed to a family suicide attempt (Parrish 1837, pp. 258–259). In this era, it was already hypothesised that the publicity given to suicide cases seemed to beget a relative amount of imitation. Publishers of newspapers and fictional works were encouraged to show care in the way they discussed the topic of suicide (Leonard 2001, pp. 460–463). Later these suggestions of care would be ratified into formal press standards in many jurisdictions.

Nevertheless, this was not a smooth transition. Worries about the press causing suicide imitation were lessened when Durkheim published *Le Suicide: Étude de sociologie* in 1897. In this seminal text, he argued that imitative suicide happened only in those who were likely to die by this method anyhow (1997, p. 141).[10] Thus, the media were absolved of the level of guilt that scholars like Parrish suggested earlier in the century. Further academic investigations into contagion also seem to have been curtailed (Leonard 2001, p. 464). This field of enquiry seems to have only emerged again in earnest with Phillips' correlation of media suicide coverage with suicide attempts amongst audiences (1974), which helped to encourage tighter media regulations to prevent mass contagion. There is now an evident decrease in suicides in jurisdictions that implement media guidelines of this kind and emphasise suicidal ideation as something treatable rather than suggesting that death by this means is inevitable (Gould *et al.* 2003, pp. 1273–1275). While it is not always easy to balance the journalistic right to inform the public of news with arguments to restrict and censor information about suicide (Canetto *et al.* 2017, p. 37, Niederkrotenthaler and Stack 2017, p. 4), or to know when suicide reporting may actually be a case of "shining a light" on a taboo topic (Collings and Kemp 2010, p. 245), careful framing does seem to be necessary for a safer media landscape.

To carry on important work in this sphere, it is important to also develop media guidelines for new media. Maloney *et al.* point out some significant lags in this area, and recommend an updated set of press guidelines including new actions such as "not referring to online suicide forums" (Maloney *et al.* 2014, p. 165). While this could be a solid start, news media is by no means the only way that people access the kind of information that can lead to harmful behaviour. Nowadays, it is very easy to access graphic content about suicide at any time on something as immediate as a personal mobile device. It is also easy to access unfettered social media discussions of known or theoretical suicide cases. This is an area that is still lacking in comprehensive research and guidelines, leading many to suggest dramatic and unhelpful solutions such as swift and comprehensive censorship of all social media chat around suicide. Indeed, Heffel *et al.* describe research into the role of online communications and suicide clusters 'extremely limited'. This is despite social networking having a broad relevance to the way in which adolescents experience and discuss peer suicide (2015, p. 286).

A way to address some of these lacunae is to reconfigure older distinctions between point and mass clusters. To this end, Heffel suggests the existence of an "online network cluster" to reflect the way technology has altered and increased direct communication – especially in the way it decreases distance between communities, thus undermining the locative clarity of traditional point clustering (2014, p. 17). The need for a new definition like this is shown clearly in Robertson *et al.*'s study of a youth suicide cluster in New Zealand, which revealed just how outdated policy and research methods had become by this stage. Traditionally, point clusters occur in single institutions such as one high school. Robertson *et al.* found a cluster stretching across multiple schools through the vehicles of mobile phone communication (primarily texting between friends to deliver news about new suicides) and online memorial sites for students lost. Of note were memorial pages on the social networking site Bebo. This linked multiple school communities and allowed the contagion to spread between them. It also created a new and significant challenge for caregivers due to the rapid rate of communication – often centring on false or exaggerated rumours about suicide pacts or methods. Students became extremely anxious about the cluster of suicides in their midst as a result. This was despite the fact that the media at the time were very careful with their coverage and adhered to all necessary guidelines to prevent any possible mass clustering or contagion (Robertson *et al.* 2012, pp. 239–242).

This event could be seen as just a bigger-than-usual point cluster, but there seems to be more at play. One such element is the use of Bebo for memorialisation. As noted, funerals have the potential to encourage point clustering. The Bebo memorial pages for the deceased students seem to have encouraged clustering beyond the typical spatial bound that is expected in a point cluster, which was due to the general accessibility of the internet. Robertson *et al.* note many similarities in the Bebo memorial pages to those lost in their suicide cluster. Typically, the deceased are remembered through photo slideshows and videos, poems, and messages shared by friends, family members, associates, and even strangers. The content shared is overwhelmingly positive, including celebrations of their lives and achievements and explanations of how much they were valued and how they would be missed. Communication chains were also established in which crosses with names of the deceased in the cluster were shared across Bebo pages of the living to remember those who had been lost (Robertson *et al.* 2012, pp. 241–242).

This is a similar structure to the Bebo pages used to memorialise those lost to suicide in other cultures, such as the aforementioned youths from the Bridgend cluster where Bebo was "placed at the centre of an internet death cult" (Bowser 2008). Since this era, there have been recommendations that social media sites be investigated when determining clusters as they may "inadvertently romanticize suicide or idealize it as a heroic deed" through tools like Bebo "memory walls" (Austin *et al.* 2011, pp. 1528, 1530). Public memorials such as these are also known to attract "emotional rubberneckers" who do not have direct ties to the deceased but who often feel an emotional connection or identify with them nonetheless (DeGroot 2014, p. 82). These features of social media can create clustering across more disparate groups of people and geographical areas than has traditionally been noted (Rezaeian 2012, p. 129).

To deal with some of these necessary changes, the model of echo clusters can give some guidance. Echo clusters were first described by Hanssens as a unique feature of communities she studied in the Northern Territory of Australia where specific indigenous communities are so entrenched in suicide and associated grief that clusters re-emerge over periods of decades – well outside of the temporal limitations of a typical point cluster (2010, p. 25). Echo clustering is also a relevant framework for harm clusters that develop online and exist somewhere outside of mass and point in their nature, such as an online network cluster. This kind of clustering inherently challenges space and time parameters of traditional cluster definitions due to the lessening re-levance of geographical region (Heffel *et al.* 2015, p. 288). Temporal boundaries are also less clear, as in echo clusters, because of the suicide and grief saturation in specific online communities (which are discussed in more detail in the following chapter). Clusters can form again and again because the original stimulus can remain. For example, detailed memorials can have an ongoing online presence and can be accessed by people across the world at any time convenient to them.

Notes

1 Bebo is a now-defunct social networking site that ran from 2005 to 2013, 2015 to 2019 with its height in c.2017. Bebo supplied each user with a profile page where they could share blogs, photographs, et cetera, and receive comments from other users. Bebo was targeted to a teenage audience and arranged users by school affiliation.

2 Due to confusion caused by misleading and sensationalist press reports, these dates are debated. For example, Jones *et al.* argue that "this cluster was smaller, shorter in duration, and predominantly later than the phenomenon that was reported in national and international print media" (2013, p. e71713).

3 For a comprehensive history of these studies, see Pirkis and Blood (2010, p. 9ff).

4 Funeral attendance is not necessarily associated with the development of a cluster. For example, Brent *et al.* found that psychopathology has a far greater impact on suicidal ideation in a high school group than attendance at the funeral of a peer lost to suicide (1989, p. 922). One differentiating factor may be the significant difference between

standard U.S. funerals in the 1980s, which tended to be more demure and sanitised, as compared with the very vibrant and participatory Māori *tangihanga* as experienced in the 2010s.

5 Even the journalists themselves can become distressed and obsessive about suicide cases, especially when they empathise or feel attachment with the person in question (Collings and Kemp 2010, p. 246).

6 At present, this definition of a cluster seems to be more niche than point and mass – tending to be favoured only by Australian academics in this field. Outside of Australia, the existence of a third type of cluster similar to echo has occasionally been hypothesised. For example, suicides on the London Underground system and at railway stations near psychiatric units have been noted as types of cluster "where there is geographical but not temporal clustering" (Haw et al. 2013, 97). While such occurrences may not be formally deemed as echo clusters, they do match this definition.

7 This cluster can also be read as a manifestation of familial contagion as well as broader community contagion as the Indigenous people on the Tiwi Islands view themselves as "one people" who share a deep relational bond (Hanssens 2010, p. 19).

8 In their survey of the field, Sisask and Värnik noted that there was considerably more research dedicated to the Werther effect than the Papageno effect (2012, p. 123). Nearly a decade later, this observation remains accurate.

9 Interestingly, participants in the Robinson study, which investigated suicide prevention via social media, enjoyed the program and 80% felt more able to provide emotional support to others as a result. No participants felt suicidal as a result of the discussions they took part in. One student described feeling upset after particpating, and 70% reported one of the texts produced lowered their mood. But, despite this, the majority still liked this text and would recommend it to someone undergoing suicidal thoughts (Robinson *et al.* 2017). This raises questions as to whether researchers need to completely avoid studies where people are exposed to potentially contagious material. Participants were able to feel upset or lowered in mood while still gaining benefit from the text in question.

10 This goes against the social learning theory underpinning this chapter, as Durkheim suggests that the main force motivating such a suicide is their own internal impulses and natural personality. In contrast, social learning argues that inner determinants of behaviour are only a part of the puzzle, and that most choices come from a kind of cultural mimesis (Bandura 1977, p. 1).

References

Abbott, C.H. and Zakriski, A.L., 2014. Grief and attitudes toward suicide in peers affected by a cluster of suicides as adolescents. *Suicide and Life-Threatening Behavior*, 44 (6), 668–681.

Austin, A.E., van den Heuvel, C., and Byard, R.W., 2011. Cluster hanging suicides in the young in South Australia. *Journal of Forensic Sciences*, 56 (6), 1528–1530.

Bandura, A., 1977. *Social learning theory*. Englewood Cliffs, NJ: Prentice-Hall.

Benn, J.A., 2012. Multiple meanings of buddhist self-immolation in China – A historical perspective. *Revue d'Etudes Tibétaines*, 25, 203–212.

Blasco-Fontecilla, H., 2013. On suicide clusters: More than contagion. *Australian & New Zealand Journal of Psychiatry*, 47 (5), 490–491.

Bonnici, T. and Dixon, S., 2008. Another girl hangs herself in death town [online]. *Daily Express*. Available from: https://www.express.co.uk/news/uk/34000/Another-girl-hangs-herself-in-death-town [Accessed 10 Mar 2020].

Bowser, J., 2008. Bebo placed at the centre of internet death cult [online]. *Campaign*. Available from: https://www.campaignlive.co.uk/article/bebo-placed-centre-internet-death-cult/778504?utm_source=website&utm_medium=social [Accessed 23 Mar 2021].

Boyce, N., 2011. Suicide clusters: The undiscovered country. *The Lancet*, 378, 1452.

Brent, D.A., Kerr, M.M., Goldstein, C., Bozigar, J., Wartella, M., and Allan, M.J., 1989. An outbreak of suicide and suicidal behavior in a high school. *Journal of the American Academy of Child & Adolescent Psychiatry*, 28 (6), 918–924.

Canetto, S.S., Tatum, P.T., and Slater, M.D., 2017. Suicide stories in the US media: Rare and focused on the young. *In*: T. Niederkrotenthaler and S. Stack, eds. *Media and Suicide: International Perspectives on Research, Theory, and Policy*. New Brunswick, USA: Transaction Publishers, 27–40.

Cheung, Y.T.D., Spittal, M.J., Williamson, M.K., Tung, S.J., and Pirkis, J.E., 2013. Application of scan statistics to detect suicide clusters in Australia. *PLoS ONE*, 8 (1), 1–11.

Cheung, Y.T.D., Spittal, M.J., Williamson, M.K., Tung, S.J., and Pirkis, J.E., 2014. Predictors of suicides occurring within suicide clusters in Australia, 2004–2008. *Social Science & Medicine*, 118, 135–142.

Collings, S.C. and Kemp, C.G., 2010. Death knocks, professional practice, and the public good: The media experience of suicide reporting in New Zealand. *Social Science & Medicine*, 71 (2), 244–248.

DeGroot, J.M., 2014. "For whom the bell tolls": Emotional rubbernecking in Facebook memorial groups. *Death Studies*, 38 (2), 79–84.

Durkheim, E., 1997. *Suicide*. Glencoe, IL.: Free Press.

Esquirol, E., 1976. *Des maladies mentales considérées sous les rapports médical, hygiénique et médico-légal*. New York: Arno Press.

Etzersdorfer, E. and Sonneck, G., 1998. Preventing suicide by influencing mass-media reporting. The viennese experience 1980–1996. *Archives of Suicide Research*, 4 (1), 67–74.

Exeter, D.J. and Boyle, P.J., 2007. Does young adult suicide cluster geographically in Scotland? *Journal of Epidemiology & Community Health*, 61 (8), 731–736.

Gould, M.S., Jamieson, P., and Romer, D., 2003. Media contagion and suicide among the young. *American Behavioral Scientist*, 46 (9), 1269–1284.

Gould, M.S., Kleinman, M.H., Lake, A.M., Forman, J., and Midle, J.B., 2014. Newspaper coverage of suicide and initiation of suicide clusters in teenagers in the USA, 1988–96: a retrospective, population-based, case-control study. *The Lancet Psychiatry*, 1 (1), 34–43.

Hanssens, L., 2008. Clusters of suicide: The need for a comprehensive postvention response to sorrow in indigenous communities in the northern territory. *Aboriginal and Islander Health Worker Journal*, 32(2), 25–33.

Hanssens, L., 2010. "Echo clusters" – Are they a unique phenomenon of indigenous attempted and completed suicide? *Aboriginal and Islander Health Worker Journal*, 34 (1), 17–26.

Hanssens, L., 2011. "Suicide (echo) clusters" – Are they socially determined, the result of a pre-existing vulnerability in indigenous communities in the Northern Territory and how can we contain cluster suicides? *Aboriginal and Islander Health Worker Journal*, 35 (1), 14–23.

Harris, K.M. and Bettiol, S., 2017. Exposure to suicidal behaviors: A common suicide risk factor or a personal negative life event? *International Journal of Social Psychiatry*, 63 (1), 70–77.

Haw, C., 1994. A cluster of suicides at a London Psychiatric Unit. *Suicide and Life-Threatening Behavior*, 24 (3), 256–266.

Haw, C., Hawton, K., Niedzwiedz, C., and Platt, S., 2013. Suicide clusters: A review of risk factors and mechanisms. *Suicide and Life-Threatening Behavior*, 43 (1), 97–108.

Heffel, C., 2014. Finding Out on Facebook: A Qualitative Analysis of Adolescents' Experiences Following a Suicide Cluster. Doctor of Philosophy. Texas: University of North Texas.

Heffel, C., Riggs, S.A., Ruiz, J.M., and Ruggles, M., 2015. The aftermath of a suicide cluster in the age of online social networking: A qualitative analysis of adolescent grief reactions. *Contemporary School Psychology*, 19 (4), 286–299.

Hughes, M., 2008. Bridgend suicides: 'I feel shaken to the core. Why are youngsters around here doing this?' [online]. *The Independent*. Available from: https://www.independent.co.uk/news/uk/home-news/bridgend-suicides-i-feel-shaken-to-the-core-why-are-youngsters-around-here-doing-this-784402.html [Accessed 10 Mar 2021].

Johansson, L., Lindqvist, P., and Eriksson, A., 2006. Teenage suicide cluster formation and contagion: Implications for primary care. *BMC Family Practice*, 7 (1), 1–5.

John, A., Hawton, K., Gunnell, D., Lloyd, K., Scourfield, J., Jones, P.A., Luce, A., Marchant, A., Platt, S., Price, S., and Dennis, M.S., 2017. Newspaper reporting on a cluster of suicides in the UK: A study of article characteristics using PRINTQUAL. *Crisis*, 38 (1), 17–25.

Joiner, T.E., 1999. The clustering and contagion of suicide. *Current Directions in Psychological Science*, 8 (3), 89–92.

Jones, P., Gunnell, D., Platt, S., Scourfield, J., Lloyd, K., Huxley, P., John, A., Kamran, B., Wells, C., and Dennis, M., 2013. Identifying probable suicide clusters in Wales using National Mortality Data. *PLoS ONE*, 8 (8), e71713.

Kleiman, E.M., 2015. Suicide acceptability as a mechanism of suicide clustering in a nationally representative sample of adolescents. *Comprehensive Psychiatry*, 59, 17–20.

Kral, M.J., 2019. *The idea of suicide: Contagion, imitation, and cultural diffusion*. Abingdon: Routledge.

Leonard, E.C., 2001. Confidential death to prevent suicidal contagion: An accepted, but never implemented, nineteenth-century idea. *Suicide and Life-Threatening Behavior*, 31 (4), 460–466.

Maloney, J., Pfuhlmann, B., Arensman, E., Coffey, C., Gusmão, R., Poštuvan, V., Scheerder, G., Sisask, M., van der Feltz-Cornelis, C.M., Hegerl, U., and Schmidtke, A., 2014. How to adjust media recommendations on reporting suicidal behavior to new media developments. *Archives of Suicide Research*, 18 (2), 156–169.

Manson, R., Lester, D., Gunn, J.F., and Yeh, C., 2013. Do suicides cluster? *OMEGA – Journal of Death and Dying*, 67 (4), 393–403.

Mercy, J.A., Kresnow, M.-J., O'Carroll, P.W., Lee, R.K., Powell, K.E., Potter, L.B., Swann, A.C., Frankowski, R.F., and Bayer, T.L., 2001. Is suicide contagious? A study of the relation between exposure to the suicidal behavior of others and nearly lethal suicide attempts. *American Journal of Epidemiology*, 154 (2), 120–127.

Mesoudi, A., 2009. The cultural dynamics of copycat suicide. *PLoS ONE*, 4 (9), e7252.

Niederkrotenthaler, T. and Stack, S., 2017. Introduction. *In*: T. Niederkrotenthaler and S. Stack, eds. *Media and Suicide: International Perspectives on Research, Theory, and Policy*. New Brunswick, USA: Transaction Publishers, 1–13.

Niederkrotenthaler, T., Till, B., Kapusta, N.D., Voracek, M., Dervic, K., and Sonneck, G., 2009. Copycat effects after media reports on suicide: A population-based ecologic study. *Social Science & Medicine*, 69 (7), 1085–1090.

Niederkrotenthaler, T., Voracek, M., Herberth, A., Till, B., Strauss, M., Etzersdorfer, E., Eisenwort, B., and Sonneck, G., 2010. Role of media reports in completed and prevented suicide: Werther v. Papageno effects. *British Journal of Psychiatry*, 197 (03), 234–243.

O'Carroll, P.W., Mercy, J.A., Steward, J.A., and Centers for Disease Control (CDC), 1988. CDC recommendations for a community plan for the prevention and containment of suicide clusters. *MMWR Supplements*, 37 (6), 1–12.

Parents Attack Suicides Coverage [online], 2008. *BBC News*. Available from: http://news.bbc.co.uk/2/hi/uk_news/wales/7253788.stm [Accessed 10 Mar 2021].

Parrish, I., 1837. Case of suicide in a child. *American Journal of the Medical Sciences*, 21, 258–259.

Phillips, D.P., 1974. The influence of suggestion on suicide: Substantive and theoretical implications of the Werther effect. *American Sociological Review*, 39 (3), 340–354.

Pirkis, J.E. and Blood, R.W., 2001a. Suicide and the media. Part I: Reportage in non-fictional media. *Crisis*, 22 (4), 146–154.

Pirkis, J.E. and Blood, R.W., 2001b. Suicide and the media. Part II: Portrayal in fictional media. *Crisis*, 22 (4), 155–163.

Pirkis, J.E. and Blood, R.W., 2010. *Suicide and the News and Information Media: A Critical Review*. Australian Capital Territory: Mindframe.

Pirkis, J.E., Burgess, P.M., Francis, C., Blood, R.W., and Jolley, D.J., 2006. The relationship between media reporting of suicide and actual suicide in Australia. *Social Science & Medicine*, 62 (11), 2874–2886.

Pirkis, J.E. and Robinson, J., 2014. Improving our understanding of youth suicide clusters. *The Lancet Psychiatry*, 1 (1), 5–6.

Randall, J.R., Nickel, N.C., and Colman, I., 2015. Contagion from peer suicidal behavior in a representative sample of American adolescents. *Journal of Affective Disorders*, 186, 219–225.

Rezaeian, M., 2012. Suicide clusters: Introducing a novel type of categorization. *Violence and Victims*, 27 (1), 125–132.

Robertson, L., Skegg, K., Poore, M., Williams, S., and Taylor, B., 2012. An adolescent suicide cluster and the possible role of electronic communication technology. *Crisis*, 33 (4), 239–245.

Robinson, J., Bailey, E., Hetrick, S., Paix, S., O'Donnell, M., Cox, G., Ftanou, M., and Skehan, J., 2017. Developing social media-based suicide prevention messages in partnership with young people: Exploratory study. *JMIR Mental Health*, 4 (4), e40.

Robinson, J., Too, L.S., Pirkis, J.E., and Spittal, M.J., 2016. Spatial suicide clusters in Australia between 2010 and 2012: A comparison of cluster and non-cluster among young people and adults. *BMC Psychiatry*, 16 (1), 1–9.

Samaritans, 2020. *Media Guidelines for Reporting Suicide*. Surrey: Samaritans Registered Office.

Scalvini, M., 2020. *13 Reasons Why*: Can a TV show about suicide be 'dangerous'? What are the moral obligations of a producer? *Media, Culture & Society*, 42 (7–8), 1564–1574.

Scherr, S. and Reinemann, C., 2013. Media depictions of suicide influence individual perceptions of health risks. *In*: M. Kulp, N. Williams Korteling, and K. McKay, eds. *Searching for Words: How Can We Tell Our Stories of Suicide*. Oxford, United Kingdom: BRILL, 73–87.

Shoumatoff, A., 2009. The mystery suicides of Bridgend county [online]. *Vanity Fair*. Available from: https://www.vanityfair.com/culture/2009/02/wales-suicides200902 [Accessed 10 Mar 2021].

Sisask, M. and Värnik, A., 2012. Media roles in suicide prevention: A systematic review. *International Journal of Environmental Research and Public Health*, 9 (1), 123–138.

Smith, R., 2008. Bride-to-be Angie Fuller is 14th suicide in death town Bridgend [online]. *Mirror*. Available from: https://www.mirror.co.uk/news/uk-news/bride-to-be-angie-fuller-is-14th-suicide-292234 [Accessed 10 Mar 2021].

Sonneck, G., Etzersdorfer, E., and Nagel-Kuess, S., 1994. Imitative suicide on the Viennese subway. *Social Science & Medicine*, 38 (3), 453–457.

Stanganelli, V., Callaghan, L., Prince, T., Hansen, B., Sutton, P., Howe, A., France, N., Cheverton, F., Lawton, J., and Travers, J., 2012. Like sparkle in sugar cane… cluster of youth suicide. *Neuropsychiatrie de l'Enfance et de l'Adolescence*, 60 (5), S58.

Staples, J., 2012. The suicide niche: Accounting for self-harm in a South Indian leprosy colony. *Contributions to Indian Sociology*, 46 (1–2), 117–144.

Stout, P.A., Villegas, J., and Jennings, N.A., 2004. Images of mental illness in the media: Identifying gaps in the research. *Schizophrenia Bulletin*, 30 (3), 543–561.

Too, L.S., Pirkis, J.E., Milner, A., and Spittal, M.J., 2017. Clusters of suicides and suicide attempts: Detection, proximity and correlates. *Epidemiology and Psychiatric Sciences*, 26 (5), 491–500.

Twenge, J.M., Martin, G.N., and Campbell, W.K., 2018. Supplemental material for decreases in psychological well-being among american adolescents after 2012 and links to screen time during the rise of smartphone technology. *Emotion*, 18 (6), 765–780.

Vandereycken, W., 2011. Can eating disorders become 'contagious' in group therapy and specialized inpatient care? *European Eating Disorders Review*, 19 (4), 289–295.

Zimmerman, G.M., Rees, C., Posick, C., and Zimmerman, L.A., 2016. The power of (mis)perception: Rethinking suicide contagion in youth friendship networks. *Social Science & Medicine*, 157, 31–38.

2 Clusters and Contagious Behaviour in Non-suicidal Harmful Activities

There is solid evidence for comparable processes of clustering and contagion in activities beyond suicide. They also seem to manifest in other areas of non-lethal, self-inflicted harm. As explained, my approach to this issue intentionally conflates any form of purposeful harm inflicted on the self. This includes suicide or suicidal gestures, self-harm, and self-starvation. This is markedly different to other analyses in which suicide and non-suicidal self-injury attempts are seen as different events, with findings disrupted by participants who may accidentally confuse the two (see, for example, Randall *et al.* 2015, p. 219). Indeed, not every study draws a strict barrier between suicide and self-harm. For example, Too *et al.* define suicide attempts as "admissions to hospital for deliberate self-harm" and suicide as "deaths due to deliberate self-harm" (2017, p. 491). Attempting to clarify terminology, Johansson *et al.* suggest the term "cluster of self-destructive behaviour" be used when suicide attempts are studied alongside completed suicide (2006, p. 3). I suggest we take this even further and use the phrase "self-harmful behaviour" to explore clustering and contagion effects associated with self-harm and disordered eating – including suicidal gestures and harmful behaviours noted in suicidal people. In cases where this behaviour is supported by intense community groups like online pro-harm forums, self-harmful behaviour can manifest an echoing clustered effect.

Social Learning in Disordered Eating and Self-Harm

The same mechanisms that support suicide as an outcome of social learning and cultural mimesis can be applied to other harmful behaviours. Studies that explore the mechanics and demographics of self-harm often focus primarily on the individual and their internal experiences. This is useful, but it paints an incomplete picture. Importantly, the antecedents to self-harm tend to have a deep connection to community and to a person's relationship with those around them. This relationship also impacts upon the techniques of harm they are likely to explore, and the kind of reaction they will be met with if their harm becomes evident to others. Self-harm is socially influenced in a number of ways, including learning the behaviour from friends or

DOI: 10.4324/9781003126065-3

engaging in it due to social motivations such as needing to fit in, or as a method for coping with the stress of social exclusion (Heath *et al.* 2009, p. 180). In order to understand why clustered self-harm can flourish, it is important to appreciate the deeply social dimensions of this behaviour. Indeed, Cowdy calls self-harm a "disease of the communal, social body" as well as a disease of the individual (2012, p. 44). Those who are most easily or excessively influenced by those around them are at the highest risk of learning and replicating self-harm behaviours. Susceptibility to self-harm is correlated with susceptibility to all social contagions (Jarvi *et al.* 2013, p. 3). Self-harm also occurs because a person has selected this method rather than other behaviour with similar functions. Social modelling is a substantial reason why this choice might be made (2009, p. 78). Thus, it operates along very similar lines to other infectious, clustering behaviours.

There is clear evidence that people who have observed self-harm amongst their friends or family are at a higher risk of developing similar coping mechanisms – often the same self-harm method that they have seen modelled (Hawton *et al.* 2002, p. 1211; Nock and Prinstein 2005; Heath *et al.* 2009, p. 183; Adler and Adler 2011, p. 60). This pre-disposition often comes from the sharing of techniques, the idea of self-harm as fashionable, or the understanding of self-harm as a beneficial technique for dealing with negative emotions. As soon as friends or family members start to discuss self-harm or show their injuries to each other, contagious behaviour can begin. Schools are an obvious source of this kind of discussion, as further explored in notes about point clustering given next. As one anonymous self-harmer explains, her behaviour happened solely due to a schoolmate confessing her own actions:

> Self injury, self mutilation, self harm...sounds grusome doesnt it … I was horrified when I found out that a friend did it, couple of weeks later I had made my first cut [sic].
>
> (Self Injury 2001)

Social learning can also help to account for the development of disordered eating. The specific cause of illnesses like anorexia nervosa is still unknown. While eating disorders are connected to body dissatisfaction, only a minority of people who are unsatisfied with their appearance will develop one (Polivy and Herman 2002, p. 205). Rates of disordered eating also seem to vary widely across time and space, suggesting a social contingent. As of the late 1990s, eating disorder professionals started to raise concerns about 'fat talk' – everyday discussions of one's body fat.[1] Catherine Steiner-Adair from the Harvard Eating Disorders Center dubbed this talk "a kind of sympathetic, sympathizing, mutual body loathing". Refusing to participate could lead to social exclusion, and many vulnerable young girls feel that they will lose their friends if they do not join in with complaints about their own body. During this era, a greater number of younger teenagers and children started to develop eating disorders. Young people, especially girls, started to rank a fear of fat above a fear of nuclear war, cancer, or death during this time (Newman 1997). Models, actresses, and pageant competitors also became on the whole "less hourglass-like, more boxy, more boyish, and more androgynous" making a curvaceous figure less desirable or elite (Thomsen *et al.* 2001, p. 51).

Fox-Kales describes this as a 'culture of eating disorders' in which food is the new taboo and scales invite a deep confrontation with one's worth and purpose. 'Sisterhood' is now constructed not through the sharing of recipes and tastes, but through a shared fear of fat. While this does not necessarily lead to a pathological eating disorder, Fox-Kales argues that the line between normative diet culture and anorexia is "razor thin" (2011, p. 1,4). Indeed, extreme versions of restriction, to the degree of mental illness, are more permitted in this culture than many would like. Young women especially have been taught that diseases like anorexia make you "skinny and special ... fragile and interesting" without too much focus on the less glamorous physical symptoms (Osgood 2013). This 'body loathing' culture is an obvious springboard for diets shared between friends, some of them extreme or within the clinical definitions of disordered eating. This has also led to the present normalisation of food restriction discussions, supporting current high rates of disordered eating due to this social learning process.

Evidence of Point Clusters of Self-Harmful Behaviour

As with suicide, self-harmful behaviour easily lends itself to the lens of point and mass clustering. Some of the older case studies in this area point to military hospitals where patients were under particular duress as locations for clustered self-harm.[2] For example, during First World War, a military hospital in Rome reported a series of incidents in which convalescing soldiers presented with particular lesions en masse. Because these lesions led them to be withdrawn from fighting, they were categorised as fraudulent injuries created to criminally fool the system (Ascarelli 1917, p. 355). Yet, the antecedents for this behaviour are strongly in line with those that lead to self-harm as it is categorised today. The 'political feeling' of a locality was blamed, along with family conditions experienced at home. Of particular risk were fathers with large families to support and soldiers who had lost brothers in battle. Young adults who were new to camp life were the most at risk of self-harm, with this risk level dropping as they became habituated to their surroundings. Soldiers who had been treated for self-inflicted injuries were likely to present again with repeat symptoms. Importantly, Ascarelli noted that particular kinds of injuries would manifest amongst specific groups of soldiers who were copying the style and location of lesions and other damage to bodily tissue from each other. Common techniques included the application of caustic substances on healed wounds, the creation of artificial swelling by incorrectly bandaging sprains, and the production of conjunctivitis symptoms in the eyes. Suspicion was often raised because soldiers from the same camps were reporting the same injuries to the same tissue at the same time, followed by abrupt cessation of these symptoms and the development of new styles to replace them (Ascarelli 1917, p. 356).

Copycat self-harm has also been reported more recently in mental health facilities or on particular wards. For example, Raine notes that contagious self-harm behaviours tend to spread when a new influential person is introduced into a clinical setting. This seminal person will often mutilate themselves in distinctive patterns that are then copied by others, albeit often in less severe forms. For example, the instigator might cut deeply, whilst others copy the formation and location of the wound but with a shallower cut or a scratch. According to her colleagues in this field, the only way to resolve these copycat outbreaks is to move patients until new group leaders arrive and change the tone of activities (Raine 1982, p. 10). This also happens in eating disorder wards where patients frequently copy ways to lose extra weight from each other, or new tricks for making clinicians think they are eating well. This can also strengthen emotional attachment to the disease and identity as an anorexic (Osgood 2013).

Arndt has observed many instances of anorexia becoming a competitive activity in hospital wards. She argues that people with chronic disordered eating can quickly spot each other. Common points of observation include the presence of thickened body hair or brittle head hair, ritualised food behaviours, unusually visible bones, or excessive layers of clothing. This leads to the question of 'who's sicker? Who's thinner?'; that is, who is 'winning' at anorexia. She sees this as especially common in people who are not yet ready for recovery and instead wish to be the "'worst anorexic' on the ward" (Arndt 2000a). She suspects this is because it is easier to devote therapy time to competitive thoughts than it is to actually focus on the emotions and struggles brought to hand in the therapeutic process (Arndt 2000b).

Unsurprisingly, schools are also a common locus of self-harm clusters. Secondary school children often describe their self-harmful behaviours as a way of coping with extreme pressure during this life stage from family, friends, or sporting teams. For example,

> I'm 15 years old. I've been bulimic for two years. Body image has always been main concern as I'm a dancer. Also, i never feel like I'm good enough. My parent think that it's easy for a teenager to be a straight A student, a school athlete and a dancer. It really isn't. They always say that i could have done better, i could have been more graceful, i could have performed a little better…could have, could have! [*sic*].
>
> (PeiPei in Hutchings 2003)

In one school, Favazza came across a 'Cut of the Month' Club where students would compete for the best wound or scar. This competition was exciting and prestigious, granting notoriety to the student who could cause the most damage to themselves. Favazza compares the Cut of the Month Club to exclusive school cliques like cheerleading teams and other athletic clubs, which students traditionally enjoy and are keen to join. Those with high achievements in these clubs receive respect from their peers, and also get attention from the wider community (2011, p. 156). Similarly, Adler and Adler have observed 'sponsorship programs' in which groups of people (usually high school students) create rituals of harm that help to form a strong sense of identity (2011, p. 168). This is both a reflection of self-harm contagion and an indication of how beneficial it can be for group members to be injured with some sense of unity and greater meaning beyond the self. Favazza believes that school-age cutting is often a way to gain notoriety from peers, and to coerce parents into behaving in a specific way. Cutters tend to get attention from school staff and medical professionals, which can lead students who feel neglected to join in as a way of getting others to focus on them. He states that many children participate in cutting clubs because of these immediate benefits and will stop once the contagion dies down or once they become bored and move on to something new. Interestingly, he warns that children with mental illnesses may not be able to cast off these behaviours with such ease, and can be haunted by them for decades – long after they leave school and disconnect from the initial source of the contagion (2011, p. 156). This suggests that students *without* any clinically notable mental illness may be harming themselves for fun and attention if the benefits seem great enough.

Similar patterns can be observed with eating disorder point contagion. Many of Arndt's patients list anorexia 'tricks' learned from close friends and people they admired at school as part of the escalation of their eating disorders. Binging and purging buddies are also common ways of adding to a "secret club" mentality surrounding extreme diets (Arndt 2000c). Exemplifying this, Singaporean teenager 'Xener' explains how a pact she made led her towards a crippling eating disorder. Xener and two of her best friends decided to skip meals together at age fourteen, starting with the morning recess meal they were expected to eat at school. Soon they were skipping several meals per day and restricting food intake during family dinners. Xener used typical tricks she gathered from pro-anorexia websites, including hiding rice from her mother so she would think it had been eaten, and drinking vast quantities of water to quieten her stomach. This pact led her towards a serious illness, which caused her mother intense grief, and only abated after she started to play more intense sports that required greater caloric intake. Her friends either encouraged or ignored the impact of this dangerous pact (Xener 2017). Similarly, Arndt developed her laxative addiction after gaining inspiration from her high school homecoming queen. This student weighed ninety-two pounds, took seventy-five laxatives per day, and was reaching out to Arndt for help. In her state of mental fragility, Arndt's support was only superficial. Instead, she secretly "thought it was a great idea" and started to buy these drugs for herself (O'Neill and Cheakalos 1999).

Disordered eating hubs also form in tertiary education institutes, especially in college dorms and similar close-knit communities. Kokaliari suspects that it may be because the college environment is intensive and goal-oriented, leading some members to seek ways to alleviate feelings of distress and pressure to succeed (2014, p. 5). This competition can be seen in first-hand accounts such as one anonymous UCSB student who had bulimia prior to arriving. She explains,

> When I got there it got worse. So many tiny little perfect blondes with their tanned thin bodies poured into these little bikinis... Walking around with a colony of Barbie dolls, or close to it, I felt so inadequate. I threw up everything.
>
> (anon. in Tabah 2002)

People reported on one American sorority house where hundreds of sandwich bags were stolen from the kitchen and later found – filled with vomit – in the basement. The competition for who could eat the least or vomit the most resulted in the plumbing being replaced due to stomach acid damage (O'Neill and Cheakalos 1999). This is an extreme example, but many young people can escalate their disordered eating in settings like this because they are free from parental supervision for the first time. Cody, a college student interviewed by the Adlers, explained, "it just gets worse because there's no outside force preventing you" (2013, p. 36). In some cases, mentors and coaches in tertiary athletics programs have been known to *encourage* disordered eating in order to help students develop very particular physiques desired at an elite level of sport.

In particular, ballet and the idealised physique of the professional ballet dancer have led people down a path of disordered eating. In one confession on *Anorexic Web*, a professional ballet dancer in New York described her industry as "the breeding ground for eating disorders. It is very hard to not get sucked in to the downward spiral" (Daisy in Arndt 2000d). This spiral is not limited to professional dancers. Recreational classes for children also seem to have a similar effect. After enrolling in a ballet class at age 10, 'Ais', who was already suffering from bulimia, started to restrict her food intake to a piece of chicken per day to mirror what she assumed the diets of other ballet dancers and teachers were like. She recalls, "I came to believe that anorexia meant being feminine, dainty, graceful, beautiful, perfect, happy, popular and outgoing – the 'perfect' person. I wanted to be that person" (Arndt 2000e). Tanya from the popular eating disorder site *Break Her Down* also blames ballet for the development of her illness. Tanya describes ballet as a 'culture of criticism' where participants share a thin ideal. This is emphasised by long practice sessions where participants perform in front of mirrors with minimal clothing, making the details of their body a focal point. At the same time, students are encouraged to make their athletic performance look effortless and hide any physical discomfort from their extreme moves or unhealed injuries. Tanya remembers gossip every time a fellow dancer gained weight, and the extra attention that was given to those who were skinnier. By the time she was fifteen, she was taking five classes a week and existing on a maximum of

500 calories per day. It was at this point that her ballet teacher praised her physique in front of the other students (Tanya 2003).

Aside from these primary sources, the connection between ballet and disordered eating has been noted in scholarly studies. The Herbrich study explored ballet as a possible zone for *anorexia athletica* (or *hypergymnasia*) – a proposed eating disorder based on extreme food regulation coupled with an exercise obsession (2011). Some sports, particularly those connected to adolescent female athletes, seem to increase the likelihood of *anorexia athletica* – both encouraging extreme thinness and preventing complete starvation due to athletic performance requirements (Afflelou 2009).[3] While this diagnosis is not an official part of the *DSM*, it is valuable when examining disordered eating patterns in athletes who feel pressure to look a certain way for their sport. Herbrich *et al.* believe that sports such as ballet lead to a high risk of disordered eating because the participants must meet rigorous physical and technical demands, and are subject to sociocultural pressures to adhere to the 'correct look' of a svelte dancer with very low body fat. As such, ballet dancers consistently show higher rates of clinically diagnosed *anorexia nervosa* and other disordered eating patterns than appear in control groups (Herbrich *et al.* 2011, pp. 1115–1116). While ballet does not necessarily lead to a clinically diagnosable eating disorder, it can create a hub of extreme eating habits, as dedicated dancers "are a highly select population, where striving for a thin body ideal is seen as normal and advantageous" (Herbrich *et al.* 2011, p. 1120). This gives participants a strong motivation to restrict their intake and does not discourage them from excessive leanness that may come from undue caloric restriction.

These pressures appear to worsen if a person aims for a professional career in dance. As with 'Daisy' mentioned earlier, professional and pre-professional dancers show a greater risk of disordered eating. Herbrich et al. note that in exclusive troops, there are only limited positions available. These positions tend to be given to dancers whose body proportions match a slender ideal (2011, p. 1116). Similar findings came out of le Grange *et al.*'s study of a tertiary ballet school where pupils who presented with anorexia nervosa-like symptoms or amenorrhea were interviewed. This study was performed at a high-level institute where degrees and diplomas in dance were awarded, as there was intense competitive pressure to "achieve a slim body shape" in this milieu. Le Grange *et al.* note that the need to restrict calories and attain a very slim physique is even more intense in this context than in the general Western population. As such, *anorexia nervosa* is also more prevalent amongst professional ballet dancers (2010, pp. 369–370). What is even more common is partial symptoms of this disease amongst dancers. Le Grange *et al.* did discover some students who met diagnostic criteria for *anorexia nervosa*, but, perhaps more revealingly, found many more whose behaviours and attitudes were close or similar to those of a person with this disease, but which remained sub-clinical.

The general perception of fatness in this group seemed unusual. Although more than half of the students had a BMI under 20, 40% described themselves as 'fat'. This perception was reflected in their eating behaviour, with many showing signs of malnourishment. Thirty-two per cent described menstrual abnormalities of some kind, including several students who stopped menstruating during term time when their athletic demands were at their highest. To keep calorie intake low, one-third of students confessed to self-induced vomiting or laxative abuse. Ninety per cent of students restricted intake to the point of feeling lethargic, faint, or dizzy on a daily basis (le Grange *et al.* 2010, p. 372). While the sport as a whole cannot be blamed and should not be discouraged on principle, the emphasis on a very slender physique has certainly led vulnerable people towards highly restrictive eating behaviours. It also demonstrates that a specific culture and group can lead to point clustering of harmful behaviour – especially when that harmful behaviour is, to a degree, endorsed.

Evidence of Mass Clusters of Self-Harmful Behaviour

As with suicide, mass clusters of self-harmful behaviour have been caused by the media. A clear example is self-poisoning through the consumption of the yellow oleander tree, which started in Sri Lanka in 1980 and was spread through graphic media reporting. Ingestion of oleander commonly leads to vomiting, light-headedness, and disruption of the heart muscles (Khan *et al.* 2010, p. 115). In some cases, death can result. The Singhalese term for consuming the poison of the oleander tree, often in liquid form, is *känēru bonnāva*. In the seminal case of 1980, two Jaffna schoolgirls died from *känēru bonnāva*. Although the yellow oleander tree is native to the region, this now common method of self-harm was relatively unknown at the time. After widespread media reports on the death of the girls, there was a notable spike in hospital admissions due to oleander poisoning. By 1981, the local hospital had dealt with 23 cases. This was followed by an increase to 46 in 1982 and 103 in 1983. By 1990, this behaviour had spread southwards and thousands of cases were reported across the nation. By 2006, 93,733 people had been admitted to hospitals across Sri Lanka over the duration of the year. Today, *känēru bonnāva* is a highly prominent and popular method of self-poisoning (Widger 2014, p. 813). Many teenagers have seen their parents and their peers engaging in this act, leading one young male to explain in a 2003 interview that harming oneself in this way "isn't a big problem and it isn't so hard". His female contemporary explained that many youths want to swallow *känēru* to see what the process is like (Ratnayake and Links 2009, p. 392). While people of all ages and genders have been known to consume this poison, the risk factor remains highest for those in the same demographic as the original victims. Young women and girls remain the most likely to consume *känēru* in stressful situations, and the most likely to die as a result (Eddleston and Warrell 1999, p. 843). Had this original story never been broadcast, it seems likely that *känēru bonnāva* would not be as systemic as it is today.

Magazines also seem to be especially inspirational when it comes to the accidental dissemination of self-harmful behaviour. Adler and Adler date the rise in a broader public knowledge of self-harm and its techniques to 1996. In this year, magazines for teenage girls started to publish articles on the dangers of self-harm. This was followed by significant feature articles on the topic appearing in *The New York Times, Newsweek,* and *Time* from 1997 to 1998 (2013, p. 18). Emblematic of this was the *New York Times* cover story (Egan 1997) concerning an "attractive, blonde, upper-middle-class cheerleader" (Favazza 2011, p. 146) which seems to have set the scene for contemporary self-harm as a "pretty girl's problem". Disordered eating also became more of a journalistic focal point at this time. Many people with eating disorders learned of their existence or picked up additional tips and tricks from magazine articles lamenting these practices. For example, one girl with bulimia explained, "I got into this mess after reading an article in a magazine about how bad it is…so, I went against them and wanted an eating disorder [sic]" (Lisbon 2002).

Similarly, some of Adler and Adler's interviewees traced back the origins of their self-harm to articles in teen magazines such as *Seventeen* that started to appear in the mid-1990s (2011, pp. 57–58). Even though these narratives did not espouse the benefits of self-harm, the interviewees were able to gain inspiration and new ideas from reading them – such as taking aspirin before cutting to prevent blood from clotting (Zahl and Hawton 2004, p. 194). While this fact about the relationship between aspirin and blood thinning was meant to be an incidental part of a narrative about recovery, this did not prevent readers from noting it down as a useful way of causing increased blood loss during cutting. The intended message of the author or the publication is not necessarily the message that the readers will focus on. Vulnerable readers also expressed a strong identification with these publicised self-harmers when they detailed their emotions and pressures prior to recovery, and less interest in the process of recovery itself. Some interviewees were heartened by the fact that none of the self-harming teenagers had died or experienced serious consequences. Quite the opposite – they had all survived and were now represented in print as popular and exciting individuals who had dabbled with cutting as a powerful solution when times were tough (Adler and Adler 2011, pp. 57–58). It appears even the glamorisation afforded to someone having their story shared in a magazine is enough to interest and inspire others, regardless of the tone.

Studies into women's fashion and beauty magazines show similar effects at play with disordered eating. Since 1980, eating disorders have been a popular theme in these publications. Bishop argues that these articles are so similar that a 'metastory' can be noted: victims of disordered eating are lonely, selfish, and obsessed with perfectionism and control. They have done something wrong and made mistakes that have led them down this path. Their obsession with starvation comes on quickly, much to the horror of family members who cannot intervene. It tends to be triggered by a single event such as a coach suggesting weight loss. (This is even though eating disorders often manifest over a period of years and are influenced heavily by relationships with other people including family and peers.) Extreme and graphic descriptions or behaviours like purging are shared. Recovery tends to happen only under coercion, with medical professionals treating protagonists as petulant children regardless of their age or attitude. The recovery journey tends to be a very lonely one as the protagonist is sent away somewhere like an expensive in-patient treatment centre. While articles written in the 1980s tended to include complex recovery journeys, by the turn of the century, this process had been sped up to something much shorter and simpler. 'The media' in an abstract sense are to blame for this pathological obsession with thinness – with little attention given to more complex issues such as food or diet advertisements in the magazines that also share conventional anorexia horror stories. Essentially, eating disorders are presented in magazine stories as a personal failing of women who are hyper-fixated with their own internalised thin ideals. Female culture as a whole is also blamed, with severe and life-threating eating disorders presented as inevitable experiences for many young women or as a generic rite of passage (Bishop 2001, pp. 221, 227–234). In this way, both people with (or at risk of) eating disorders and their peers and family are dictated a normative narrative about what causes an eating disorder, how it might progress, and who to blame. Any obsession with celebrity thinness is thus seen as a by-product of self-obsession and compulsiveness, not a milieu encouraged by magazines themselves.

Nevertheless, Thomsen *et al.* found that such publications were central in "reinforcing the sociocultural preference for thinness" so popular at the turn of the century (2001, p. 50). When discussing magazines with those recovering from eating disorders, these researchers found very similar behaviours to those noted in pro-ana online communities where users share 'thinspiration' images of very slender models, often competing with them and each other to reach the highest levels of emaciation or 'perfect' certain body parts. A high drive for perfectionism is also present with the idea that a thin body can solve deeper social and psychological problems (Alderton 2018, p. 6ff). Thomsen *et al.*'s interviewees used magazine images as a 'how-to manual' for extreme slenderness and assumed perfection in order to fight against problems in life. In addition, many used these magazines to model adult roles, learn developmental skills, and feel mature. Much of this adult modelling is maladaptive, with readers enjoying content such as the weight of models and a perceived competition to weigh even less than them (2001, pp. 54–57). This is coupled with the apparent addictive qualities of magazines with some anorexia sufferers describing themselves as "addicted to" or "obsessive" about this text type (Carney and Louw 2006, p. 962). The slenderness of the models featured also allowed for the development of an interesting cognitive dissonance. Readers frequently saw models who had, or were close to, dangerously low BMIs. This made starvation seem less like a disease or a painful psychological disorder. One woman explained, "I mean on one page, you got the girl with the disease. On the other page, you've got the model. And they look exactly the same". Others saw this trend as ammunition against family members who thought they were too thin; magazines suggested this level of thinness and restriction was glamorous (Thomsen *et al.* 2001, p. 58).

In terms of thinspiration, fashion magazines seem to have provided a pre social media avenue for collecting the obsessive images of extreme slenderness and emaciation that would later be popular on Tumblr (Alderton 2018, p. 9). Multiple interviewees told Thomsen *et al.* that they cut out images of thin models and placed them in scrapbooks, displayed them around their houses, or stuck them to refrigerators. One called her collection an 'obsession book'. These were often used as tools of comparison as the readers tried to be as similar as possible to the ideal figures of models, often describing extreme frustration or even bouts of self-harm when they fell short (2001, pp. 56–57). They also picked up a range of tips and tricks from articles intended as eating disorder scare pieces. One woman remembers struggling to develop bulimia because she was unable to make herself vomit. She learned how to trigger her gag reflex by seeking out stories with tag lines like "Bulimia ruined my life, a true story" as they would contain content about purging (Thomsen *et al.* 2001, pp. 57–58). The 'life-ruining' dimension of the narrative could, it seems, be easily ignored.

Despite these issues, something important to note is that many of the women who spoke to Thomsen *et al.* were already engaged in disordered behavioural patterns with eating and body image *prior* to becoming interested in fashion magazines. This comparison and drive for thinness often started at elementary school and childhood sports or social activities – not in teen years or adulthood when they became the demographic for such magazines (Thomsen *et al.* 2001, p. 55). Others who speak of their disordered eating struggles are not especially impacted by magazines but used them to discover other avenues of pro-starvation content. One writes, "I read in a magazine about horrible things called pro-anorexic sites. So of course I looked for them" (Joe 2005). Magazines can also be antecedents or descendants of a broader interest in celebrity culture, which has also been connected to self-harmful behavioural clustering.

In a broader sense, celebrity culture and imitation of celebrities has led to echoing clusters of self-harmful behaviour. Celebrities who have self-harmed are often used as examples of successful people who have this habit, and articles exploring their self-harm have inadvertently educated their readers on new techniques for causing injury. Some celebrities have also been very open with their disordered eating. For example, in a celebrity profile in *Page Six* magazine (which was subsequently deleted), blogger and beauty columnist Cat Marnell celebrated her drug-taking habit and her bulimic behaviours. She explained, "I'm not a happy person. I'm a narcissist, but I hate myself". Marnell describes bulimia, something she learned from her mother, as "part of being a woman" and claims that "Real girls know how to do it" (Karni 2012). Hollywood celebrity culture has even led to people in the broader Los Angeles area being susceptible to this trend. Arndt feels that growing up in this city played a direct role in my disordered eating, as the shadow cast by the Hollywood sign engulfed me and the other hundreds of young people at my high school. We all wanted to be Somebody and we were told that in order to fulfill such dreams we must look the part.

(Arndt 2000f)

Arndt attended Santa Monica High where this drive to thinness, coupled with life stressors, created a 'perfect storm' for the initial onset of her disordered eating. Her parents went through a bitter divorce, which left Arndt traumatised and meant that daily activities like her mealtimes were not readily scrutinised. After being dumped by a boyfriend who told her she needed to lose five pounds, Arndt started to use powdered diet drinks to impress her celebrity-obsessed cohort (O'Neill and Cheakalos 1999).[4] This seems to be a case of mass contagion via celebrity culture encouraging point starvation clusters in communities with a close connection to them.

Well-known and beloved celebrities. including Princess Diana, Johnny Depp, Angelina Jolie, and Christina Ricci. have all admitted to self-harming in the past and have all given reasons why it worked for them at the time. Whitlock *et al.* believe that none of them actually intended to promote self-harm, but that their high-profile disclosures "may serve as vectors for contagion" (2009, p. 140). Indeed, many pro-self-harm websites list celebrities who have disclosed this behaviour (Lewis and Baker 2011, p. 393). These celebrities are usually contextualised as examples of self-harmers who have done well in life, or as evidence that self-harm does not stop a person from succeeding. For example, one pro-self-harmful behaviour blog *Ana saved me* explores the example of Princess Diana who cut her wrists, threw herself down stairs, and starved herself to "distract from the pain she felt for not being validated by those she loved", including her parents and her husband. The author of this blog sees openness about self-harm as a positive because "Princess Diana was so perfect….she openly addmitted to it…. i want to be perfect…just like Di [sic]" (Ana saved me 2004).

Presently, one of the most popular celebrities who has been open about self-harm is Demi Lovato – a singer and actor who has grown up with many members of the online self-harm community. Born in 1992, many of her fans were first introduced to her in the children's television program *Barney & Friends*. She was then signed to the Disney Channel and became a major celebrity, eventually starring in the popular show *Sonny with a Chance*. Meanwhile, her pop career was booming. Despite her success, Lovato was battling a drug addiction and intense negative emotions, which saw her hospitalised in 2010. She then confessed to having an eating disorder and self-harming in order to relieve tension and make her body match the torment she felt on the inside (Larkin 2012). She has since become a figurehead for the public discussion of mental illness, which is especially resonant with members of her generation.

Tumblr contains thousands of images of Lovato with a direct connection to self-harm content. The most popular of these are black and white gifs of Lovato being interviewed about her mental struggles and using self-harm as an answer. Some gifs contain words from her music or her interviews that are profoundly relatable such as, "Hard as I try I know I can't quit" (Jasmine Laurel 2016a), and "I looked so happy on the outside but, I was a mess on the inside" (Tasha 2016). Others have added commentary from those who posted them on Tumblr. Jasmine Laurel (2016b) agrees and empathises with Lovato's confession that she was not actively planning to kill herself but "if I had gone too far I wouldn't care". In reference to an image of Lovato grimly nodding when asked if she remembered the first time she cut, Tumblr user Tyler adds, "its just not something you can forget" (2014). All of these posts have been shared and liked more than twenty thousand times each. Although Lovato has now been diagnosed with bipolar disorder and is in recovery and ongoing treatment for her behaviour, she is not contextualised as a figure who should necessarily encourage others to do the same. Instead, she is seen on Tumblr as someone who is relatable and who mirrors and amplifies the feelings of pain and unworthiness in young self-harmers. She is also a figurehead for looking good while feeling terrible. None of these functions are especially recovery-oriented and seem to imply that even the most beautiful and successful people are plagued by cutting and self-hate.

Watching TV programs has also been an introduction to disordered eating and pro-ED communities for many. Documentaries on self-harm started to run on *The Learning Channel* in 1997 (Adler and Adler 2013, p. 18). In 2001, an episode of *The Oprah Winfrey Show* featured Holly Hoff discussing pro-ED communities online. This was the first major broadcast on this topic (Singler 2011, p. 19) and was followed by many other stories about young girls battling disordered eating.[5] Although these episodes were clearly meant to be warnings about a very dangerous illness, this did not stop the people featured from becoming role models. Osgood recalls being an "emotionally confused adolescent" who wanted to transform herself into the anorexic teens on *Oprah* who were "models of self-regulation" (Osgood 2013). Webmistress 'Mrs. Slim' learned about the 'pro-ana underworld' when she was flipping through channels and happened upon the Holly Hoff special. Until that point, she had felt 'very alone' in her starvation. After seeing that other people were interested in a similar lifestyle, she decided to use her professional web design skills to "help other 'Anas' out there not feel alone either" (Mrs. Slim in Druley 2002b). Similarly, a teenager called Abbey explained to *Teen People* magazine how the Holly Hoff episode introduced her to the world of pro-ana sites, which she quickly searched for and joined (Mackeen 2002, p. 149).[6] This is a notably common reaction to what was supposed to be a warning. The media – including news reporting, television shows, magazines, and celebrity culture more broadly – has the ability to inspire mass clusters of self-harmful behaviour simply by exploring its existence.

Notes

1 This was not the beginning of the notable rise in eating disorders but does reflect a new way of fostering them in everyday conversation. The emergence of anorexia nervosa as a prevalent Western illness is dated to the 1960s, with bulimia nervosa emerging en masse in the 1970s (Polivy and Herman 2002, p. 187).

2 In some cases, self-harm may have been a pragmatic choice to gain respite or additional care. For example, prisoners in Japanese internment camps during the Second World War inflicted minor injuries upon themselves in order to gain a few days of rest from hard labour (Curtin 1946, p. 586).

3 While ballet seems to be the most prevalent example of this behaviour, it also occurs in other sports such as track and field. One sixteen-year-old runner confessed to vomiting while running so that she could avoid doing so at home. After returning from her run, she will often eat, then feel guilty, fat, and bloated as a result. She explains, "Sometimes I've gone to bed and I've ate and I can't let myself fall asleep because I feel so fat so I'll do sit ups or something just to feel like I burned off something". These feelings seem unwarranted and paranoid, as her interviewer describes her as "petite and slim". Her teammates, who also appear fit and healthy, describe intense pressure to slim down from their parents and peers (Druley 2002a).

4 Los Angeles is not the only region where a culture of thinness is taken to the extreme. Another example is given by Hamshaw who moved to Washington, DC, and noted how many executive women were very thin and very muscular. While many are simply fit, others strike her as "hauntingly thin". She notes, "I wouldn't be surprised if you told me that there is a link between DC's culture of hyper-achievement and Type A tendencies and the fact that many of its professionals are *very* slender and *very* into fitness" (Hamshaw 2011). These local body norms provide an opportunity for shared fitness and diet behaviours to be taken to the extreme in similar patterns. Many other examples of extreme thinness culture in specific geographic locations exist on a global scale.

5 Disordered eating was already a popular topic on *Oprah*, with seminal episodes including "Rudine Howard's 17-Year Battle with Anorexia" (1994).

6 It should also be noted that many of the people who modelled eating disorders off television programs also describe other negative experiences in their life that took place prior or concurrently. For example, Sica saw a *Dr. Phil* episode about eating disorders and recalls "the girl with bulima [sic] sounded like she had a good idea to me". Although this episode did give Sica the idea to purge, her interest in doing so came from a summer spent with her anorexic father who made fun of her weight and restricted her eating so much that she became severely underweight under his care ("Sica" in Free Butterfly 2008).

References

Adler, P.A. and Adler, P., 2011. *The Tender Cut: Inside the Hidden World of Self-Injury.* United States of America: NYU Press.

Adler, P.A. and Adler, P., 2013. Self-injury and the internet: Reconfiguring the therapeutic community. *Reset*, 2, 16–40.

Afflelou, S., 2009. Place de l'anorexia athletica chez la sportive intensive. *Archives de Pédiatrie*, 16 (1), 88–92.

Alderton, Z., 2018. *The Aesthetics of Self-Harm: The Visual Rhetoric of Online Communities.* Abingdon: Routledge.

Are they perfection?...yes [online], 2004. *Ana saved me*. Available from: https://web.archive. org/web/20050318102659/http://www.freewebs.com/anasavedme/aretheyperfectionyes. htm [Accessed 18 Aug 2020].

Arndt, L., 2000a. Restricted Access: Page 1 [online]. *Anorexic Web*. Available from: https://web. archive.org/web/20000823224156fw_/http://www.anorexicweb.com:80/InsidetheFridge/ restrictedaccess.html [Accessed 28 Mar 2018].

Arndt, L., 2000b. Restricted Access: Page 2 [online]. *Anorexic Web*. Available from: https://web. archive.org/web/20000823224200fw_/http://www.anorexicweb.com:80/InsidetheFridge/ restrictedaccess2.html [Accessed 28 Mar 2018].

Arndt, L., 2000c. Table For Two [online]. *Anorexic Web*. Available from: https://web.archive. org/web/20000823224246fw_/http://www.anorexicweb.com:80/InsidetheFridge/ tablefortwo.html [Accessed 14 Mar 2018].

Arndt, L., 2000d. EDU: The eating disordered underground Page 4 [online]. *Anorexic Web*. Available from: https://web.archive.org/web/20000928235507/http://www.anorexicweb. com:80/EatingDisorderedUnderground/edupage4.html [Accessed 22 Mar 2018].

Arndt, L., 2000e. Food for thought: Page 5 [online]. *Anorexic Web*. Available from: https://web. archive.org/web/20001219114100/http://www.anorexicweb.com:80/FoodForThought/ foodforthoughtpc.html [Accessed 13 Mar 2018].

Arndt, L., 2000f. Starving for attention [online]. *Anorexic Web*. Available from: https://web.archive.org/web/20000823224316/http://www.anorexicweb. com:80/StarvingforAttention/starvingforattent.html [Accessed 15 Mar 2018].

Ascarelli, A., 1917. Self-inflicted injuries among soldiers. *The Lancet*, 190 (4905), 355–356.

Bishop, R., 2001. The pursuit of perfection: A narrative analysis of how women's magazines cover eating disorders. *Howard Journal of Communications*, 12 (4), 221–240.

Carney, T. and Louw, J., 2006. Eating disordered behaviors and media exposure. *Social Psychiatry and Psychiatric Epidemiology*, 41 (12), 957–966.

Cowdy, C., 2012. Resistant rituals: Self-mutilation and the female adolescent body in fairy tales and young adult fiction *Bookbird: A Journal of International Children's Literature*, 50 (1), 42–52.

Curtin, A.P., 1946. Imprisonment under the Japanese. *BMJ*, 2 (4476), 585–586.

Druley, L., 2002a. Starving for perfection [online]. *Minnesota Public Radio*. Available from: http://news.minnesota.publicradio.org/features/200205/08_druleyl_lifestyle-m/index. shtml [Accessed 6 Dec 2018].

Druley, L., 2002b. An interview with 'Mrs. Slim' [online]. *Minnesota Public Radio*. Available from: http://news.minnesota.publicradio.org/features/200205/08_druleyl_lifestyle-m/ interview.shtml [Accessed 6 Dec 2018].

Eddleston, M. and Warrell, D.A., 1999. Management of acute yellow oleander poisoning. *QJM*, 92 (9), 483–485.

Egan, J., 1997. The thin red line. *The New York Times*, 27 Jul., Section 6, Page 21.

Favazza, A.R., 2011. *Bodies Under Siege: Self-mutilation, Nonsuicidal Self-injury, and Body Modification in Culture and Psychiatry*. 3rd ed. Baltimore: Johns Hopkins University Press.

Fox-Kales, E., 2011. *Body Shots: Hollywood and the Culture of Eating Disorders*. Albany: State University of New York Press.

Free Butterfly, 2008. Life with ED [online]. *~ free the butterfly within ~: the haven of an ana butterfly*. Available from: https://web.archive.org/web/20080218052723/http://www. freewebs.com:80/free-the-bfly/lifewithed.htm [Accessed 6 Mar 2018].

Hamshaw, G., 2011. Eating disorders and the executive woman [online]. *The Full Helping*. Available from: https://www.thefullhelping.com/eating-disorders-and-the-executive- woman/ [Accessed 7 Dec 2018].

Hawton, K., Rodham, K., Evans, E., and Weatherall, R., 2002. Deliberate self harm in adolescents: Self report survey in schools in England. *BMJ*, 325, 1207–1211.

Heath, N.L., Ross, S., Toste, J.R., Charlebois, A., and Nedecheva, T., 2009. Retrospective analysis of social factors and nonsuicidal self-injury among young adults. *Canadian Journal of Behavioural Science/Revue canadienne des sciences du comportement*, 41 (3), 180–186.

Herbrich, L., Pfeiffer, E., Lehmkuhl, U., and Schneider, N., 2011. Anorexia athletica in pre-professional ballet dancers. *Journal of Sports Sciences*, 29 (11), 1115–1123.

Hutchings, M., 2003. Your emails and insights 4 [online]. *Body Cage*. Available from: https://web.archive.org/web/20030207083948/http://www.bodycage.com/yourinsights4.html [Accessed 8 Apr 2021].

Jarvi, S., Jackson, B., Swenson, L., and Crawford, H., 2013. The impact of social contagion on non-suicidal self-injury: A review of the literature. *Archives of Suicide Research*, 17 (1), 1–19.

Joe, 2005. [m]y story [online]. *Fragile Innocence*. Available from: https://web.archive.org/web/20041212013218if_/http://winkin.phpwebhosting.com:80/~joeic/privet/thin/me/mystory.html [Accessed 15 Nov 2018].

Johansson, L., Lindqvist, P., and Eriksson, A., 2006. Teenage suicide cluster formation and contagion: Implications for primary care. *BMC Family Practice*, 7 (1).

Karni, A., 2012. Up all night… With a drug addict [online]. *Page Six*. Available from: https://web.archive.org/web/20120910140228/http://www.nypost.com:80/pagesixmag/issues/20120906/all+night+Drug+Addict?page=1 [Accessed 14 Mar 2018].

Khan, I., Kant, C., Sanwaria, A., and Meena, L., 2010. Acute cardiac toxicity of Nerium oleander/indicum poisoning (Kaner) poisoning. *Heart Views*, 11 (3), 115.

Kokaliari, E.D., 2014. An exploratory study of the nature and extent of nonsuicidal self-injury among college women. *International Journal of Population Research*, 2014, 1–7.

Larkin, M., 2012. Demi Lovato reveals why she used to self-harm [online]. *Daily Mail*. Available from: http://www.dailymail.co.uk/tvshowbiz/article-2174674/Demi-Lovato-reveals-used-self-harm.html [Accessed 21 Sep 2016].

Laurel, J., 2016a. *Tumblr*. Available from: http://stillsomewhatsane.tumblr.com/post/74721986431 [Accessed 21 Sep 2016].

Laurel, J., 2016b. *Tumblr*. Available from: http://stillsomewhatsane.tumblr.com/post/74934291277/you-and-me-both-demi [Accessed 21 Sep 2016].

le Grange, D., Tibbs, J., and Noakes, T.D., 2010. Implications of a diagnosis of anorexia nervosa in a ballet school. *International Journal of Eating Disorders*, 15 (4), 369–376.

Lewis, S.P. and Baker, T.G., 2011. The possible risks of self-injury web sites: A content analysis. *Archives of Suicide Research*, 15 (4), 390–396.

Lisbon, L., 2002. Wednesday ~ June 26, 2002 [online]. *~*~Lux Lisbon~*~*. Available from: https://web.archive.org/web/20030204103613/http://studio_26.tripod.com/Home.html [Accessed 18 Aug 2020].

Mackeen, D., 2002. Waifs on the web. *Teen People*, 5(3), 147–149.

Newman, J., 1997. Little girls who won't eat. *Redbook*, 189 (6), 120–127.

Nock, M.K., 2009. Why do people hurt themselves?: New insights into the nature and functions of self-injury. *Current Directions in Psychological Science*, 18 (2), 78–83.

Nock, M.K. and Prinstein, M.J., 2005. Contextual features and behavioral functions of self-mutilation among adolescents. *Journal of Abnormal Psychology*, 114 (1), 140–146.

O'Neill, A.-M. and Cheakalos, C., 1999. Out of control. *People*, 51 (13), 52.

Osgood, K., 2013. Anorexia is contagious, and I wanted to catch it. *Time*. https://ideas.time.com/2013/11/15/anorexia-is-contagious-and-i-wanted-to-catch-it/

Polivy, J. and Herman, C.P., 2002. Causes of eating disorders. *Annual Review of Psychology*, 53 (1), 187–213.

Raine, W.J.B., 1982. Self mutilation. *Journal of Adolescence*, 5 (1), 1–13.

Randall, J.R., Nickel, N.C., and Colman, I., 2015. Contagion from peer suicidal behavior in a representative sample of American adolescents. *Journal of Affective Disorders*, 186, 219–225.

Ratnayake, R. and Links, P., 2009. Examining student perspectives on suicidal behaviour and its prevention in Sri Lanka. *International Journal of Social Psychiatry*, 55 (5), 387–400.

Self Injury [online], 2001. *MY secret PAGE*. Available from: https://web.archive.org/web/20011006000443/http://www.angelfire.com:80/pq/tynd/si.html [Accessed 28 Mar 2018].

Singler, B., 2011. "Skeletons into Goddesses": Creating Religion, the Case of the Pro-Ana Movement and Anamadim. MPhil Theology and Religious Studies. United Kingdom: The University of Cambridge.

Tabah, S., 2002. Your thoughts [online]. ~ *Anorexics Anonymous* ~. Available from: https://web.archive.org/web/20021127105423/http://www.anorexicsanonymous.com/ [Accessed 9 Apr 2021].

Tanya, 2003. Ballet [online]. *Break Her Down*. Available from: https://web.archive.org/web/20030616092009/http://www.break-her-down.org:80/famine/ballet.html [Accessed 19 Nov 2018].

Tasha, 2016. I looked so happy on the outside. *Tumblr*. Available from: https://www.tumblr.com/dashboard/blog/imperfect-panda/102744856869 [Accessed 21 Sep 2016].

Thomsen, S.R., McCoy, J.K., and Williams, M., 2001. Internalizing the impossible: Anorexic outpatients' experiences with women's beauty and fashion magazines. *Eating Disorders*, 9 (1), 49–64.

Too, L.S., Pirkis, J.E., Milner, A., and Spittal, M.J., 2017. Clusters of suicides and suicide attempts: detection, proximity and correlates. *Epidemiology and Psychiatric Sciences*, 26 (5), 491–500.

Tyler, 2014. its just not something you can forget.... *Tumblr*. Available from: http://truly-unstable.tumblr.com/post/78726693338/its-just-not-something-you-can-forget [Accessed 21 Sep 2016].

Whitlock, J., Purington, A., and Gershkovich, M., 2009. Media, the Internet, and non-suicidal self-injury. *In*: M.K. Nock, ed. *Understanding Nonsuicidal Self-Injury: Origins, Assessment, and Treatment*. Washington: American Psychological Association, 139–155.

Widger, T., 2014. Reading Sri Lanka's suicide rate. *Modern Asian Studies*, 48 (03), 791–825.

Xener, 2017. Struggling with eating disorders as a teen: 'We skipped meals together' [online]. *Yahoo! Lifestyle*. Available from: https://sg.style.yahoo.com/struggling-eating-disorders-teen-skipped-meals-together-091244116.html [Accessed 2 Oct 2018].

Zahl, D.L. and Hawton, K., 2004. Media influences on suicidal behaviour: An interview study of young people. *Behavioural and Cognitive Psychotherapy*, 32 (2), 189–198.

3 Echoing Self-Harmful Contagions from Fiction

Why do we have this morbid fascination with Everything ED related…what makes it so important that we watch every single episode, movie, interview, talk show, news broadcast there is on eating disorders?…This fascination…seems to be part of every eating disordered individuals psyche…we are simply collecting ammunition to show that we are the 'best' the most knowledgeable people out there. and when sick, but diagnosed, perhaps it is the desire to be the perfect anorectic, to have the anorectic personality down to a tee.

(Tabah 2002)

There are many movies on the topic of disordered eating and self-harm – most of which are produced in the United States as 'made-for-TV' items (later, streaming services). These seem to have formed perceptions about who is vulnerable to these behaviours. It has also introduced these diseases and their symptoms to curious viewers who have gone on to model what they observed in fiction. One of the earliest examples of this genre is *Kate's Secret* (1986), which explores a seemingly perfect housewife who develops bulimia as a way of coping with the hidden pressures of her life. As the genre developed, middle-aged characters were swapped for younger protagonists while retaining a common theme of the drive for female perfection. For example, *For the Love of Nancy* (1994) follows the story of a teenager who loses weight after minor surgery. Her interest in her new slim physique develops into anorexia once she leaves for college. *A Secret Between Friends* (1996) tells the story of two teenage best friends who encourage each other down the path of disordered eating so they can be more like a famous model they admire. Both girls have issues in their family lives, and one is told to lose weight by their volleyball coach. *Perfect Body* (1997) focussed on a young gymnast who is training for the Olympics. Her new coach suggests she loses weight, which soon leads her down the path of extreme restriction. A teammate teaches her how to induce vomiting so she can eat while still losing weight.[1]

This genre carried on into the present century with the addition of more storylines exploring self-harm in addition to starvation. *Sharing the Secret* (2000) follows the story of a popular and beautiful high school ballet dancer who develops bulimia. Her binge and purge cycles give her a sense of control over

DOI: 10.4324/9781003126065-4

her life. In a similar narrative, *Dying to Dance* (2001) tracks an aspiring ballerina who has been accepted into a New York ballet company and asked to lose five pounds. She soon loses far more than this during an addiction to diet drugs and disordered eating. *Painful Secrets* (2000) tells the story of a 16-year-old who feels unable to communicate her authentic feelings. When stressed by this, she cuts herself as a secret means of exploring and expressing her emotions. The next group of films in this category becomes a little more artistic with higher production values. *Perfection* (2009) explores the world of a young woman who cuts herself in order to feel alive. This is contrasted with the story of her mother who is addicted to plastic surgery for similar reasons. *Likeness* (2013) is a psychological drama tracking a young girl obsessed with beauty. The plot and style of the film become increasingly chaotic in line with the protagonist's advancing bulimia.

In the late 1990s and early 2000s, TV series also started to incorporate self-harm subplots into standalone episodes. In 1998, *Beverly Hills 90210* broadcast 'Skin Deep', an episode briefly focussing on guest character Monica, a friend of regular character Donna Martin, who cuts herself. Donna encourages Monica to get professional help when she discovers her secret. In this same year, *7th Heaven* released the episode 'Cutters' where main character Lucy Camden's new best friend Nicole is discovered cutting herself. Nicole is sent to rehab and Lucy's father educates the audience on the dangers of this behaviour. Later, main characters in fictional programs were given self-harm plots. In 2003, *Degrassi: The Next Generation* featured the episode 'Whisper to a Scream' where popular character Ellie Nash starts to cut herself in response to family pressures and poor academic performance.[2] In these episodes, self-harm is easily identified and treated by professionals who can make the problem go away and allow the dramatic universe to progress to the next 'problem of the week'.

The more recent films covering these topics have incorporated the increasing role of the internet in fostering harmful behaviours. *Starving in Suburbia* (2014) tells the story of a teenage dancer who becomes obsessed with Thinspiration sites and a founding community member called ButterflyAna. Her anorexia worsens the more her obsession grows. Similarly, *Little Miss Perfect* (2016) chronicles the freshman year of a straight-A student who suffers through family dramas, academic pressure, and her own high expectations. She discovers pro-ED blogs and uses calorie restriction as a way of gaining back a sense of control. Netflix's *To the Bone* (2017), discussed in the final chapter of this volume, also has a significant internet subplot as the protagonist is wracked with guilt over her pro-ana art leading to the death of another girl.

While there is diversity in style, era, and production values, all these films and TV episodes share important similarities. All protagonists are White and female. The vast majority are teenagers. The actresses who play these roles are all very beautiful and slim prior to the development of eating disorders. In terms of their motivation to cut or starve themselves, perfectionism is a major factor. Their enviable lives are revealed to be sources of pressure as they are asked to maintain very high academic or sporting performance. Many of the protagonists harm themselves in pairs or have friends and teammates who give advice on matters such as effective purging. More recent films include online friendship groups such as pro-ana circles. In contrast to enabling friends, these protagonists are often in conflict with family members who do not understand why they would cut or starve themselves. In many of these films, it is family members who push the protagonists into treatment programs where we get to witness their painful and often non-linear recovery journeys at the hands of medical professionals. The overall message of these films is that a person who cuts or starves themselves is likely to be a pretty, White, slim, sporty teenager whose close female friends have knowledge of purging techniques. She is probably a perfectionist whose behaviour is a desperate attempt to break free from high standards, family problems, or express inner turmoil in conflict with her public image. She may be encouraged to lose weight by a mentor such as a sport coach and is likely to want a slim body to improve her performance in a sport like ballet or gymnastics. Eventually her family will notice her problem and force her into treatment. In doing so, she will achieve freedom from her restrictive sport academy or her obsession with her grades. She is likely to recover before adulthood with the help of normative treatment options such as temporary residential therapy.

As explained earlier, celebrities can be powerful sources of self-harm ideation because they are appealing to people who seem successful, cute, glamourous, or charismatic. Many fictional characters have a similar effect on audiences. Whitlock *et al.* put together a comprehensive list of characters who harm themselves in movies, books, and songs. These characters tend to have numerous positive attributes. They are likely to be strong, engaging, and have a high level of character appeal for their audience (2009, p. 146). One example of this is *Girl, Interrupted* (1999), which follows the story of 18-year-old Susanna Kaysen who has a nervous breakdown and is placed in a psychiatric ward for a year and a half. Played by the beautiful Winona Ryder, Susanna is a kind, compassionate, and thoughtful protagonist who is easy to empathise with. She also takes an overdose of pills in order to convey her deep anxiety and discomfort with her surroundings. There is evidence that vulnerable people have learned from Susanna's behaviour. For example, one participant in the Zahl and Hawton study watched this film over seventy times, and obsessively read the book it was based on. She enjoyed this story because it made her feel less alone, but it also gave her the idea that taking an overdose would be an acceptable response to her negative feelings (2004, p. 193).

She is not the only person to have learned about self-harmful behaviour or its social functions via fictional treatments. In the late 1990s, Favazza rightly predicted that "with increased media attention it is probable that the number of self-mutilators seeking help will increase greatly" (1998). This seems to have been because of storylines where fictional cutters were shown receiving counselling, therapy, and outpatient treatments. At the same time, there is also evidence of people picking up negative harmful traits after modelling what was seen on television. For example, Williams argues that memoirs of illness and recovery and "pearl-clutching cautionary tales" are rife with tips and tricks for eating disorders. After watching a lifetime movie about an anorexic woman in college, she picked up the idea that 1,000 crunches were the right amount to burn off dessert (Williams 2014). This was not what the movie intended to teach, but it was the lesson she took away from it. One of Sales' teenage informants experimented with suicidal gestures she had seen in movies when she was feeling acutely depressed. She would gather up a handful of pills from her parents' bathroom cabinet and swallow them. Usually this resulted in her developing a headache and nausea after passing out, but she did once have her stomach pumped to save her life (2016, p. 169). It is very easy to find comprehensive lists of films on topics such as eating disorders, often assembled to help people trigger themselves or engage more deeply in a lifestyle structured around illness (see, for example, azula 2019).

Fictional characters, and their framing on the screen, can also have a significant impact on viewer's feelings about ideal bodies and feminine relationships with food. Fox-Kales (2011) argues that women and girls derive their "dream bodies" – often those of an unhealthy weight – via the movies. One young woman starved herself to look like Jennifer Aniston in *The Break-Up* (2006) in order to gain a sense of power and control during a breakup of her own relationship. Another dealt with her insecurities about her height by developing bulimia to be more physically akin to Reese Witherspoon and Sarah Michelle Geller in *Cruel Intentions* (1999). Cinema is an immersive environment where viewers receive a very immediate sense of what femineity, desire, love, and power should look like. Based on contemporary cinema, women are presented with a very narrow idea of bodily slenderness as perfection and a marker of success (2011, pp. 3, 21–23).

An example of this is noted by Wooden in her analysis of 1990s film adaptations of Jane Austen novels. In these films, part of the personal and moral development of Austen's heroines is their self-discipline when it comes to food. Their 'rigorous self-denial' of food is tied into their femineity, while less likeable female characters are seen overeating and chewing inelegantly as a way of framing their more selfish or impulsive traits. Wooden believes that this message is very clear and impactful to young women watching these films and aiming to model themselves on the protagonists: beautiful and successful ladies have discipline over their intake. She calls this symbolic function of food a kind of contagion that "replicates the energies that propel anorexia and tacitly endorses modern cultural forces that produce particularly female eating disorders" (Wooden 2002, pp. 222–223).

Even when food or the female physique is not an abiding theme in a film, an anorexic lens can be applied in order to highlight ways the text supports or illuminates experiences of starvation, perfectionism, the role of 'good' women in society, and so on. An example of a more oblique film used to further anorexia dialogue is Disney's *Frozen* (2013).[3] Holmes, a scholar in recovery from anorexia, was surprised when she was deeply affected by the film's popular track 'Let It Go' and discovered that many other people had made a connection between *Frozen* and the female experience of disordered eating. She argues that people engaged in pro-anorexia draw from a wider range of texts to construct their identity than may be anticipated. On the community site *MyProAna*, Holmes found many voices exploring Princess Elsa as an anorexic icon or 'Let It Go' as an anthem for the community. Interestingly, the specific meaning of these texts is not agreed upon. Some see them as an inspiring prompt for recovery while others use them to sure up anti-recovery sentiments. Of particular importance are the lyrics "Don't let them in, don't let them see/ Be the good girl you always have to be" and "Let it go, let it go/ That perfect girl is gone!", which speak to the common pressure felt by anorexic females to be the "good"/"perfect" girl (Holmes 2015, pp. 98–105). While this is a more abstracted reading of a text ostensibly about princesses reuniting and recovering their royal birthright, even hints of the anorexic mindset can be powerful forces in the reading of filmic texts.

Even without cinematic representations, classic literature aimed at women is awash with comparisons between the 'good' characters who are chaste in morals and appetite versus 'bad' characters whose gluttony or attachment to the sensual is reflected in the way that they eat. Giobbi notes this symbolism in canonical texts including Christina Rossetti's poem *Goblin Market* (1862) where the sisters Laura and Lizzie embody two pathways of weak, profane sensuality versus strong and sacred reason – played out in the purchasing of food and the temptations of taste. Giobbi observes similar themes in Emily Brontë's *Wuthering Heights* (1847) where extreme self-denial is inherent in the human experience and becomes a pertinent expression of internal pain. Protagonist Catherine fears adulthood, pregnancy, and the confines of bourgeois patriarchal adulthood. She starves herself to death in a fit of grief. Later, Heathcliff is so troubled by his own culpability that he follows a similar path of death by implied anorexia. Giobbi argues that both characters "seem to be killed by something within themselves. Their souls will their bodies into a slow and painful death by starvation". Food, or its denial, is an important expressive device of morality and selfhood in these foundational texts of the Western corpus (1997, pp. 77, 81, 88). While the physical bodies of characters like Catherine or Laura are only conjured in the reader's mind when engaging with written texts, there are still many clues as to who is thin, chaste, and strong versus who succumbs to sensual urges and is punished accordingly – much as there are in the Jane Austen novels that inspired the 1990s adaptations. This is more than just a case of the popular media encouraging skinniness. It is part of a long-term psychodrama played out in both factual reporting and fiction in which skinniness is representative of aspects of human achievement and morality – especially for females.

Contemporary Anorexia Books

> Had you recently read *The Best Little Girl in the World*, just as I had? Was *Wasted* your bible, as was mine?
>
> (Melissa in Arndt 2000a)

More modern books contain overt themes of self-starvation in the form of clinically diagnosable anorexia nervosa. Both fiction and memoir feature in this genre often read without too much attention paid to relative veracity. Popular anorexia books include Levenkron's *The Best Little Girl in the World* (1978), Wilson's *Girls Under Pressure* (1998), Hornbacher's *Wasted* (1999), Cullis and Bibb's *Bronte's Story* (2004), Kaslik's *Skinny* (2006), Howard-Taylor's *Biting Anorexia* (2009), Anderson's *Wintergirls* (2009), Hutchings's *Why Can't I Look the Way I Want?* (2010), and de Rossi's *Unbearable Lightness* (2010) (Shaw and Homewood 2015, p. 592, Troscianko 2018a, p. 6).[4] Much like the fictional films and TV shows mentioned earlier, these books are the stories of protagonists who are generally very engaging and interesting. Many are popular and talented people, and some are real celebrities such as Portia de Rossi whose svelte physique has seemingly earned her significant success as an actress. As such, it seems that several vulnerable people have hoped to copy them on their eating disorder journeys. For example, during her "search for an anorexic role model", Arndt came across a variety of books with anorexic themes designed for young adults. In her junior high days, she was especially taken by *Second Star to the Right* (1981) by Deborah Hautzig (Arndt 2000b). The lead character Leslie is smart, talented, attractive, and loved by her family and friends. She also models techniques like chewing and spitting her food into napkins to avert suspicion form her concerned friends.

It is plot points such as this that have proven inspirational – not in terms of teaching people to seek help but in terms of teaching them how to worsen their behaviours and take in fewer calories. Osgood, author of the memoir *How to Disappear Completely* (2013a), notes how she and other patients she met during treatment had "doggedly pursued anorexia" by seeking out memoirs on the topic and "becoming enamored with the idea" of starvation (Osgood 2013b). Similarly, Arndt calls herself a "student of starvation" who "sought out information on anorexia in an effort to learn how to be the 'best' at being the 'least' (in weight)" (2000c). She argues that books about anorexia, especially personal accounts, are well-loved for a reason. Because of the details contained in these texts, other people with the same illness can "study our disease not to free ourselves from it, but to become experts" (Arndt 2000d). Readers describe using these books "as a guide" and also because it is comforting to read about people with the same illness as oneself thus "not eating bread or potatoes or feeling holy about refusing a food no longer felt like a habit that was unrelatable" (Salman in Farah 2014). Instead, engaging protagonists also engage in habits and beliefs that outsiders would read as eccentric or worrisome.

This trend was also observed by Troscianko in her study of eating disorder patients. A significant portion of her respondents deliberately sought out fiction or memoirs about disordered eating in order to knowingly trigger an exacerbation of symptoms, even though they also knew that this genre would have negative effects on their mood and body image (2018a, pp. 8, 11). Reflecting on these findings, Troscianko hypothesises that feedback loops have a large role to play. For example, a person whose eating disorder has caused very low self-esteem is likely to read a text with this mindset guiding them. They may become fixated on associations of thinness with positive things, which makes them feel more determined to lose weight, and subsequently directs them towards more literature on this topic (Troscianko 2018b). Similarly, participants in the Shaw and Homewood study used eating disorder memoirs to help them feel entrenched in their disorder. The negative effects of this were recognised, but no respondents stopped reading. One called memoirs "almost porn for my ED". Participants enjoyed details such as low weights of protagonists, number of times hospitalised, or images taken of them at the peak of their illness. They felt a sense of achievement if they were 'worse' than the authors, or guilt and motivation to restrict more if not. Some decided they would need to lose more weight before deserving help. Memoirs also helped some with normalisation of their pathological behaviours by making disordered eating feel commonplace. They also taught readers new tips for restriction, purging, ideal daily calorie counts, extreme exercise routines, and deceiving others (Shaw and Homewood 2015, pp. 593–594). All of this occurred despite most memoirs ending with the recovery of the protagonist and ostensibly functioning as cautionary tales.

Unfortunately, Troscianko's and Shaw and Homewood's studies are some of the only ones to focus on this area. There is less research focus on contagious dimensions of self-harm in fiction, how this might vary from nonfiction reporting, or how individuals may be impacted differently (Scalvini 2020, p. 1564). Troscianko suspects this may be because of two main albeit contradictory factors. One is the belief that creative works cannot be seriously impactful on human health. The other is a reticence to see that literature can harm when there is evidence of it also having great healing powers (2018a, p. 15). Whatever the motivations, this is quite an oversight, as eating disorder fiction is an enduringly popular genre. In 2015, there were 245 matches for 'eating disorder memoir' on Amazon (Shaw and Homewood 2015, p. 591). In 2021, I found over 1,000 results using the same search criterion. To help address this lacuna, next I explore some of the seminal contributors to this genre of eating disorder fiction and memoir and how they have encouraged echoing self-harmful behaviour in fans (and sometimes in authors as well).

Steven Levenkron's *The Best Little Girl in The World* (1978)

Levenkron's novel *The Best Little Girl in the World* tells the story of a fifteen-year-old called Kessa who develops an eating disorder when her parents are distracted by her sister's disruptive behaviour. The story opens with Kessa in a ballet class where she obsessively compares herself with the other students and her teacher, Madame, in a hall filled with mirrors. Kessa finds her own physique wanting, noting her various failings such as the "grotesque bulges" of her thighs. Soon after, Madame asks her to slim down a little for a chance to become a real dancer (Levenkron 1996, pp. 1–3). Her quest to lose a small amount of weight quickly spirals into a full-blown eating disorder and obsession with perfection for which she eventually receives professional inpatient treatment. Throughout the book, her parents are baffled by her choices and fight with her to encourage recovery. Under the guidance of the understanding Dr Sandy Sherman, arguably based on Levenkron himself, Kessa slowly comes to terms with her place in her family and cements her recovery journey. *The Best Little Girl in the World* is generally taken to be the first major novel explicitly about anorexia nervosa.

There are several cases of this book inspiring readers to worsen their disordered behaviours. Arndt used it as a way of learning how to become a "good anorexic" in her formative years after first reading the book at age twelve (Arndt 2000e).[5] 'K' has a similar story of reading *The Best Little Girl in the World* as a child. When she was eleven, she discovered a copy of the book in a local supermarket. She read it, a few pages at a time, while accompanying her parents on their weekly shopping trip. Even though she was already slim, she became fascinated with anorexia and saw it as 'such an exotic disease'. In 1981, *The Best Little Girl in the World* was adapted into a primetime movie. K's schoolmates all watched the film. This was the point at which she decided to become anorexic because it would be 'neat'. She wanted to attract the attention of her drama teacher, and "loved the idea of getting so thin that my parents would freak out and just care about my life without my having to fulfill all their expectations". She succeeded in her aim of cultivating the illness, and ended up with a lifetime addiction to starvation that refuses to entirely abate even though she is now an adult with many years of therapy completed ('K' in Arndt 2000f). In reviews of the book, it is easy to find comments like "I read this book when i was about 11 and it honestly became part of my downfall. For me it was more of 'how to' then a 'dont be like her' [sic]" ("Sarah" in *The Best Little Girl in the World* 2008).

This infection was probably quite accidental, as Levenkron is a psychotherapist with expertise in eating disorders and self-harm. Major pro-ana commentators such as AnaGirlEmpath (2012) see him as the father of modern anorexia treatment. Twenty years after writing this book, Levenkron was still working eight-hour days delivering therapy in New York. He is known for treating patients across America and receiving cards and letters from former patients who owe him their recovery. He is also famous because "the vast majority of girls Levenkron treats get better" (Sheffer 1999). This is an interesting contrast to the impact of *The Best Little Girl in the World*, which seems to have made girls worse. Arndt feels that she would have been helped if the author or publisher had included a statement designed for people who were reading the book to find 'ways to practice' their eating disorder. She believes that a small note of understanding could have helped to encourage self-analysis as to why she and others were choosing to be so destructive and using their intelligence towards a dangerous act (Arndt 2000g). Further methods of handling potentially contagious ideas without excessive censorship will be discussed later in this volume.

Marya Hornbacher's *Wasted* (1998)

Wasted is perhaps the most popular and impactful memoir of anorexia and bulimia. Hornbacher's story is a painful, disturbing, and vivid recollection of a fourteen-year battle with eating disorders started at age nine. Her healing journey is non-linear as she goes through residential treatment, therapy, and moves across America – moving between moments of healing and relapse. Reflecting on her experiences, Hornbacher promotes the idea that eating disorders are deeply complex and caused by a variety of inter-secting factors. In her own case, she sees her behaviours emerging from a chaotic home life, cultural interest in thinness, and inherent personality features like perfectionism. As such, she also shows that there is no clear path for treatment or set moment at which a person is 'recovered'. Her main claim at the book's conclusion is that she, at least, remains alive. Hornbacher found the book very painful to write and did so mainly out of anger with herself and a "culture that celebrated eating disorders" and made them seem like "a mysterious, glamorous illness" when they are quite the opposite (Hornbacher in Ronan 2014).

Another thing Hornbacher had hoped was that her book could "speak *only against* eating disorders" but realised this was not possible (Hornbacher in Ronan 2014). This was not helped by her publishers. A popular edition of Hornbacher's *Wasted* shows the author looking very thin in a pair of jeans – a piece of clothing that she felt a great fear towards during the heights of her disease. Her publisher, HarperCollins, requested what she describes as "all the garish, train-wreck type photos of me at a really low weight" for the book, but she refused to give over these highly sensitive images. She com-promised on a less extreme picture, but still found their decision to use it as a cover image "incredibly distressing...I was mortified. It felt like, 'Do you not see how this replicates what I'm fighting against?'" (Hornbacher in Ronan 2014). Images such as this are likely to attract people who are interested in creating a physique like this for themselves, or who feel attracted to this sickly aesthetic.

Indeed, there are numerous examples of copycat behaviour caused by this detailed book. Osgood was inspired by Hornbacher's rigorous 202-calorie-per-day diet. When she was hospitalised for anorexia, Osgood discovered other patients who had also used this book as a catalyst and guide for re-stricted eating (2013b). Indeed, it is easy to find diets based on food consumption mentioned in this book online such as the 'Marya Hornbacher Diet' (Faux 2008). Others found nostalgia for the worst days of their disorders sparked. One commentator writes, "after reading just a few pages I realised how strong I used to be…how beautiful I was inside when I wasn't eating. I miss it". (Beauty is Bones 2003). Reviews on sites like *Goodreads* echo similar sentiments. One reviewer warns that the book reversed her recovery and left her in a worse condition. This was due to Hornbacher's perceived gloating and presentation as 'the worst and most ill anorexic/ bulimic in the world'. In response, she felt like Hornbacher was smarter and stronger than her with tips for weight loss. Her unincumbered discussion of disordered eating techniques "gives out secrets and tips that could easily kill you, glorifies it and makes it seem like its no big deal [sic]" (Ashley in Wasted 2018). Another reviewer sees *Wasted* as the source of anorexia tricks for the pre-Tumblr generation (Stephanie in Wasted 2018). Hornbacher is aware of people using her memoir in this way and found it 'heartbreaking' to discover this fact. She explains, "I was stunned. It makes me tear up just thinking about it". But despite her sadness, she does not feel guilt. She believes that "you're misusing it" if you use her book to trigger yourself or as a how-to guide; "that's your problem" and not hers to solve (Hornbacher in Ronan 2014).

Laurie Halse Anderson's *Wintergirls* (2009)

Wintergirls follows the story of Lia Overbrook who uses anorexia and self-harm to cope with the pressures of her blended family and her guilt over the death of her estranged best friend Cassie. Prior to her death from complications of bulimia, Cassie and Lia helped each other in their quest to be the skinniest girls in school. Anderson was inspired in this narrative by classical mythology, which she sees as a way of making difficult life issues clearer for children. In this sense, Lia is modelled on Persephone who was abducted into the underworld – sending the earth into permanent winter until her rescue. Anderson decided to write *Wintergirls* in response to her readers who felt safe sharing their own experiences with disordered eating and cutting with her. These stories were touching and showed her that many young people turned to this behaviour when faced with overwhelming pain. She was also encouraged by a doctor friend who saw large volumes of patients with eating disorders and thought a good novel on this topic could help. Anderson was aided by her medical advice, and also read medical journals and chatted with psychiatrists and eating disorder survivors to get a fuller picture of this behaviour. Anderson was initially uncomfortable writing eating disorder fiction as 'it hit too close to home'. While she does not feel she was anorexic, she did 'eat in an unhealthy way' in response to teasing about her body. The experience of writing *Wintergirls* helped her to "get rid of the snakes in my head and love my body", which is something she also hopes her readers can achieve (Anderson 2019).

Regardless of Anderson's intentions, it seems clear that *Wintergirls* has been used as a 'how-to manual' for starvation and self-harm rather than simply a cautionary tale or emotional support for those at risk. *TV Tropes* notes that the text is gruesome, dark, and ugly – aiming to show the destructive impacts of Lia and Cassie's behaviour. Nevertheless, "much to the author's dismay, *Wintergirls* is held up in certain circles as the pro-anorexia bible, its self-destructive and deeply disturbed protagonist an inspiration rather than a warning" with *TV Tropes* dubbing it as an example of "misaimed fiction" where fans, often en masse, interpret a book differently to its intended authorial aims (Wintergirls 2021). One reader claims that *Wintergirls* "made my eating disorder worse – and I'm not the only one". She was recommended this book by a friend when she was suffering from a breakup, her chronic depression was severe, and she altered between having no appetite and vomiting up the food she consumed. After finishing the book in one day, s he was smitten. She was especially drawn to Lia's power to effectively starve herself. She started to ask herself, "Why couldn't I be as thin as her? Why didn't I have the willpower to be her size?". To try and become more like Lia, she copied her compulsive calorie counting, extreme starvation methods, goal weight obsession, and time spent on pro-ana websites. She also learned how to cut herself for emotional relief and hide the evidence from family and friends. While she feels that books about eating disorders are needed in order to raise awareness, she believes *Wintergirls* has caused more harm than good (Ricks 2019).

One of the reasons Ricks find *Wintergirls* so persuasive is the evocative and immersive prose. She suggests that the high-quality writing is what makes the content contagious. This includes the mythological dimensions that Anderson wove into the tale. She notes,

> I was certainly enthralled by this 'fairy tale' about a fragile, porcelain girl on her quest to become 'the skinniest girl in school'. It is easy to forget that you are reading about a person with an eating disorder.
>
> (Ricks 2019)

Her informant 'Camille' agrees that the story is 'very romantic', even when discussing graphic and uncomfortable themes ('Camille' in Ricks 2019). Ricks also notes ways in which the text lends itself perfectly to the thinspo genre. One is the unique formatting of the book, which is stylized to match Lia's obsessive and intrusive thoughts like "Empty is good, empty is strong". She calls these "a collection of destructive mantras" akin to the experience of reading thinspo (Ricks 2019). Indeed, much thinspo has been created from this content. The term 'wintergirl(s)' is used on numerous Pinterest boards to collect images relating to starvation. For example, Lucy Moss's board 'WINTERGIRLS' contains quotes from the book, images of very thin, White abdomens, guides to calories, and text about darkness, pain, and monsters (Moss 2021). 'Em's' 'Wintergirls' board has a Soft Grunge aesthetic and focusses on emaciated, pale female bodies. A recurrent theme is girls who are able to circle their upper thighs with the fingers of one hand (Em 2021). There are also standalone pro-ED sites like *Wintergirls Wonderland* with an overt eating disorder theme. Exploring both anorexia and bulimia, this site reads:

> Mia – the close friend of Ana. Sometimes there is overlap between the two. It doesn't matter what you are we're all the same. We're all wintergirls.
>
> (Mia 2021)

This site provides the kind of tools that help a Wintergirl, such as tips and tricks for starvation and thinspiration quotes.

As with Hornbacher, Anderson has become aware of people using her book to trigger themselves. Even while writing *Wintergirls,* Anderson was aware that texts dealing with disordered eating have a potential for contagion. Taking this responsibility seriously, she spoke with mental health professionals who warned her that some readers might indeed use the text as inspiration for weight loss. Nevertheless, they encouraged her to continue as 'starvation tips are one click away on the internet' and many vulnerable people are triggered by everyday texts like magazine covers and billboards. These professionals led her to conclude that there was inherent value in 'books that tell the whole story' about eating disorders and which educate people and spark discussion on taboo topics. By telling an unglamorous story about starvation and cutting, Anderson believes she has created a 'positive tool' in *Wintergirls*. Indeed, many readers have contacted her to say that the book gave them courage to talk to their parents and doctors about their struggles (Anderson 2019). One wrote to her saying "thank you for talking about the destruction of eating disorders because if I had never read your book, I might be in trouble right now" (Anderson 2016), which is clearly her intended outcome.

Regarding those who use her book for pro-ED purposes, Anderson is "furious". She visited many pro-ana websites as inspiration for Wintergirls, dubbing them as places that "foolishly promote anorexia as a lifestyle choice" (Anderson 2014). While one reviewer notes that "in Lia's barren world, the warmest voices come from the anorexia chat rooms" (Feinberg 2009), this is meant to be more of a reflection of her sickness and isolation than an actual validation of these places. Anderson is very upset "with pro-ana people ripping out quotes from *Wintergirls* and posting them to help others starve themselves" as she wrote *Wintergirls* to showcase the fatal, horrifying aspects of anorexia and to point readers towards sources of help. As for pro-ana communities, Anderson understands their depression, loneliness, and desperate need for support but argues that they have not found real care in a space that advocates for the worsening of their disease (Anderson 2014). More dimensions of this debate will be considered in the following chapters, but overall, Anderson's frustrations over her book being used as thinspo have done very little to stop this from happening.

Conclusion

A fundamental dimension of human culture is our ability to learn from, and imitate, one another. This human drive to mimic is not always positive and constructive. It can lead us towards copying destructive and self-harmful behaviours – especially from people whose demographics or situation seem to mirror our own. It can also lead us to learn harmful social scripts from fictional sources. As Kral notes in this theory of suicide, feelings of perturbation are part of the human experience and happen when a person's tolerance threshold is crossed. While people who are suicidal are in a state of perturbation, perturbation does not lead every person to such lethal acts. Ideas about lethal responses to emotional duress come from our cultural surround (Kral 2019, p. 7). This means that when a person feels acutely unhappy and wishes to behave in a manner that reflects this, they can find behavioural models from people or texts that show behavioural responses to similar levels of perturbation. This does not necessarily mean just suicide. For example, Millard notes that self-harm in the media, especially after the seminal self-harm decade of the 1990s, carries with it an entrenched idea of young, attractive women who cut. This, he believes, gives women a socially recognised script to act out when they feel distressed. This, in turn, creates a looping effect where more people act in keeping with the script, thus making it more prominent (2013, p. 136). We learn such scripts from the media or close associates. While the idea that pain, or even death, can be a relief is something that we often realise through personal somatic exploration, the way in which we cause this pain to occur can be determined through powerful social factors.

To this end, this chapter has explored theories underpinning clusters, contagions, and other ways that damaging human behaviour can be spread across groups. While it is typical to use these methods as a lens for understanding suicide, I have outlined many ways in which they also shed light on other auto-aggressive acts such as self-harm or eating disorders. Magazines, celebrities, fictional works, the news, and memoirs all have the potential to model self-harmful behaviours and encourage them to echo through time and space – especially with the advent of the internet collapsing prior barriers between communities and weakening the temporal limits of clusters. This leads to a very difficult situation for anyone aiming to censor problematic media. In a world where people's triggers and sources of damaging information include texts developed by the National Eating Disorder Association (Shaw and Homewood 2015, p. 592), or when they find themselves painfully obsessing over food themes in *The Hobbit* (1937) (Troscianko 2018a, p. 12), there is only so much that can be done to lessen this complex web of contagion.

This is even more difficult now that the internet is such a core factor in human communication. For young people in particular, in-person and on-line social spaces are deeply intertwined. Ignoring this contemporary change will limit our understanding of patterns of suicide in this demographic

(Heffel *et al.* 2015, p. 296). Pirkis and Blood point out a significant *lacuna* in the area of suicide and suicide-framing in online media for teenagers and young people (2001, p. 169), which this volume aims to resolve. One area that will be discussed is the fact that internet groups often feel like the safest place to disclose 'dark' feelings. In the Blum study, the majority of young people surveyed indicated that they would opt to talk to their peers if they were feeling suicidal. The second most popular answer was to speak to nobody (2012, p. S42). More reputable sources of information such as school counsellors were not a common choice, nor were parents. It seems that many younger people are learning how to act and how to self-soothe from their peers, from strangers online, and from stories that they hear on the news, watch on TV, or read in books.

At present, there is also difficulty in determining postvention strategies for young people exposed to a contagion or cluster of harmful behaviour. The internet has made traditional strategies less efficacious, as it is harder to create a safe and controlled environment in the wake of tragedy. When examining their youth suicide case study, Heffel *et al.* noted that many students were confused by the actions of the school. Using recognised best practice at the time, the school launched awareness programs about bullying and suicide, and provided resources for working through grief. They also adhered to guidelines suggesting limited memorialisation of the deceased to avoid accidental glamourisation of their loss. Unfortunately, many students were at odds with this choice and took it as a sign that they were expected to return to 'business as usual'. Not being ready, many turned to social networking as a space where they could carry on processes of grief and memorialisation (Heffel *et al.* 2015, p. 296). This is an understandable response, but it still places them in a context where contagion can have a powerful effect through, for example, explicit discussion of suicide method. This youth-generated content is not shaped by media professionals or those with awareness of safe suicide discussions (Robinson *et al.* 2017). This is also happening in a context where young people who are close to epicentres of suicide bereavement are unhopeful about prevention and the impact of help-seeking behaviour (Abbott and Zakriski 2014, p. 679). In the following chapters, I explore online content deemed problematic and censorship efforts aiming to limit contagion and keep discussions of self-harm, eating disorders, and suicide in the hands of professionals. While intentions are usually good, there are multiple flaws and misunderstandings that need to be addressed in order to develop new best practices with the internet in mind.

Notes

1 These texts were all produced concurrently with similar non-fiction stories in the same genre. For example, *An Anorexic's Tale: The Brief Life of Catherine* (1988) is a true biopic of a fifteen-year-old who develops anorexia and her seven-year-struggle as the disease steals her health and independence. *The Secret Life of Mary-Margaret* (1992) is also a biopic,

exploring the eponymous character's growing obsession with beauty and the modelling world. Mary-Margaret learns to binge and purge from another aspiring model, and the disease slowly takes over her life.

2 For a comprehensive analysis of this episode, see Sternudd (2018).

3 While this film does not focus on any specific discussions of weight, eating, or restriction, the idealised and impossible physiques of protagonists Anna and Elsa and Disney Princesses as a whole have been reflected upon as "thinspiration" (e.g., see, Holmes (2015, p. 111ff)).

4 Even Stephen King/Richard Bachman's *Thinner* (1984) where the protagonist loses weight rapidly after a Gypsy curse is regularly cited as an appropriate addition to this list. For example, although Joe is aware that the book is about unintentional, supernatural weight loss, she still found it "quite triggering" and suggests this is because "It's perhaps every hungry anorexics dream, to be able to eat up to 8 000 calories a day and still lose two pounds" (Joe 2005).

5 Remembering this, Arndt was concerned about the impact of telling her own story of anorexia and recovery, which was broadcast on *Dateline NBC* and written up in *People Magazine* in 1999. Nevertheless, from her own experience, she knows that anyone using it as thinspo would have been struggling before taking tips from her story (Arndt 2000e).

References

Abbott, C.H. and Zakriski, A.L., 2014. Grief and attitudes toward suicide in peers affected by a cluster of suicides as adolescents. *Suicide and Life-Threatening Behavior*, 44 (6), 668–681.

AnaGirlEmpath, 2012. Understanding the ProAna Movement I: Background & precipitating factors [online]. *YouTube*. Available from: https://www.youtube.com/watch?v=GYy1_zNvkHA [Accessed 29 Aug 2018].

Anderson, L.H., 2014. I'm furious with pro-ana people ripping out quotes [online]. *Tumblr*. Available from: https://lauriehalseanderson.tumblr.com/post/68575414912/im-furious-with-pro-ana-people-ripping-out-quotes [Accessed 24 Feb 2021].

Anderson, L.H., 2016. Letter from a fan [online]. *Laurie Halse Anderson's Tumblr*. Available from: https://lauriehalseanderson.tumblr.com/post/117732893001/letter-from-a-fan-who-gave-permission-for-me-to [Accessed 2 Apr 2021].

Anderson, L.H., 2019. Wintergirls Q&A [online]. *Mad Woman in the Forest*. Available from: https://madwomanintheforest.com/wintergirls-qa/ [Accessed 23 Feb 2021].

Arndt, L., 2000a. EDU: The eating disordered underground Page 4 [online]. *Anorexic Web*. Available from: https://web.archive.org/web/20000928235507/http://www.anorexicweb.com:80/EatingDisorderedUnderground/edupage4.html [Accessed 22 Mar 2018].

Arndt, L., 2000b. The edible digest: Books [online]. *Anorexic Web*. Available from: https://web.archive.org/web/20001121062900fw_/http://www.anorexicweb.com:80/InsidetheFridge/edibledigest.html [Accessed 7 Mar 2018].

Arndt, L., 2000c. Mission & explanation statement: Why I do what I do at the anorexic web [online]. *Anorexic Web*. Available from: https://web.archive.org/web/20000522063507/http://www.anorexicweb.com:80/Taste/missionstatement.html [Accessed 21 Mar 2018].

Arndt, L., 2000d. Restricted access: Page 1 [online]. *Anorexic Web*. Available from: https://web.archive.org/web/20000823224156fw_/http://www.anorexicweb.com:80/InsidetheFridge/restrictedaccess.html [Accessed 28 Mar 2018].

Arndt, L., 2000e. Introduction to taste [online]. *Anorexic Web*. Available from: https://web. archive.org/web/20000823224118/http://www.anorexicweb.com:80/Taste/taste.html [Accessed 7 Mar 2018].

Arndt, L., 2000f. Wishbone: The secret wish to be or continue to be anorexic (Part 4) [online]. *Anorexic Web*. Available from: https://web.archive.org/web/20000823224419/ http://www.anorexicweb.com:80/Wishbone/wishbonepage4.html [Accessed 8 Mar 2018].

Arndt, L., 2000g. Methods of madness [online]. *Anorexic Web*. Available from: https://web. archive.org/web/20000615191459fw_/http://www.anorexicweb.com:80/InsidetheFridge/ methodsofmadness.html [Accessed 8 Mar 2018].

azula, 2019. thread of ED movies!!! [online]. *Twitter*. Available from: https://twitter.com/ fatandrepulsive/status/1083072681438699520 [Accessed 8 Jul 2020].

Beauty is Bones, 2003. The artist in you [online]. *Beauty is Bones' Journal*. Available from: https://web.archive.org/web/20060718022601/http://www.blurty.com:80/users/ beautyisbones/ [Accessed 9 Oct 2018].

Blum, R., Sudhinaraset, M., and Emerson, M.R., 2012. Youth at risk: Suicidal thoughts and attempts in Vietnam, China, and Taiwan. *Journal of Adolescent Health*, 50 (3), S37–S44.

Em, 2021. Wintergirls [online]. *Pinterest*. Available from: https://www.pinterest.com.au/ estrat570/wintergirls/ [Accessed 24 Feb 2021].

Farah, S.H., 2014. Ramadan is tough for Muslims with eating disorders [online]. *Munchies*. Available from: https://munchies.vice.com/en_us/article/nz9x97/ramadan-is-tough-for-muslims-with-eating-disorders [Accessed 29 Aug 2018].

Faux, M., 2008. Marya Hornbacher diet [online]. *Fading Obsession:: Pro Ana Mia Website plus Forum*. Available from: https://web.archive.org/web/20080 724115050/http://www.fading-obsession.com/diets/marya-hornbacher-diet.php [Accessed 5 May 2021].

Favazza, A.R., 1998. The coming of age of self-mutilation. *Journal of Nervous & Mental Disease*, 186 (5), 259–268.

Feinberg, B., 2009. Skin and bone. *The New York Times Book Review*, 2009-05-10, p. 19.

Fox-Kales, E., 2011. *Body Shots: Hollywood and the Culture of Eating Disorders*. Albany: State University of New York Press.

Giobbi, G., 1997. 'No bread will feed my hungry soul': Anorexic heroines in female fiction – from the example of Emily Brontë as mirrored by Anita Brookner, Gianna Schelotto and Alessandra Arachi. *Journal of European Studies*, 27 (1), 073–092.

Heffel, C., Riggs, S.A., Ruiz, J.M., and Ruggles, M., 2015. The aftermath of a suicide cluster in the age of online social networking: A qualitative analysis of adolescent grief reactions. *Contemporary School Psychology*, 19 (4), 286–299.

Holmes, S., 2015. 'That perfect girl is gone': Pro-ana, anorexia and Frozen (2013) as an 'eating disorder' film. *Participations*, 12 (2), 98–120.

Joe, 2005. [t]hinner – stephen king [online]. *Fragile Innocence*. Available from: https://web. archive.org/web/20041216094649if_/http://winkin.phpwebhosting.com:80/~joeic/ privet/thin/media/book2.html [Accessed 14 Nov 2018].

Kral, M.J., 2019. *The Idea of Suicide: Contagion, Imitation, and Cultural Diffusion*. Abingdon: Routledge.

Levenkron, S., 1996. *The Best Little Girl in the World*. London: Puffin.

Mia [online], 2021. *Wintergirls Wonderland*. Available from: http://wintergirlswonderland. weebly.com/mia.html [Accessed 2 Apr 2021].

Millard, C., 2013. Making the cut: The production of 'self-harm' in post-1945 Anglo-Saxon psychiatry. *History of the Human Sciences*, 26 (2), 126–150.

Moss, L., 2021. WINTERGIRLS [online]. *Pinterest*. Available from: https://www.pinterest.com.au/llluuucccyyy/wintergirls/ [Accessed 24 Feb 2021].

Osgood, K., 2013a. *How to Disappear Completely: On Modern Anorexia*. London: Duckworth Overlook.

Osgood, K., 2013b. Anorexia is contagious, and I wanted to catch it. *Time*. https://ideas.time.com/2013/11/15/anorexia-is-contagious-and-i-wanted-to-catch-it/

Pirkis, J.E. and Blood, R.W., 2001. Suicide and the media. Part III: Theoretical issues. *Crisis*, 22 (4), 163–169.

Ricks, E., 2019. 'Wintergirls' by Laurie Halse Anderson made my eating disorder worse — And I'm not the only one [online]. *Bustle*. Available from: https://www.bustle.com/p/wintergirls-by-laurie-halse-anderson-made-my-eating-disorder-worse-im-not-the-only-one-15649710 [Accessed 23 Feb 2021].

Robinson, J., Bailey, E., Hetrick, S., Paix, S., O'Donnell, M., Cox, G., Ftanou, M., and Skehan, J., 2017. Developing social media-based suicide prevention messages in partnership with young people: Exploratory study. *JMIR Mental Health*, 4 (4), e40.

Ronan, A., 2014. 'Like seeing a ghost': Wasted, 15 years later [online]. *The Cut*. Available from: https://www.thecut.com/2014/07/like-seeing-a-ghost-wasted-15-years-later.html [Accessed 27 Aug 2018].

Sales, N.J., 2016. *American Girls: Social Media and the Secret Lives of Teenagers*. First edition. New York: Alfred A. Knopf.

Scalvini, M., 2020. *13 Reasons Why*: Can a TV show about suicide be 'dangerous'? What are the moral obligations of a producer? *Media, Culture & Society*, 42 (7–8), 1564–1574.

Shaw, L.-K. and Homewood, J., 2015. The effect of eating disorder memoirs in individuals with self-identified eating pathologies. *The Journal of Nervous and Mental Disease*, 203 (8), 591–595.

Sheffer, S., 1999. Eating disorders: Cracking the code – An interview with Steven Levenkron [online]. *New Moon Network*. Available from: https://www.susannahsheffer.com/uploads/1/1/6/7/11672632/levenkroninterview.pdf [Accessed 21 Jul 2020].

Sternudd, H.T., 2018. Ellie's first time: Constructing self-cutting in a teen drama. *Journal of Gender Studies*, 27 (5), 574–588.

Tabah, S., 2002. ED Specials [online]. *~ Anorexics Anonymous ~*. Available from: https://web.archive.org/web/20021218133950/http://www.anorexicsanonymous.com/whats_on_tv.htm [Accessed 9 Apr 2021].

The Best Little Girl in the World [online], 2008. *goodreads*. Available from: https://www.goodreads.com/work/best_book/1082053-the-best-little-girl-in-the-world [Accessed 1 Apr 2021].

Troscianko, E., 2018a. Literary reading and eating disorders: Survey evidence of therapeutic help and harm. *Journal of Eating Disorders*, 6 (1), 1–17.

Troscianko, E., 2018b. New research explores how reading affects eating disorders – For good and ill [online]. *The Conversation*. Available from: http://theconversation.com/new-research-explores-how-reading-affects-eating-disorders-for-good-and-ill-93040 [Accessed 27 Jan 2021].

Wasted [online], 2018. *goodreads*. Available from: https://www.goodreads.com/work/best_book/1256238-wasted-a-memoir-of-anorexia-and-bulimia [Accessed 1 Apr 2021].

Whitlock, J., Purington, A., and Gershkovich, M., 2009. Media, the internet, and nonsuicidal self-injury. *In*: M.K. Nock, ed. *Understanding Nonsuicidal Self-injury: Origins, Assessment, and Treatment*. Washington: American Psychological Association, 139–155.

Williams, M., 2014. Unpopular opinion: Pro-Ana websites were a positive influence in helping me recover from my eating disorder [online]. *xoJane*. Available from: http://www.xojane. com/issues/unpopular-opinion-pro-ana-websites-were-a-positive-influence-in-helping-me-recover-from-my-eating-disorder?utm_medium=facebook [Accessed 3 Jan 2017].

Wintergirls, 2021. *TV Tropes*. https://tvtropes.org/pmwiki/pmwiki.php/Literature/ Wintergirls

Wooden, S.R., 2002. 'You even forget yourself': The cinematic construction of anorexic women in the 1990s Austen films. *Journal of Popular Culture*, 32 (2), 221–235.

Zahl, D.L. and Hawton, K., 2004. Media influences on suicidal behaviour: An interview study of young people. *Behavioural and Cognitive Psychotherapy*, 32 (2), 189–198.

Section II

Harmful Ideas Online

4 An Overview of Echoing Self-Harmful Behaviours and the Internet

Introduction

> The only people that understand are you people, here in the online world and if I didn't have that then I know I would not be here. But the 'outsiders' see, they just don't understand that. I don't know whch way to turn, I don't know what to do. Suicidal thoughts are frequently entering my mind, a screaming noise seems to be nested inside my head [*sic*].
>
> (Lou 2003)

People who turn to self-harmful online spaces tend to be in significant pain. This pain, and its symptoms, can be very isolating experiences. Those who cut, starve, or otherwise hurt themselves to communicate distress are generally met with horror or misunderstanding by those who have not experienced this depth of pain or the responses to pain they have chosen. The internet is a place where people who make deviant choices can come together and find support and empathy. It is also a place where self-harmful behaviours can echo, teaching individuals dangerous new techniques, normalising secrecy in the face of distress, or leading to competitive behaviour over the question of who is the sickest, bravest, or the furthest from health. In this chapter, I explore a more nuanced take on the content and functions of pro-self-harmful behaviour groups. Some elements are acutely dangerous, while others are very supportive. There is a complex spectrum of content and outcomes, meaning there is no singular way to interpret or 'deal with' these spaces.

A key question when examining online groups is whether discussions about the positive aspects of self-harmful behaviour, and explicit images and instructions, can lead to an increase in echoing self-harmful behaviour. There are valid concerns that young people who are prone to self-harm and risky behaviours will see information about suicide online, thus making them vulnerable to suicidal ideation (Kirmayer 2012, p. 1016). The same can be said of activities like cutting or purging. Certainly, there are users in these spaces who believe such problematic things as "THIN IS THE ONLY WAY WORTH LIVING! so… starve me, please!;)" (Becca 2007), and who communicate such mantras with others. Nevertheless, despite suggestions from the media, only a

DOI: 10.4324/9781003126065-6

minority of pro-ana bloggers actually describe their illness as a lifestyle choice (Yeshua-Katz 2015, p. 1352). Engaging with pro-ana spaces does not necessarily lead to increased levels of disordered behaviour (Mulveen and Hepworth 2006, p. 283). While echoing self-harmful behaviour certainly occurs in these spaces, its actual manifestation is more subtle and unpredictable than might be initially imagined. In this chapter, I explore common themes and behaviours in self-harmful internet communities, and examine how actions like scripting facilitate hubs of resistance against stigmatisation and normative medical belief.

An Overview of Online Dangers

Overall, research is inconsistent about the relative dangers of the online space. As Hanson notes, proactive self-harmful communities would not exist without the internet and its boundless, asynchronous nature. Nevertheless, while it is incorrect to say that the internet can do something like "evoke eating disorders in women ... the electronic frontier [may be] complicit in the provocation of certain pre-existing behavior" (Hanson 2003, p. 37). This has happened through the creation of online spaces where eating disorders (and other self-harmful behaviours) could be given new social and discursive attention. In such online spaces, the pathological status of self-harmful behaviour does not stop discussions or articulations of distress and other complex feelings amongst participants (Burke 2012, p. 43). To explain this phenomenon, Haas *et al.* use the terminology "Online Negative Enabling Support Group" (ONESG). Such groups thrive due to the anonymity of the internet protecting them during the expression of extreme or stigmatised views. In this safe space, participants can have their negative behaviours and self-images viewed in an affirming way and discussed without challenge. This is in contrast to typical support groups where participants are encouraged to reframe their self-image in a positive light and work towards constructive and socially accepted behaviours (Haas *et al.* 2011, pp. 51–52). Similarly, Pater *et al.* use the term "support networks" to denote groups that support actions associated with disease (2016, p. 1187). These groups can be in support of actions as significantly deviant and dangerous as suicide and can lead to outcomes including completed suicide pacts (Seko 2008).

As internet usage has grown, self-harmful activities have increased alongside greater awareness of such emotional issues (Adler and Adler 2011, p. 168, Le *et al.* 2012, p. 344). Discussions between participants have become international and asynchronous, transcending older temporal boundaries (Hanson 2003, p. 38). These experiences are intimate but also free or very low-cost, making them an accessible way of connecting deeply with others (Swannell *et al.* 2010, p. 178). Disembodied communication of this kind can be appealing to those who struggle with close social contact (Brady 2014, p. 219). Nevertheless, these discussions have the potential to be extremely damaging and dangerous, such as guides for effective suicide plans and access to lethal drugs from unregulated pharmacies (Luxton *et al.* 2012, p. s196). Online communities are both a sanctuary for deviant behaviours like self-harm or -starvation and a place where these harmful behaviours become exacerbated over time (Maratea and Kavanaugh 2012, p. 105). They can lead to blurring of online and offline behaviours and identities, which can be problematic in terms of the spread of deviance (Hipple Walters *et al.* 2016, p. 223). They can also feed the transmutation of individual suffering into group suffering, thus spreading negative affect and fostering distressed worldviews (Alderton 2018, p. 6).

A significant perceived threat of the internet is the ability for "web 2.0"[1] users to create and share their own content without needing the external approval of governing bodies like book publishers or censorship boards. On a more domestic level, this means children creating and sharing ideas without the consent and control of their parents. This has led to a new area of concern, which Boyd *et al.* dub "youth-generated problematic content" (including sexting, spreading videos of gang fights, and creating communities to promote eating disorders and self-harm). They specify that teens have contributed to online problematic content since the 1990s, which has often been of concern to adults and parents. But through the rise of social media and social networking, this content has become more socially prominent and more impactful on everyday lives (2011, p. 3). It has also raised questions about the impact of unregulated, interactive new media on mass and point clusters (Pirkis and Robinson 2014, p. 6). Increasingly, young people have opportunities to gather spectators and drive discussion or feedback on their original content.

If their expression is stigmatised or marginalised, there is a greater chance of social disapproval in their offline lives than there is in a uniquely curated online space. Discrimination and sanction are less likely on the internet where those with similar beliefs and behaviours can be found (Bell 2007, p. 451). Web 2.0 has thus facilitated highly personalised social media content that can stand against normative mass media. Social media is increasingly visually rich and engaging, allowing users to feel genuine connection with others and challenge the values and behaviours they have gained from offline socialisation. This can often be dysfunctional and lead to activities like increased body surveillance (Perloff 2014, p. 366) and distorted belief systems within networks of peers (Peebles *et al.* 2012, p. s62). Overall, evidence suggests that adolescents who invest their time in electronic communications and internet browsing have lower psychological wellbeing than those who also devote time to in-person social activities, sports, community groups, and so on (Twenge *et al.* 2018, p. 765). While these in-person interactions are not necessarily free from negative interactions like bullying, the online manifestations of such interactions are broader reaching, harder to detach from, and last longer as digital artefacts (Pater *et al.* 2016, pp. 1195–1196). Deviant ideas and practices are preserved. Next, I draw on the example of pro-ana communities where deviant anti-medical ideas and behaviours are shared, creating a space that offers both genuine and much-needed support alongside echoing clusters of harmful behaviour.

Online Scripting in Echoing Self-Harmful Behaviour

A significant way in which self-harmful behaviour can form an echoing contagion is through online scripting. Communities dedicated to activities like starvation or cutting render these actions as deeply communal pursuits used to communicate with and connect to others. This idea draws on research from Lewis and Baker who proposed that repeated discussion of self-harm can lead to what they call "NSSI[2] scripts". These scripts can lead vulnerable people to decide that self-harm is functional and justifiable since other people who they talk to online present it in this way. Repeatedly reading about self-harm experiences, especially from favourable protagonists like online friends or idols, reinforces the idea that self-harm is justifiable or that it is a useful tool for the reduction of distress (2011, pp. 390–391). As such, many self-harmers see the exchange of images showing their scars and injuries as normal. This is because sharing pictures of all aspects of life is now a typical online activity (Sternudd 2012, p. 430). Adolescents are growing less judgemental about suicidal and self-harm behaviours due to the manner in which these activities are portrayed in modern youth culture (Fortune and Hawton 2007, p. 443). Self-harm can even seem glamourous and exciting in this kind of context. Most people have several options available to them when they feel distressed. If self-harm is thought to be the most useful or appealing option, then it is the most likely behaviour to occur.

Scripting can also support a common 'us versus them' mentality, as many people who feel welcomed in self-harmful communities have suffered rejection and negative scripting in mainstream social groups. Many people who starve or injure themselves report being bullied at school for their size, feeling generally rejected, or feeling highly uncomfortable with reactions to their body in the wake of puberty (Castro and Osório 2013, p. 327). As demonstrated further, participants in groups like pro-ana tend to feel lonely and report general negative affect, often mentioning alienation from social and familial bonds. This fits with Haas *et al.*'s observations that ONESGs can facilitate strong-tie networks that turns participants away from traditional cultural values and sources of support (2011, p. 53). This seems especially tempting to someone who is already alienated and who lacks resources for dealing with periods of emotional distress. As one pro-ana participant explains,

> Eating disorders are diseases of silence. We are all silently screaming for something: attention, love, help, escape or forgiveness. Although we might be looking to fill different voids, we never ask for the things we need. We feel unworthy, that for some reason we don't deserve them. So, we play the game of guess what I need from you. You're inability to guess just feeds our feelings of worthlessness [sic].
>
> (Martel 2003)

This worthlessness then, in turn, feeds interest in dangerous online spaces. People who have experienced high-intensity or repeated victimisation experiences tend to have negative self-schemata and prefer content that reinforces this (Oksanen *et al.* 2016, p. 4). Bardone-Cone and Cass found that viewing just a single pro-ana website can result in negative affect, lower self-esteem, drive to exercise, and less reliable perception of one's own weight (2007, p. 544). Similarly, Harper *et al.* found that visitors to these sites have high levels of body dissatisfaction and eating disturbance (Harper *et al.* 2008, p. 92). As such, the more that a person feels bad about their body and place in their community, the more likely they are to search out new supportive spaces with alternative behavioural scripting. While these alternative communities tend to be supportive, the support they provide feeds greater emotional distress and poorer self-image.

Pro-Ana

Pro-ana is a powerful manifestation of online self-harmful behaviour that can help us to analyse the degree to which these potentially contagious ideas echo, and how this echoing manifests. It also appears to be the most common form of self-harmful online content (Oksanen *et al.* 2016, p. 7). Pro-ana is a community containing echoing self-harmful behaviour that has received substantial attention from the academic community.[3] It has been described as a "community of practice" (Giles 2006, p. 464) and a "powerful cultural movement" (Wooldridge *et al.* 2014, p. 97) that seeks to reframe disordered eating and provide a controlled space for the exploration of stigmatised identities and ideas (Yeshua-Katz 2015, p. 1352). By allowing people to be open about their disordered eating and encouraging a kind of radical tolerance against a stigmatised illness, those in the community can feel hope, stability, and acceptance. This acceptance can be quite radical, with participants coming to terms with disordered eating as a core of their life and identity that should not be fought against (Layton 2016). Instead, participants recognise that their illness gives them some sense of stability and purpose and try to find "safe" ways of existing with it (Ward 2007, p. 7). Through processes like scripting, this community does indeed support a lifestyle where people can resist normative medical treatment and see their starvation as more than just a disease. This is a very complex philosophical process that seems to be misleadingly truncated into 'teaching girls to starve' by many public commentators. The reality of the contagion at play within this community is far more complex and not wholly evil.

Pro-ana (rendered without capitalisation) is ostensibly a shortening of pro-anorexia, but this does miss some important nuance. Many commentators, especially in the popular press, have interpreted 'pro-' as meaning a positive or even encouraging attitude towards anorexia and other eating disorders. This is something that most participants actively disagree with. One of the main emic commentators on the history and definition of 2000s-era pro-ana is Mandi

Faux who ran numerous popular community groups in this space. She is clear that 'pro' refers to a 'proactive approach' to eating disorder communities and discussions. It does not stand for "promotion" of disordered eating "in any way, shape or form" (Faux 2008a). Rather, 'pro-' refers to an inherent acceptance of the existence of anorexia without the typical pressure to render it as a disease that must be immediately cured. In discussing the identity of pro-ana, adherents often make claims like "I accept my eating disorder as a lifestyle and not a disease" (Layton 2016) or "Ana... *Is a lifestyle choice, it is your choice to live with out food* [sic]" (Ana is Love 2016).

Later in the movement, 'pro-acceptance' gained popularity as a way of describing specialised support for long-term anorexics to discuss their unique experience in opposition to that of 'newbies' (Lavis 2016, p. 27). While these philosophies may be somewhat inconsistent across members, a shared value is the importance of a judgement-free space where non-normative thoughts about eating can be shared (Overbeke 2008, p. 57). This proved appealing for long-term anorexia sufferers who have not achieved recovery and need somewhere understanding where they can live "life with a disordered mind" (Enter 2007). While recovery is accepted as an option, pro-ana rejects this as the sole objective of those with disordered eating (Fox *et al.* 2005, p. 959). This support is in contrast to the often critical opinions of family and friends or the one-dimensional food focus of medical professionals (Brotsky and Giles 2007, p. 99). Pro- seems to exist in contrast to the anti- of these discourses.

'Ana' is a shortening of anorexia, but is seen by participants as "a more benign descriptor of behaviour" as opposed to the full medicalised word (Uca 2004, p. 2). Faux agrees that "using the words ana mia to describe anorexia bulimia allows for a friendlier atmosphere" (Faux 2006a). Indeed, Giles argues that the pro-ana space is such a unique manifestation that "anorexia" may not actually be the same discursive object as "ana" (2006, p. 476). He feels that over the duration of pro-ana online, this concept and community have undergone so much radical transformation that ana is ontologically distinct from normative medicine's psychiatric diagnosis of anorexia nervosa. Ana is a fetish category that frames the practice of starvation very differently. Medical frameworks are insufficient for understanding ana, which is more than simply an online manifestation of disordered eating. Rather, ana is a complex media product that has an online genesis and unique community characteristics (Giles 2016, pp. 232, 309–312). It is important to explore pro-ana as it is framed by participants rather than assuming it is an uncomplicated promotion of anorexia nervosa.

Faux's comprehensive historical accounts of pro-ana are a good way of understanding its construction from the perspective of participants – most of whom have a very different take on its level of danger from the mainstream perspective. According to Faux, pro-ana started in 2001 as a way of people with eating disorders connecting and discussing their lives "so as not to suffer in silence" (Faux 2008b). Prior to these communities, individuals had few options for discussing eating disorders – often having to rely on consultations with health professionals or "emotionally charged encounters with friends and family" where the nuances of their feelings could not necessarily be expressed (Brotsky and Giles 2007, p. 93). Similarly, non-anorexia topics like personal fears, family, clothing, or education can be explored through a pro-ana lens with guidance and friendship given by those who calmly accept anorexia as an underlying presence (Cantó-Milà and Seebach 2011, pp. 150–151). Pro-ana participants generally seek acceptance of who they are as individuals and the feeling of family and global togetherness that comes from close relationships with people in similar mindsets (Faux 2007a). Community structure seeks to "provide a safe, stable online home for those who are eating disordered". It also rejects "intolorence towards eating disorders [sic]" from the broader public (Faux 2007b). Other sites of the era like *Anna's Place* similarly aimed for users to "at least feel normal about ourselves, and hopefully pass on those attributes to others who are at their last shred of hope" (Robbins 2007).

The media quickly became aware of this community and spread what Faux calls "blatent lies about the movement [sic]" and its drive to recruit people into illness.[4] Conversely, she says that "an honest pro ana" will wish anyone seeking to recover the best of luck and never try to drag them back – supposedly leading to better recovery rates than formal medical programs. At the same time, they will not *force* recovery to happen. Instead, the general philosophy is that people with eating disorders are not inherently bad and wrong, nor are their processes of help-seeking and coping (Faux 2008b). Pro-ana spaces are known for making room for people with eating disorders who are not seeking treatment (Tong *et al.* 2013, p. 408). Faux criticises mainstream medical treatments for focussing too much on the disorder of anorexia and ignoring the individual. She believes that eating disorders "will just come back again instantly" if they are "cured" through the kind of traditional programs she and her community have experienced. Instead, pro-ana "treats the person" by valuing their individual needs and encouraging gentle and thorough means of recovery such as journaling on community forums (Faux 2006b).[5] The idea of cathartic journaling is central to the early-to-mid-2000s experience of pro-ana.

These forums were semi-restricted spaces, often locked with passwords and accessible only after an arduous audition process. As such, Cantó-Milà and Seebach believe these communities are a kind of secret society linked by a special friendship bond that offers relief from strained relationships with peers and loved ones. In these forums, it was safe to share emotions, beliefs, and fears without an underlying pressure to reject anorexic behaviours and recover (2011, p. 151). Via this semi-public journaling, pro-ana participants could see other people believing in them, which was designed to help with self-belief and self-esteem (Faux 2006a). They were also allowed to move at a slower pace than may be required to meet clinical recovery goals (Faux 2007b). In a study of such pro-ana blogs, Tong *et al.* found that processes of reciprocal self-disclosure have been central in creating a sense of community whether they become focussed overtly on disordered eating or about more mundane life activities and feelings. Blogging in the pro-ana sphere provided self-expression and catharsis while allowing others to empathise (2013, p. 419). Indeed, many users were prompted to share experiences similar to those they read about thus strengthening community binds via self-disclosure and a reciprocal feedback loop (Tong *et al.* 2013, p. 411). They were spaces where people could be "heard and believed" when disclosing serious and painful experiences like sexual violence (McLellan 2010, p. 235). They also allowed for acceptable confessions of guilt when users inevitably deviate from their pro-ana goals (Haas *et al.* 2011, p. 47). Indeed, fear of weight gain and an obsession with food was one of the most popular topics discussed (Sheldon *et al.* 2015, p. 179). Whether they be significant confessions, memories of trauma, or mundane ruminations, forums were a safe place for sharing content that seemed too contentious for an unfiltered audience. As such, they were central to forming the idea of what pro-ana really is – a space for powerful disclosure of stigmatised ideas and experiences.

On "Becoming" Anorexic

The question then is whether discussing stigmatised behaviours can glamorise them or make others wish to copy them. The issue of converting people to eating disorder lifestyles is vital in the understanding of contagion and, interestingly, is something that is vehemently denied by website creators of the early- to mid-2000s. Faux herself declares, "We are not cults, we do not encourage anyone to develop eating disorders, we do not encouage deathly behaviours [*sic*]" (Faux 2007b). Similarly, popular webmistress Arianna explains: "This site isn't meant to draw people into the hellish worlds of disordered eating. It's meant to provide people who already have eating disorders with support to do what they feel they need to do. Some people are happy with their eating disorders". She argues that no one can "just become" anorexic, rather people accidentally enter into an anorectic lifestyle and then struggle to let it go once they realise it has happened (Arianna 2002a). This reflects a community rejection of the idea that pro-ana content converts victims or begets more anorexic behaviour.

Faux argues that no one can "become" anorexic by choice, thus reading about anorexia online can, at most, encourage a person to skip a few meals before they return to more sustainable diets (Faux 2006b). This sentiment against contagion is echoed by other users such as Torri who claims, "I in no way want to 'give' someone an eating disorder". Rather, she built her own pro-ana site to educate and "help out people who suffer from them" because "I suffered by myself for so many years" (Torri 2007a). Like Faux, she does not want to convert (and even doubts this is possible) but would like to diminish lonely feelings. This is a real outcome of pro-ana spaces, where evidence suggests that the most common participatory activity is the provision of support – even though that support sometimes comes when a person fails at a restrictive fast and feels stressed as a result (Wooldridge *et al.* 2014, p. 103).

Pro-ana is an important sanctuary against medical and social discourses that disapprove of starvation activities, focussing instead on ways to manage this "all-consuming condition" in a place of empathy (Ward 2007, p. 11). Uca agrees that pro-ana spaces cannot sustain attitudes of hostility, as the general push towards support and acceptance creates a "genuine state of sisterhood" and ethos of care in the face of emotional strife (2004, pp. 21–22).

Nevertheless, there is a large body of evidence to show that contagion does occur, and these communities do encourage a worsening of symptoms and a shoring up of an anorexic identity. For example, Riley *et al.* note how "problematic bodily experiences" on pro-ana sites, such as hair loss due to starvation, are seen as measures of success. Participants experiencing frightening symptoms such as this will often initially be alarmed but will then gauge a more positive meaning from interaction with other anorexics in the community. This helps to reframe their personal experiences and encourage uncommon thoughts such as seeing hair loss as a sign of progress or correct behaviour (Riley *et al.* 2009, p. 356). Indeed, research shows that increased exposure to pro-ana sites leads to increased sensation seeking and disinhibition – potentially coupled with appearance-related teasing (Almenara *et al.* 2016, p. 478). Adherence to these embracive and immersive communities can lead to psychological changes. Coupled with explicit instructions for the worsening of behaviour (discussed below), this has created echoing contagions.

Common Pro-Ana Content

To unpack some of the complexities at play in this online contagion, next I provide a summary of the themes, content, and philosophies evident in pro-ana across the past twenty years. Pro-ana spaces are so amorphous and dynamic that they are hard to speak of with numerical data. To give some sense of their nature, Gwizdek *et al.* provided some statistics from 2012. At this time, the structure of sites was tallied at 60% blogs, 34% forums, and 6% informational resources. In terms of access, 78% were totally unrestricted with 18% for approved people only and 4% with a mixture of open and restricted content (Gwizdek *et al.* 2012, p. 159). These statistics are unlikely to remain accurate a decade after the fact – due primary to a major shift towards social media hosting. Nevertheless, they do provide a good picture of what the initial 2000 to early 2010s pro-ana space looked like. So too does Sharpe *et al.*'s summary of repeated features. These include: tips on weight loss, guidelines for secrecy and deception regarding body or diet changes, tips for purging (commonly through vomiting or laxatives), thinspiration (defined further in the chapter), personification of eating disorders, and lists of religious commandments for the eating disorder lifestyle (Sharpe *et al.* 2011, p. 34). To this I would also add lists of formal diagnostic criteria for conditions like anorexia nervosa, NSSI, or borderline personality disorder. Blogging content tended to include the site owner's personal blog and discussion boards with discussions between participants. Of all the aforementioned content, support forums and thin-spiration are the most common elements (Overbeke 2008, p. 52). Common linguistic features in these blogs included referring to the more intimate and colloquial "ana" and "mia" rather than anorexia and bulimia (Day and Keys 2008, p. 7). Pro-ana websites of the 2000s were known for having very similar formats, structures, and subheadings – including those that are pro-recovery or designed as warnings (Uca 2004, p. 10). Content was so frequently copied without attribution that many texts have become completely decontextualised and are the products of multiple uncredited authors (Ullyatt 2010, p. 84).

While some sites were mainly an amalgamation of replicated content, other creators communicated their own personal takes on the topic. It was common in this era to find disagreements about what it meant to be eating disordered, how "ana" should be viewed, and whether this behaviour is a lifestyle choice and positive or a medical illness and negative (Giles 2006, p. 464). Even within specific sub-communities these disagreements were rife (Brotsky and Giles 2007, p. 102) and there is no evidence of a unifying ideological stance (Giles 2016, p. 321). This also encouraged a space of innovation where unique ways of expressing the anorexic identity flourished. For example, the "University of EdNos" (2006–2007) was established as an online space where students "learn about themselves and achieve the goals that they set for themselves"; these goals being related to disordered eating. The University promised spiritual and emotional growth for participants and encouraged people with eating disorders to love themselves and choose healthier options than "purging, laxies, or extreme fasting" (Misa 2007a). Part of this growth is through enrolment in one of 36 month-long graded programs. Functioning as quite a direct mani-festation of fears that pro-ana teaches anorexic behaviours, classes include the "Next Thinspo Program" where participants are pushed to become thin-spiration models for others through eating 1000 calories per week and ru-minating on their favourite emaciated images of others (Misa 2007b). The University of EdNos also contained resources like a health clinic (vitamin advice), gym (exercise routines), lunchroom (diet tips), library (list of thin-spiration books), sororities (buddy systems), and even a counselling program (for help with recovery and higher calorie eating plans).

At present, most of these communities and sites are outdated and aban-doned. When exploring pages from the first and second waves, Cobb found what she calls "a pro-ana graveyard". Some site owners have left messages about their shift towards recovery while many other sites and forums are frozen or abandoned (2020, p. 67). Despite this, discussions of pro-ana often view the community as somehow monolithic and eternal, still frozen in the form they were found in back in 2005. As Giles notes, internal community evolutions (e.g., irony and use of humour) have not always been understood by commentators in a nuanced and temporal way – especially in media coverage. He feels that many have "nailed down the community at a specific point in time and generalised accordingly", rather than appreciating its often-rapid evolution (Giles 2016, p. 319). In the 2020s, the aforementioned community structure is looked back upon with embarrassment, humour, and some sympathy. This is especially true as regards religious pro-ana content. On one *Reddit* post, people who engaged with these older spaces commented "Pro ana websites really turned ED's into a religion lmao i am sorry", "Y'all ever pretend to see/talk to ana back in the day? Man I was wild at 13. Just had a big kid imaginary friend", and "i have had moments where i was like 'yes lord ana i must obey' [*sic*]" (I_am_the_flower 2021). Not all reminiscences are negative. ED content on Tumblr, particularly aesthetic posts, is now looked back upon by as a positive, nostalgic, comforting memory (∗.·∵.)✧ **e the re al** ✧℃.·∵.∗ 2021).

With newer social media platforms trending towards video and photo content, pro-ana is now more image-centric and text-light. Discussion is more limited, with a greater focus on elements like hashtags (discussed below). This is less conducive to the layered conversation seen in older formats (Cobb 2017, pp. 75, 191). Nevertheless, these visual mediums still allow the community to produce and negotiate their shared identity (Burke 2012, p. 44). Thinspo image boards are popular across social media sites like Tumblr, Pinterest, and Instagram. The idea of thinspo has also evolved with users obscuring the pro-ana origin of this content by claiming it is "healthy" or pro-fitness rather than pro-ana (Cobb 2020, p. 70).

One of the most significant contemporary spaces for anorexic community formation is the microblogging site *Twitter* where connections are primarily formed through shared hashtags and mutual following. Users in this space use the term 'edtwt' in opposition to the now-outdated 'pro-ana'. This has allowed them to reject some of the baggage from older eras.[6] Nevertheless, participants describe remarkably similar benefits to those of earlier spaces. Like many others, sola finds her eating disorder "incredibly taboo and alienating" and uses her Twitter to journal feelings that cannot be discussed in broader society (sola 2020). katrin sees hers as one of the few resources she has to help cope with mental illness and would prefer to connect with other people in a similar situation than to suffer alone. She notes that she and many others lack the resources to get proper professional support and resort to social media instead (katrin 2020). Most text-based community discussion happens on Twitter, often employing tools like threads to increase word count and allow commentary from others. This inherent need for the community to evolve was anticipated by Faux who believes that static pro-ana spaces can become "tired and boring" and users risk becoming "a parody" of themselves (Faux 2008b). Nevertheless, despite community change, there is still a great deal to be learned from observation of pro-ana in all its manifestations across the past two decades.

Tagging

Content tagging has become increasingly important with the rise of microblogging social media platforms. Because sites like Instagram lack formal community structures such as forums or private groups, ad-hoc communities have clustered around tags like #proana (Chancellor *et al.* 2016, p. 1171). Tags are presently used to summon the attention of others with similar interests and behaviours. For example, the self-harm Twitter community often address each other with tags: "@ Shtwt, do y'all get proud when you make a cut deeper than usual? #shtwt" (syx♡ 2021). Eating-disorder Twitter users are addressed similarly with #edtwt. Tags also add important commentary to visual posts on sites like Instagram. While images shared may be fairly benign, tags are a way of making their emotional content heard by the right audience. For example, a selfie can take on special meaning through the inclusion of #ed, #fat, or #selfharmmm (Cobb 2020, p. 113). Tags are so cogent in this sense that they can even be used as a diagnostic tool. Chancellor *et al.* argue that Mental Illness Severity (MIS) can be rated based on the tags a person uses. High MIS is associated with extreme weight control tags like #purge and #starve, self-harm activity tags like #cutting and #blades, or suicidal ideation tags like #killme. Medium MIS is associated with tags that discuss these actions or reveal negative opinions about the self, but are a little more abstract like #mia, #bdp, or #uglyandfat (2016, p. 1173).

As discussed in the following chapter, censorship has impacted significantly on the way pro-self-harmful spaces operate. One major adaptation has been in the vocabulary used for tagging. Many pro-ana participants see their friendships and communities as secret societies (Cantó-Milà and Seebach 2011, p. 154). Indeed, #secretsociety has become a popular pro-ana tag (Chancellor *et al.* 2016, p. 1171). As Cobb observes, blacklisted tags like #thinspo, #bonespo, or #proana have also been swapped out for more obscure spellings like #thynspooo, #spo, and #proanna. This process continues to evolve as tags are added to blacklists and new forms of them develop in response. She also notes the rise of more innocuous hashtags with more covert pro-ana undertones like the popular #sexy and obtuse #blithe. Through this secret lexicon, users can evade detection by caregivers and censors while still signalling content to insiders. These insiders have their own lexical knowledge where they understand 'blithe' not as a state of being carefree and happy but as one of lacking care for oneself. Because this meaning is hard to discern, it functions as a useful hidden hashtag for a community hampered by censorship (Cobb 2020, pp. 73, 75). As shown in Table 4.1, tags range from very direct (#proana) to very obscure (#ricecaketwt – rice cake referring to a staple of highly restrictive diets).

Thinspiration

A perennial concern with pro-ana is the possibility of thinspiration directly functioning as an inspirational device for dangerous levels of food restriction. Thinspiration, or 'thinspo', is any kind of text (primarily visual) that helps to motivate viewers towards extreme thinness. Thinspiration will often be used to help people imagine their ideal body, or to keep themselves focussed on

Table 4.1 Samples of overt and covert tags used to identify self-harmful content and groups

Common Pro-Ana Hashtags	Common Self-Harm Hashtags
#ana	#barcodetwt
#anamia	#blades
#anorexia	#catscratchtwt
#beantwt	#catscratchtwt
#blithe	#cutter
#blythe	#cutting
#bodycheck	#madeofbeans
#bonespo	#madeofstyrofoam
#chestbones	#ouchietwt
#collarbones	#ouchytwt
#donteat	#owietwt
#ednos	#secretsociety123
#edproblems	#self-harm
#edtwt	#self-injury
#flatstomach	#selfhate
#hipbones	#selfmutilation
#hipbones	#slicetwt
#needtobethin	#sliceytwt
#pro-mia	#slit
#proana	#styrofoamtwt
#proanna	#suicidal
#promia	#yeettwt[7]
#purge	
#ricecaketwt	
#secretsociety123	
#size00	
#skinnylegs	
#spo	
#starve	
#suicidal	
#thighgap	
#thighgap	
#thin	
#thinspo	
#thynspo	
#thynspooo	
#uglyandfat	

Note: Some of these tags overlap with other groups such as the use of #flatstomach in fitness circles.

starvation when tempted by food. In this way, it is an imaginative tool that helps those wishing to starve to visualise themselves in a new and better body where their fears and insecurities will be released. This can function as a meditative exercise that temporarily calms negative affect with a happy dream of the future (Alderton 2018, pp. 9–10). It can also be used as a tool to berate oneself for failing to be thin enough and thus gain a burst of fresh motivation for starvation. Thinspo allows viewers to "get a good shock into thinking thin; very, very thin" (Delicate Sylph 2009). These images tend to be shocking because they often show bodies in a state of cachexia – the irreversible muscle wastage seen in late-stage starvation. Those outside of the pro-ana community tend to perceive such skeletal forms as deviant and startling, lacking in the classic attributes of beauty (Reichel *et al.* 2014, p. 168). In-group members do not necessarily disagree but tend to prize these images as representation of atypical beauty or enjoy the spectacle of a body near to death as something they too wish to achieve.

As explored in the previous chapter, fashion magazines provided the first version of thinspiration now popular in a digital form. People who lived with eating disorders in the 1990s commonly note cutting out pictures of very skinny people and sticking them up as motivation, for example, on a fridge to prevent eating (Carney and Louw 2006, p. 961). The internet made the sharing and viewing of such images far easier. An estimated 82% of pro-ana sites contained thinspiration in the 2000s (Gwizdek *et al.* 2012, p. 158). Celebrity images were the most popular content type (Watts and Crowe 2014), especially if the celebrity in question has admitted to eating disturbances or has gone into treatment for their disorder. This makes their images more genuine and worthy of competing with (Lavis 2016, p. 21). Even if they seem negative and off-putting, stories about celebrities who have died from eating disorders or who have experienced significant negative impacts on their lives and bodies have also been perennial thinspo favourites (Castro and Osório 2013, p. 325). Manipulation of photos to make their subjects seem even skinner is well known and accepted (Polak 2007, p. 89). The idea of extreme emaciation is still highly motivational even when viewers know it to be more fantasy than reality.

More recently, thinspo has become a recurring theme on social media plat-forms. On edtwt, there are multiple accounts dedicated to frequent reblogging of thinspo content such as extreme weight loss progress pics, very thin people in poses that emphasise this like closing their fingers around their upper thighs, thematic groupings like #legs, and photo sets of recognisable thin celebrities such as KPop idols. These accounts have titles like @THINSPOFILES and @ thinspo_for_u. Written thinspo is also shared by such account with motivational tweets such as "you could have so much potential if only you were skinny" (thinspo archive 2021). In this way, thinspo remains just as prevalent and im-portant to the pro-ana community in the present day as it has been throughout the history of the movement.

Thinspo is relatively diverse and has traditionally been understood as either positive or negative. The former includes aspirational images like catwalk models or extreme weight loss success stories. The latter refers to images of obesity or stories about death by overeating (often called 'fatspo'). Thinspo is also divided by its intensity. Some people prefer images of extreme emaciation (or 'onespo') while others gravitate to images of those who are very slim but still socially acceptable such as pop stars. Those who prefer more extreme imagery tend to view such celebrities as "too fat" to be properly inspirational (Uca 2004, pp. 13–16). Bell calls fatspo a kind of "reverse trigger" where "near-pornographic" images of overweight women are captioned to express pity and shame or derisive humour. Conversely, she notes that bonespo tends to be uncaptioned as though it can speak for itself (2014, p. 54). Fatspo is more actively contextualised, often used as a form of revenge or an expression of self-disgust. An account of this is given by edtwt user @dukecals who shares content including an overweight woman eating marshmallows and making a bath full of hot chocolate to soak in, TikTok videos of people eating grotesquely, and images where there is a 'fat friend' amongst skinnier peers. She explains that this content appeals due to lingering resentment over her experiences as an obese child where she felt encouraged to maintain her higher weight, be body positive, and accept a larger physique – a stance that now angers her (duchess 2021). Fatspo allows her to reclaim disgust towards fat bodies including the one she herself inhabited during childhood. The specific variety of thinspo engaged with is a matter of personal taste and need with a whole portfolio of diverse styles available for the choosing.

Thinspo has a quantifiable impact on the perceptions and bodies of those who engage with it. Repeated exposure to images of very thin people typically leads to 'thin ideal' internalisation. Pro-ana community members can succumb to dysfunctional and incapacitating idealisation of emaciation, which impacts on the development and maintenance of their eating disorders (Smith *et al.* 2014, p. 138). People who use thinspo note feeling guilty when they eat normally (Haley in Coggan 2017). Thinspo can also alter perceptions of who is or can be anorexic. Despite the recent popularity of Korean celebrities on a broader cultural level, most thinspo favours White, female bodies. Images of male bodies are uncommon and harder to find (Wooldridge *et al.* 2014, p. 105, Branley and Covey 2017, p. 1356). Cobb notes that bodies used for thinspo are overwhelmingly White with the biggest skin tone diversity created by degrees of fake tan. This creates belief in the White body as the most (th) inspirational and erroneously implies that anorexia is an issue for White women only (2020, p. 91). This can inhibit accurate diagnoses both due to a person's self-image as a possible anorexic or the degree to which they will be read as such by medical professionals.

Finally, thinspo encourages the performance and observation of starvation as something shocking, powerful, and addictive. This is something Gooldin explores in her appraisal of fasting as a *performed* text observed by spectators in a social relationship. In the Victorian Era, fasting girls were an object of interest and a focus of the public gaze due to their supposed ability to live for long periods of time with no nourishment (2003, pp. 32, 35). In the present era, starvation still holds the public attention and still functions as a mechanism for social relations. Starvation as represented through thinspo allows for visible bodily distress to be observed. People are admired for having the capacity to withstand this distress to the degree that similar discomfort is often longed for by viewers (Burke 2012, pp. 45–47). The feelings of obsession and a desire for perfection that are engendered in a pro-ana audience when viewing tend to already be excessive amongst this group (Polivy and Herman 2002, p. 200).

This leads to many viewers of thinspo also desiring to be performers of star-vation, not just consumers. It is easy to find 'homemade' thinspo by viewing content amalgamated under the #bodycheck tag. This tag is used for frequent check-ins to make sure one's emaciation is increased or maintained. While many people with eating disorders are not acutely starved,[8] #bodycheck is replete with images such as concave stomachs and protruding rib bones or people circling their upper arms with thumb and middle finger. In this way, anyone who is starved enough can earn the honour of their own thinspo performance and carry on the echoing contagion in this manner.

Instructions for the Worsening of Behaviour

Pro-ana communities have been hosting 'tips & tricks' pages since their inception, designed to teach people how to cultivate disordered eating and hide this behaviour from others. A good representative example is *Free the Butterfly*, which shares common tips for the evasion of detection. Readers are encouraged to hide pale skin and dark circles with make-up, brush hair in a volumising way to hide a thinning scalp, wear extra layers to give a false silhouette, wax lanugo hair, and paint discoloured nails. For trips to the doctor, *Free the Butterfly* recommends hiding weights in clothing and un-derwear to gain a false reading, and consuming large volumes of water to appear both plumper and heavier. For bulimics who wish to hide vomiting, the website recommends purging in the shower or vomiting in bushes. To throw off suspicion about restrictive eating, readers were told to announce to parents how much they liked high-calorie treats like Pop Tarts and "drop into the conversation how gross Nicole Richie [a popular underweight celebrity of the era] looks etc.". Finally, a large portion of the page was dedicated to excuses that will allow a teenager under parental and school supervision to avoid eating. Most involve claiming to have eaten large meals at other times during the day, while others involve claims about medical or religious/ethical prohibitions against certain foods. Readers are encouraged to become vegetarian or claim lactose intolerance in order to reject pre-made food in a family or restaurant setting. There are also tips to be used when the aforementioned fail and one is forced to eat some amount of food. Chewed mouthfuls can be spat into a drinking glass or napkin, and eating very slowly often means no one will notice how little food is consumed during the meal (Free Butterfly 2006a). While none of these 'tricks' is likely to hide a serious change in behaviour indefinitely, it seems quite possible that such behaviours can conceal a developing disorder and prolong the amount of time a person can avoid suspicion or medical treatment.

Instructions for dangerous behaviours like purging are also common. This same website also includes very detailed instructions on how to purge food through vomiting. The author describes where one's fingers should be placed, when to take a breath, and what motions to expect from your body as the reflex is triggered (Free Butterfly 2006b). A popular website of the same era,

Fragile Innocence, contains similar advice. Owner Joe suggests that her readers look at sickening images like autopsies on *Rotten.com* if purging proves difficult. She believes that people who have 'done well' with purging can lose up to two pounds per day for a total loss of fourteen pounds a week. Although she notes that water weight can disrupt this process, she suggests that her readers will "never really know how much weight can be lost in a week until you try to find out for yourself" (Joe 2005). This is a blatant invitation for reader participation.

For those who prefer starvation over purging 'excess' calories, it is also easy to find instructions on pro-ana sites such as those run by Faux. Like Joe, she suggests using negative associations. Readers are instructed to find an image of something unpleasant that makes them feel ill, then place this image beside their food and look at it intensely while eating. This should make food associated with unpleasantness and thus "make you less inclined to eat". She also recommends sabotaging food by using bad ingredients or over-seasoning. If food tastes unpalatable, less will be consumed. Faux suggests that it is easier to control food intake gradually and recommends setting a series of strict rules to achieve this. Each rule should be mastered before a new one is added, thus allowing you to "sneak up on yourself in tiny little stages" (Faux 2008c). Instructions are also available for people who live with others and need to be more secretive about their starvation behaviours. Faux emphasises the importance of secrecy and the value of hiding anorexic behaviours before others realise they are happening and start to monitor them. She recommends keeping friends and family 'clueless' for as long as possible. To achieve this, she suggests actions such as:

> Check the fridge when nobody else is around. Find foods that you would have eaten and get rid of them, for example, three eggs and a piece of butter. Then if someone asks, you can say you had scrambled eggs and are really full. And if they check, the ingredients are gone, which reinforces your story. Consider dishes and silverware as well.
>
> (Faux 2008d)

When eating is necessary, it is easy to find pro-ana extreme diets. These tools are often based on alleged eating habits from ultra-thin celebrities like the "Nicole Richie Diet/Workout" with suggestions like "*Breakfast:* 2 Egg Whites; 1 Scoop of Protein Powder mixed with Water" followed by an intense cardio regimen (Torri 2007b). Advice for strength and cardio training also tends to be quite dangerous and excessive with recommendations like "do reps until your arms give out" or run backwards and forwards "until you can't stand up any longer" (Arianna 2002b). These extreme diets, purging tips, and starvation advice are explicit, repeated across pro-ana sites, and simple to understand and follow even if the processes of starvation themselves are not easy. The difficulty of learning to despise food and lie to others is not necessarily off-putting, as rising to the challenge of arduous processes is central to the competitive, elitist core of the pro-ana movement.

Notes

1 'Web 2.0' refers to a newer version of the internet based on user-generated content and rapidly changing participatory spaces. This is in contrast to 'Web 1.0', the older version of the internet environment based on more static text and images with less interactivity (DiNucci 1999, p. 32).
2 'Non-Suicidal Self-Injury'.
3 'Pro-ana' is a broad, generic term used to encompass a wider range of eating disorders beyond anorexia nervosa. This term is most commonly found on websites and thus through search engines when looking for this material (Polak 2007, p. 87).
4 A more comprehensive history of this censorship is presented in the final section of this book.
5 This diary focus is not just apparent on sites owned by Faux. Across other sites, "diary-like reports" where users are encouraged to "record your own personal progress with your ana" have been observed as the most popular forum element (Mulveen and Hepworth 2006, p. 286).
6 There are some interesting lexical debates in this space. In 2021, the Twitter account 'edtwt confessions' shared the anonymous question: "whats yall opinion on pro ana ppl?". Answers included the extremely negative: "attack kill", "most loud and wrong ppl" mixed in with a suggestion that everyone engaging with edtwt might actually be pro-ana themselves: "if we mean people saying anorexia is good then fuck them, if you mean ppl with ana not in recovery, then that's most of edtwt" and the realisation that "proana has referred to a wide range of ideologies over time" (edtwt confessions 2021). A popular conclusion was "if ur on edtwt for a restrictive ed, u are proana [sic]" (mads 2021).
7 More detail about unique self-harm tags like #madeofbeans is discussed in the following chapter.
8 This is very challenging to quantify, but based on data provided by pro-ana participants, around 20% are "severely malnourished" (Yom-Tov *et al.* 2016, p. 109).

References

Adler, P.A. and Adler, P., 2011. *The Tender Cut: Inside the Hidden World of Self-Injury.* United States of America: NYU Press.

Alderton, Z., 2018. *The Aesthetics of Self-Harm: The Visual Rhetoric of Online Communities.* Abingdon: Routledge.

Almenara, C.A., Machackova, H., and Smahel, D., 2016. Individual differences associated with exposure to "Ana-Mia" websites: An examination of adolescents from 25 European countries. *Cyberpsychology, Behavior, and Social Networking*, 19 (8), 475–480.

Ana is Love, 2016. Ana loves us [online]. *Ana loves us.* Available from: https://web.archive. org/web/20160615232258/http://anaislove.weebly.com:80/ [Accessed 23 Apr 2021].

Arianna, 2002a. About Me [online]. *AnOreXiC AdDiCt.* Available from: https://web.archive. org/web/20030407043209fw_/http://myweb.ecomplanet.com/bouc2329/pageaboutus. htm [Accessed 24 May 2021].

Arianna, 2002b. Exercise tips [online]. *AnOreXic AdDiCt.* Available from: https://web. archive.org/web/20030407050249fw_/http://myweb.ecomplanet.com/bouc2329/ mycustompage0017.htm [Accessed 24 May 2021].

Bardone-Cone, A.M. and Cass, K.M., 2007. What does viewing a pro-anorexia website do? An experimental examination of website exposure and moderating effects. *International Journal of Eating Disorders*, 40 (3), 537–548.

Becca, 2007. Profile [online]. *angelicgirl21.* Available from: https://web.archive.org/web/ 20130802025922/http://angelicgirl21.xanga.com/profile/ [Accessed 20 May 2021].

Bell, M., 2014. "Virtual" autobiography? Anorexia, obsession, and Calvin Klein. *In*: S. Brophy and J. Hladki, eds. *Embodied Politics in Visual Autobiography*. University of Toronto Press, 48–63.

Bell, V., 2007. Online information, extreme communities and internet therapy: Is the internet good for our mental health? *Journal of Mental Health*, 16 (4), 445–457.

Boyd, D., Leavitt, A., and Ryan, J., 2011. Pro-self-harm and the visibility of youth-generated problematic material. *I/S: A Journal of Law and Policy for the Information Society*, 7 (1), 1–32.

Brady, M.T., 2014. Pro-anorexia websites through an adolescent development lens: Commentary on paper by Tom Wooldridge. *Journal of Infant, Child, and Adolescent Psychotherapy*, 13 (3), 217–223.

Branley, D.B. and Covey, J., 2017. Pro-ana versus pro-recovery: A content analytic comparison of social media users' communication about eating disorders on Twitter and Tumblr. *Frontiers in Psychology*, 8, 1356.

Brotsky, S.R. and Giles, D., 2007. Inside the "Pro-ana" community: A covert online participant observation. *Eating Disorders*, 15 (2), 93–109.

Burke, E., 2012. Reflections on the Waif: Images of slenderness and distress in pro-anorexia websites. *Australian Feminist Studies*, 27 (71), 37–54.

Cantó-Milà, N. and Seebach, S., 2011. Ana's friends. Friendship in online pro-Ana communities. *Sociological Research Online*, 16 (1), 149–161.

Carney, T. and Louw, J., 2006. Eating disordered behaviors and media exposure. *Social Psychiatry and Psychiatric Epidemiology*, 41 (12), 957–966.

Castro, T.S. and Osório, A.J., 2013. "I love my bones!": Self-harm and dangerous eating youth behaviours in Portuguese written blogs. *Young Consumers*, 14 (4), 321–330.

Chancellor, S., Lin, Z., Goodman, E.L., Zerwas, S., and De Choudhury, M., 2016. *Quantifying and Predicting Mental Illness Severity in Online Pro-Eating Disorder Communities*. ACM Press, 1169–1182.

Cobb, G., 2017. "This is *not* pro-ana": Denial and disguise in pro-anorexia online spaces. *Fat Studies*, 6 (2), 189–205.

Cobb, G., 2020. *Negotiating Thinness Online: The Cultural Politics of Pro-anorexia*. 1st ed. Abingdon, Oxon; New York, NY: Routledge.

Coggan, M., 2017. Body positivity hasn't defeated the thinspo blog [online]. *Vice*. Available from: https://www.vice.com/en/article/8xxnqk/body-positivity-hasnt-defeated-the-thinspo-blog [Accessed 20 May 2021].

Day, K. and Keys, T., 2008. Starving in cyberspace: A discourse analysis of pro-eating-disorder websites. *Journal of Gender Studies*, 17 (1), 1–15.

Delicate Sylph, 2009. Fighting the battle of our lives: When recovery becomes an option—But a very shaky one [online]. *Haven of the Delicate Sylph*. Available from: http://www.geocities.ws/haven_of_the_delicate_sylph/prorecoveryessay.html [Accessed 5 May 2021].

DiNucci, D., 1999. Fragmented future. *Print*, 53 (4), 32, 221–222.

duchess, 2021. I spew so much 'fatphobia' because I've been keeping in so much of my vitriol [online]. *@dukecals*. Available from: https://twitter.com/dukecals/status/1384066703189889024 [Accessed 20 Apr 2021].

edtwt confessions, 2021. whats yall opinion on pro ana ppl? [online]. *@e_twtconfess*. Available from: https://twitter.com/e_twtconfess/status/1371922125406277638 [Accessed 21 Apr 2021].

Enter [online], 2007. *Pro-Ana Nation*. Available from: https://web.archive.org/web/20070225014906/http://www.pro-ana-nation.com/ [Accessed 10 May 2021].

*.∴.)✧ **e the re al** ✧℃.∴.*, 2021. ED Tumblr Vibes: A Thread [online]. *@tsukicals*. Available from: https://twitter.com/tsukicals/status/1380745066470240257 [Accessed 5 May 2021].

Faux, M., 2006a. Welcome to House of Thin [online]. *House Of Thin*. Available from: https://web.archive.org/web/20070702075229/http://www.houseofthin.com/ [Accessed 7 Mar 2018].

Faux, M., 2006b. Pro-Ana myths exposed [online]. *House of Thin*. Available from: http://www.houseofthin.com/library/pro-ana-myths.php [Accessed 6 Sep 2016].

Faux, M., 2007a. Secret closets – Outcasts unite [online]. *House of Thin*. Available from: https://web.archive.org/web/20070702075529/http://www.houseofthin.com/ newsroom/secret-closet.php [Accessed 10 May 2021].

Faux, M., 2007b. House of thin mission [online]. *House of Thin*. Available from: https://web. archive.org/web/20070702075910/http://www.houseofthin.com/entrance/mission.php [Accessed 6 May 2021].

Faux, M., 2008a. Pro-Ana acronyms, ect. [online]. *Fading Obsession:: Pro Ana Mia Website plus Forum*. Available from: https://web.archive.org/web/20080724115101/ http://www.fading-obsession.com/information/acronyms.php [Accessed 23 Apr 2021].

Faux, M., 2008b. Pro-Ana definition [online]. *Fading Obsession:: Pro Ana Mia Website plus Forum*. Available from: https://web.archive.org/web/20080724114538/http://www. fading-obsession.com/information/pro-ana-definition.php [Accessed 23 Apr 2021].

Faux, M., 2008c. Self control tips [online]. *Fading Obsession:: Pro Ana Mia Website plus Forum*. Available from: https://web.archive.org/web/20080724114858/http://www. fading-obsession.com/tips-tricks/self-control.php [Accessed 23 Apr 2021].

Faux, M., 2008d. Secrecy tips [online]. *Fading Obsession:: Pro Ana Mia Website plus Forum*. Available from: https://web.archive.org/web/20080724114602/http://www.fading-obsession.com/tips-tricks/secrecy.php [Accessed 23 Apr 2021].

Fortune, S. and Hawton, K., 2007. Suicide and deliberate self-harm in children and adolescents. *Paediatrics and Child Health*, 17 (11), 443–447.

Fox, N., Ward, K., and O'Rourke, A., 2005. Pro-anorexia, weight-loss drugs and the internet: an 'anti-recovery' explanatory model of anorexia. *Sociology of Health and Illness*, 27 (7), 944–971.

Free Butterfly, 2006a. Tips & Tricks [online]. *~ Free the butterfly within ~: the haven of an ana butterfly*. Available from: https://web.archive.org/web/20061029050933/http://www. freewebs.com:80/free-the-bfly/tipstricks.htm [Accessed 5 Mar 2018].

Free Butterfly, 2006b. Fasting & Purging 101 [online]. *~ Free the butterfly within ~: the haven of an ana butterfly*. Available from: https://web.archive.org/web/20061028225847/http:// www.freewebs.com:80/free-the-bfly/fastingpurging101.htm [Accessed 6 Mar 2018].

Giles, D., 2006. Constructing identities in cyberspace: The case of eating disorders. *British Journal of Social Psychology*, 45 (3), 463–477.

Giles, D.C., 2016. Does ana=Anorexia? Online interaction and the construction of new discursive objects. *In*: M. O'Reilly and J.N. Lester, eds. *The Palgrave Handbook of Adult Mental Health: Discourse and Conversation Studies*. Houndmills, Basingstoke, Hampshire; New York: Palgrave Macmillan, 308–326.

Gooldin, S., 2003. Fasting Women, living skeletons and hunger artists: Spectacles of body and miracles at the turn of a century. *Body & Society*, 9 (2), 27–53.

Gwizdek, A., Gwizdek, K., and Koszowska, A., 2012. Pro-ana, murderous face of the Internet. *Progress in Health Sciences*, 2 (1), 158–161.

Haas, S.M., Irr, M.E., Jennings, N.A., and Wagner, L.M., 2011. Communicating thin: A grounded model of Online Negative Enabling Support Groups in the pro-anorexia movement. *New Media & Society*, 13 (1), 40–57.

Hanson, L., 2003. Pro-ana, a culture remediated in cyberspace. *Proceedings of the Media Ecology Association*, 4, 36–46.

Harper, K., Sperry, S., and Thompson, J.K., 2008. Viewership of pro-eating disorder websites: Association with body image and eating disturbances. *International Journal of Eating Disorders*, 41 (1), 92–95.

Hipple Walters, B., Adams, S., Broer, T., and Bal, R., 2016. Proud2Bme: Exploratory research on care and control in young women's online eating disorder narratives. *Health: An Interdisciplinary Journal for the Social Study of Health, Illness and Medicine*, 20 (3), 220–241.

I_am_the_flower, 2021. Pro ana websites really turned ED's into a religion [online]. r/ *EDanonymemes*. Available from: https://www.reddit.com/r/EDanonymemes/comments/ m0gj2f/pro_ana_websites_really_turned_eds_into_a/ [Accessed 15 Apr 2021].

Joe, 2005. [f]requently asked questions [online]. *Fragile Innocence*. Available from: https:// web.archive.org/web/20041212013047if_/http://winkin.phpwebhosting.com:80/ ~joeic/privet/thin/help/faq.html [Accessed 14 Nov 2018].

katrin, 2020. thread on why you should not expose ed twt [online]. *Twitter*. Available from: https://twitter.com/7AEGl/status/1276321266291671040 [Accessed 17 Jul 2020].

Kirmayer, L.J., 2012. Changing patterns in suicide among young people. *Canadian Medical Association Journal*, 184 (9), 1015–1016.

Lavis, A., 2016. Alarming engagements? Exploring pro-anorexia websites in/and the media. *In*: K. Eli and S.J. Ulijaszek, eds. *Obesity, Eating Disorders and the Media*. London: Routledge, 11–35.

Layton, A., 2016. Interview: Pro ANA, an easy concept? [online]. *A Culture Starved for Love*. Available from: http://starvedlove.blogspot.com/2016/04/interview.html [Accessed 21 Nov 2018].

Le, M.T.H., Nguyen, H.T., Tran, T.D., and Fisher, J.R.W., 2012. Experience of low mood and suicidal behaviors among adolescents in Vietnam: Findings from two national population-based surveys. *Journal of Adolescent Health*, 51 (4), 339–348.

Lewis, S.P. and Baker, T.G., 2011. The possible risks of self-injury web sites: A content analysis. *Archives of Suicide Research*, 15 (4), 390–396.

Lou, 2003. someone, somewhere must know the answer [online]. *LiveJournal*. Available from: https://web.archive.org/web/20030731170927/http://www.livejournal.com/ users/loopylou/98336.html [Accessed 7 Apr 2021].

Luxton, D.D., June, J.D., and Fairall, J.M., 2012. Social media and suicide: A public health perspective. *American Journal of Public Health*, 102 (S2), S195–S200.

mads, 2021. if ur on edtwt for a restrictive ed [online]. *@frailcals*. Available from: https://twitter.com/frailcals/status/1384550324657135617 [Accessed 21 Apr 2021].

Maratea, R.J. and Kavanaugh, P.R., 2012. Deviant identity in online contexts: New directives in the study of a classic concept: Deviant identity in online contexts. *Sociology Compass*, 6 (2), 102–112.

Martel, K., 2003. How it feels [online]. *Caring Online*. Available from: https://web.archive. org/web/20030413103146/http://caringonline.com/feelings/byvictims/martel.htm [Accessed 9 Apr 2021].

McLellan, K., 2010. 'Is THAT what they are so afraid of?': The popular media and pro-anorexia websites. *In*: C. Chaput, M.J. Braun, and D.M. Brown, eds. *Entertaining Fear: Rhetoric and the Political Economy of Social Control*. New York: Peter Lang, 223–243.

Misa, 2007a. University of EdNos [online]. *University of EdNos*. Available from: https://web. archive.org/web/20070322203254/http://www.freewebs.com/uenway/generalrules.htm [Accessed 3 Jun 2021].

Misa, 2007b. Programs [online]. *University of EdNos*. Available from: https://web.archive. org/web/20070323083238/http://www.freewebs.com/uenway/degrees.htm [Accessed 3 Jun 2021].

Mulveen, R. and Hepworth, J., 2006. An interpretative phenomenological analysis of participation in a pro-anorexia internet site and its relationship with disordered eating. *Journal of Health Psychology*, 11 (2), 283–296.

Oksanen, A., Näsi, M., Minkkinen, J., Keipi, T., Kaakinen, M., and Räsänen, P., 2016. Young people who access harm-advocating online content: A four-country survey. *Cyberpsychology: Journal of Psychosocial Research on Cyberspace*, 10 (2).

Overbeke, G., 2008. Pro-Anorexia websites: Content, impact, and explanations of popularity. *Mind Matters: The Wesleyan Journal of Psychology*, 3, 49–62.

Pater, J.A., Haimson, O.L., Andalibi, N., and Mynatt, E.D., 2016. "Hunger hurts but starving works": Characterizing the presentation of eating disorders online. *In: Proceedings of the 19th ACM Conference on Computer-Supported Cooperative Work & Social Computing*. Presented at the CSCW '16: Computer Supported Cooperative Work and Social Computing, San Francisco, California, USA: ACM, 1185–1200.

Peebles, R., Harrison, S., McCown, K., Wilson, J., Borzekowski, D., and Lock, J., 2012. Voices of pro-Ana and Pro-Mia: A qualitative analysis of reasons for entering and continuing pro-eating disorder website usage. *Journal of Adolescent Health*, 50 (2), S62.

Perloff, R.M., 2014. Social media effects on young women's body image concerns: Theoretical perspectives and an agenda for research. *Sex Roles*, 71 (11–12), 363–377.

Pirkis, J.E. and Robinson, J., 2014. Improving our understanding of youth suicide clusters. *The Lancet Psychiatry*, 1 (1), 5–6.

Polak, M., 2007. 'I think we must be normal… There are too many of us for this to be abnormal!!!': Girls creating identity and forming community in pro-Ana/Mia websites. *In*: S. Weber and S. Dixon, eds. *Growing Up Online: Young People and Digital Technologies*. New York, NY: Palgrave Macmillan, 83–96.

Polivy, J. and Herman, C.P., 2002. Causes of eating disorders. *Annual Review of Psychology*, 53 (1), 187–213.

Reichel, V.A., Schneider, N., Grünewald, B., Kienast, T., Pfeiffer, E., Lehmkuhl, U., and Korte, A., 2014. "Glass fairies" and "bone children": Adolescents and young adults with anorexia nervosa show positive reactions towards extremely emaciated body pictures measured by the startle reflex paradigm: Glass fairies and bone children. *Psychophysiology*, 51 (2), 168–177.

Riley, S., Rodham, K., and Gavin, J., 2009. Doing weight: Pro-ana and recovery identities in cyberspace. *Journal of Community & Applied Social Psychology*, 19 (5), 348–359.

Robbins, A., 2007. About [online]. *Anna's Place*. Available from: https://web.archive.org/web/20070526084315/http://www.annasplace.us/enter.html [Accessed 10 May 2021].

Seko, Y., 2008. "Suicide machine" seekers: Transgressing suicidal taboos online. *Learning Inquiry*, 2 (3), 181–199.

Sharpe, H., Musiat, P., Knapton, O., and Schmidt, U., 2011. Pro-eating disorder websites: Facts, fictions and fixes. *Journal of Public Mental Health*, 10 (1), 34–44.

Sheldon, P., Grey, S.H., Vickery, A.J., and Honeycutt, J.M., 2015. An analysis of imagined interactions with pro-ana (anorexia): Implications for mental and physical health. *Imagination, Cognition and Personality*, 35 (2), 166–189.

Smith, A.R., Joiner, T.E., and Dodd, D.R., 2014. Examining implicit attitudes toward emaciation and thinness in anorexia nervosa: Implicit attitudes in anorexia. *International Journal of Eating Disorders*, 47 (2), 138–147.

sola, 2020. thread on why 'exposing' ed twitter is so dangerous + what you can do to stay safe! (please rt!!) [online]. *Twitter*. Available from: https://twitter.com/avenoira/status/1276336854971940865 [Accessed 15 Jul 2020].

Sternudd, H.T., 2012. Photographs of self-injury: Production and reception in a group of self-injurers. *Journal of Youth Studies*, 15 (4), 421–436.

Swannell, S., Martin, G., Krysinska, K., Kay, T., Olsson, K., and Win, A., 2010. Cutting on-line: Self-injury and the internet. *Advances in Mental Health*, 9 (2), 177–189.

syx♡, 2021. @ Shtwt, do y'all get proud when you make a cut deeper than usual? [online]. @ *suicidesyx*. Available from: https://twitter.com/suicidesyx/status/1384768158783787012 [Accessed 23 Apr 2021].

thinspo archive, 2021. you could have so much potential if only you were skinny [online]. *@THlNSPOFILES*. Available from: https://twitter.com/THlNSPOFILES/status/1380969563832090628 [Accessed 20 Apr 2021].

Tong, S.T., Heinemann-LaFave, D., Jeon, J., Kolodziej-Smith, R., and Warshay, N., 2013. The use of pro-ana blogs for online social support. *Eating Disorders*, 21 (5), 408–422.

Torri, 2007a. The Red Bracelet Project [online]. *The Red Bracelet Project*. Available from: https://web.archive.org/web/20070706152716/http://quodmenutritmedestruit.bravehost.com/ [Accessed 24 May 2021].

Torri, 2007b. Nicole Richie Diet / Workout [online]. *The Red Bracelet Project*. Available from: https://web.archive.org/web/20070624065854/http://quodmenutritmedestruit.bravehost.com/nicolediet.html [Accessed 24 May 2021].

Twenge, J.M., Martin, G.N., and Campbell, W.K., 2018. Supplemental material for decreases in psychological well-being among American adolescents after 2012 and links to screen time during the rise of smartphone technology. *Emotion*, 18 (6), 765–780.

Uca, E.R., 2004. *Ana's Girls: The Essential Guide to the Underground Eating Disorder Community Online*. Bloomington: Authorhouse.

Ullyatt, G., 2010. "Dwelling in fear of the scales forever": Religious diction in Pro-Anorectic websites from a discourse-analytic perspective. *Journal for Language Teaching*, 44 (2), 69–86.

Ward, K.J., 2007. 'I Love you to the bones': Constructing the anorexic body in 'pro-ana' message boards. *Sociological Research Online*, 12 (2), 1–14.

Watts, M. and Crowe, N., 2014. Anorexia advocates turn medical condition into self-expression [online]. *The Conversation*. Available from: http://theconversation.com/anorexia-advocates-turn-medical-condition-into-self-expression-23955 [Accessed 20 May 2021].

Wooldridge, T., Mok, C., and Chiu, S., 2014. Content analysis of male participation in pro-eating disorder web sites. *Eating Disorders*, 22 (2), 97–110.

Yeshua-Katz, D., 2015. Online stigma resistance in the pro-ana community. *Qualitative Health Research*, 25 (10), 1347–1358.

Yom-Tov, E., Brunstein-Klomek, A., Hadas, A., Tamir, O., and Fennig, S., 2016. Differences in physical status, mental state and online behavior of people in pro-anorexia web communities. *Eating Behaviors*, 22, 109–112.

5 Further Behavioural Observations in Pro-Ana Communities

Competitive Behaviours

Fri, Oct 1, 1999, 4:03 PM
Dying. That's what I am. The scale reads 51.1. The numbers are magical, bright florescent against the digital scale. And the joy I feel, the euphoric, lighter than-air joy, makes me want to fly, soar above the sky. I am the thinnest. The thinnest. ... I am 5'4 and 51 pounds. Clinically dying. and if that's what gets me the thinnest, thinner than every other anorexic, then so be it. I live for the emaciation.

(Arndt 2000a)

Perhaps the most impactful phenomenon on contagion is a trend towards competition within self-harmful communities. The idea of being 'the best anorexic' is common in pro-ana spaces. One user describes this quest as "my only priority in life", yet she was never able to be satisfied. Every time she reached her newest emaciated goal weight she still felt unhappy and triggered herself with more "proof" that other anorexics were skinnier and thus better (Jessica in Hutchings 2003a). Another agrees that "the thinner you get, the fatter you feel" with the "wish" of feeling thin never coming true and being inherently impossible under the anorexic mindset (Michele in Arndt 2000b). Indeed, it is common for anorexics to express that losing weight only makes them want to lose more and more (Dignon et al. 2006, p. 950). Because satisfaction is always deferred, there is an attitude if dissatisfaction and intense competitiveness in the pro-ana sphere. This competition can be with the general public, with each other, or simply with oneself.

Competition with wider society tends to manifest in displays of elitism. Cantó-Milà and Seebach note an "aristocratic motive" that makes members of the secretive pro-ana community feel special and valued due to their control and striving to perfection. This is especially valuable considering worthlessness is a common feeling amongst individuals in this group (2011, p. 157). Elitism is established through being able to withstand high levels of distress (Burke 2012, p. 38). In these circles, anorexia is often discussed as a skill to be boasted about and refined; something possessed by the talented and the dedicated

DOI: 10.4324/9781003126065-7

(Knapton 2013, p. 467). By viewing starvation as a competitive pursuit, those who are successful gain a sense of elitism and are granted respect by other community members. One of the earliest observations of pro-ana called it a "negative marathon" where participants earn cachet by being amongst the only people who are able to voluntarily starve for long periods (Reaves 2001). Persistence and endurance are important values in the pro-ana community. Because the uncomfortable symptoms of starvation are very hard to live with, this allows those who can endure it a feeling of superiority over those who cannot (Uca 2004, pp. 70–71). As one participant explains, the anorexic mindset convinces you that you are a hero and an elite who deserves to "feel better than the other mere mortals who dig in to their cereal and their donuts" (Misa 2007). Websites commonly ask users to "stay strong" and reinforce this with claims like "we are the strongest of them all" (Mayli 2007), or "volitional anorexics possess the most iron-cored, indomitable wills of all. Our way is not that of the weak" (Ana is Love 2016).

Within the pro-ana community there are also degrees of elitism based on starvation method with abstinence from food seen as the most pure and re-spectable of paths. Bulimia is perceived as a weaker pathway because it in-volves succumbing to hunger urges and needing to purge as a result. Giles notes how mia is perceived of as "cheating" with "dirty" outcomes like vo-miting unlike the "purity" of ana (2006, p. 468). Tools like laxatives are also seen as crutches, showing messiness and weakness or a loss of control in the face of appetite (Warin 2006, p. 49). Similarly, Uca describes mia as having less positive connotations than ana, and as a state that is often suffered through rather than celebrated like its counterpart (2004, p. 5). As one participant explains,

> As for the moment I wouldn't call myself Anorexic under any circumstances. I'm trying to shift in that direction, but I'm a bulimic. I hate it, and I'm trying really hard to change over and to be more disciplined with myself.
>
> (Arianna 2002)

Indeed, bulimia is often rendered in this manner as a mere temporary state until one can achieve the ideal of anorexia (Giles 2006, p. 470). As can be seen from the dates of these sources, the conceptualisation of anorexia as the most elite state was most important in the early- to mid-2000s. Nevertheless, this hierarchy does still lurk in community attitudes and manifests in some of the forthcoming discussions on the religious aspects of pro-ana.

Another major aspect of intra-community competition comes from efforts to make bodies as public and physically manifest as possible despite the primacy of supposedly anonymous and disembodied digital communication (Alderton 2018a, p. 18). Users will often post vast quantities of personal data such as their body measurements, exercise duration, calorie consumption, speed of weight loss, and size of thigh gap. In the earlier days of pro-ana, participants would often use forum signatures to note their current weight, high weight, goal weight, and height. About 70.8% of bloggers during this era also disclosed weight data (Tong *et al.* 2013, p. 414). Often several goals were provided, sometimes with ideal time periods (Ward 2007, p. 5). Unsurprisingly, these goals tended to be unhealthy, with most aiming for a BMI between 17.5 and 15 (Uca 2004, p. 3). Some would choose to represent goals via clothing size instead, or with a more abstract state like "perfection" or "pride" (Mulveen and Hepworth 2006, p. 289). Current stats often had bracketed commentary like "(ew!)" or "(disgusting!)" (Uca 2004, p. 18). Supporting a contagion hypothesis, current and goal weights differ based on communities with forums like *Proanorexia* having some of the lowest and most dangerous figures listed (Yom-Tov *et al.* 2016, p. 110), presumably due to members encouraging each other in this extreme direction.

In more recent years, this behaviour has shifted onto social media/micro-blogging sites to similar effect. Edtwt users will often have an indication of how long they have been fasting for. This is probably an inheritance from mid-2000s ED forums where users would commonly attach information to their sign-in names like "←hr63!" (Uca 2004, p. 20). It is also common to have pinned tweets that are unpinned when a specific weight is reached, for example, "unpinning at gw <3 (114lbs)" (kat 2021a). Participant Overw8y believes that participants share this kind of physical information to make themselves feel better via validation and approval from others, even if they present this data as simply motivation for themselves. She gets frustrated when friends send her information like readouts from gym equipment or pictures of skinny legs, as they make her feel jealous and angry. She explains,

> Everyone seems to be constantly trying to 'one-up' each other. "You fasted for 13 hours? Oh, I just passed hour 37." "You ate 746 calories today? God, I already feel full when I eat 200!" "You eat healthy to lose weight? Well I am vegan and I don't eat sugar or carbs and never touch KFC."
>
> (overw8y 2018)

Because of this discourse, she finds herself envious of people who seem to be more skilled at their eating disorders, even though she knows it is wrong. This puts her in a mindset of constant failure as knows there is always someone eating less than her or exercising more (overw8y 2018).

Potential rivals in the quest to be the best anorexic can be met with extreme hostility. For example, a blogger called Becca was angered by a co-worker losing weight through means rumoured to be unhealthy such as purging. In response, Becca wrote:

> If she starves for a day, im doing 2 days! She starves for a week…im doing 2 weeks! She works out for an hour, im doing 2 hours! She gets to 90lbs… im getting to 80lbs! She can't beat me…after all…she's 'playing' with ana

and mia...I FUCKING LIVE WITH THEM!...IM THE BETTER ANA...IM THE BETTER MIA...IM MORE PERFECT! [sic].

(Becca 2006a)

This spirit of antagonism seems to have a tangible impact on the mental health of participants. While pro-ana can be a comforting community, its other reality is as a source of stressful competition (Rich 2006, p. 286). Despite this, many seem to use the pain and anger they feel as further motivation, sometimes even seeking it out through meanspo and aggressive challenges.

Online starvation challenges are a perennial part of the community. The traditional format for this involves one participant establishing a stringent set of rules for a diet lasting from a few days to a few weeks. These contests often take place around important dates like public holidays or the school calendar (Charlotte 2002). In the more intensive contests, those who cannot stick to the rules will be disqualified and the person who gets closest to their goal weight during the period will win (Castro and Osório 2012, p. 177). Fasting challenges frequently persist beyond their original stated time period in order to allow elite-level competition (Uca 2004, p. 17). At present, most of these organised contests take place in private group chats recruited on Twitter as exemplified in the following 'advertisement': "does anyone wanna join a toxic/competitive ed gc? -do not join if you're sensitive -turn receive messages on -13+ -weekly weigh ins -fasts together -be okay with fatspo(problematic ppl only), meanspo, thinspo etc -there will be ranks! RT IF INTERESTED IN JOINING! #edtwtgc" (bee 2020) (see also Fig. 5.1).

In addition to these broader and more transient groups, users will often find 'buddies' with whom they can both compete and bond closely. These buddies are designed to offer the "highest level of support" (Uca 2004, p. 22). Some forums called this a 'twin' relationship. Twins were expected to be each other's primary relationship and a source of moral wisdom and support. Depending on needs, twins were assigned to help each other lose more weight quicker, effectively hide their disease, fast together in a small contest, cope with negative symptoms, or in some cases to recover together. Primarily, twins help foster a sense of intimacy during a disease that tends to alienate people from their family and friends (Cantó-Milà and Seebach 2011, pp. 149–150, 156). By coming together with a buddy under these terms, followers of pro-ana are promised they will find themselves in the "optimal conditions of human perfection" (Free Butterfly 2008).

One user explains her relationship with her texting buddy: "We remind each other to exercise, and even get competitive. Sometimes we tell each other we are stronger than our hunger, and chastise each other for eating. It is nice to have someone that understands and tells me what I want to hear". She explained that most people in her life tell her she is skinny and needs to eat. Her texting buddy gives her the message she wants, which is that she is still fat and that she needs to stay motivated to lose weight and work harder on starvation. She specifies, this is

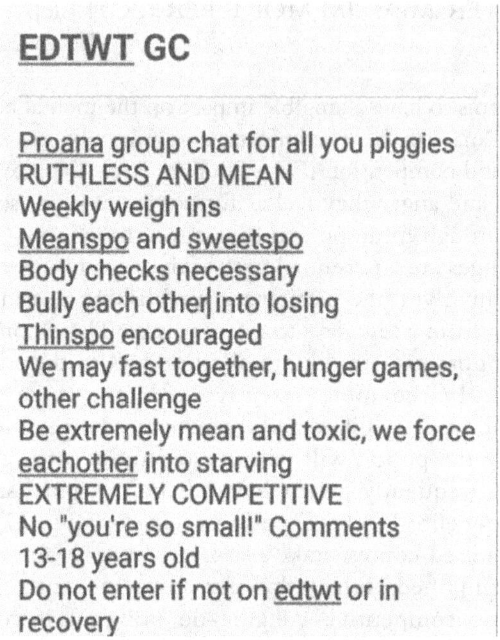

EDTWT GC

Proana group chat for all you piggies
RUTHLESS AND MEAN
Weekly weigh ins
Meanspo and sweetspo
Body checks necessary
Bully each other into losing
Thinspo encouraged
We may fast together, hunger games,
other challenge
Be extremely mean and toxic, we force
eachother into starving
EXTREMELY COMPETITIVE
No "you're so small!" Comments
13-18 years old
Do not enter if not on edtwt or in
recovery

Fig. 5.1 215 people asked publicly to join this group before the tweet it was advertised
on was deleted (bunny 2021).

"how I keep myself motivated, and this is a lifestyle that I want to continue" (Layton 2016). Participants describe additional starvation behaviours to keep up with their buddies' progress (Lilly 2011) and motivate each other through phrases like "stay strong" and "starve on" (Lavis 2016a, p. 42) or "stay strong, think thin, live ana" (Lilly 2011). Misa agrees that buddies help you "swap tips and indulge in your little sordid anorexia world together, force each other to exercise, pat each other on the back when you reach goals, etc.". Most importantly, they encourage you to move out of a mainstream consciousness and "completely surround yourself with all thoughts of anorexia" (Misa 2007). It is under these conditions that contagions can be supported through intimate social reinforcement.

Anorexia Personification

> Your voice in my head,
> sweet when I'm good,
> severe when I'm bad,
> you sing your song,
> "It'll all be ok when you're thin…"

and I try to sing along, off key, but you cut me off with a glare.
I feel like imposition on your greatness. (P O E M S 2001)

The characters "ana" and "mia" are often referred to as independent beings within pro-ana discourse – sometimes literally and sometimes as a metaphorical device for understanding mental illness. A common approach is to see ana as a friend. Many individuals see this friend as a part of themselves (Lavis 2017, p. 202), which is more common than the alternative of viewing her as a genuinely external character. This perception seems to be an inheritance from the Foucauldian Narrative Therapy popular in the 1990s that helped patients to place less blame on their own personalities and see diseases like anorexia as external influencing forces (Singler 2011, pp. 28–30). In a somewhat bastardised version of this approach, ana is often positioned as a guide who leads her followers toward a more effective starvation praxis. This is often against their own desires and bodily sensations. For example, "Does Ana want to go in the fridge? No she does not. Its time youy started paying attention to what Ana wants, not what you want [*sic*]" (Misa 2007).

The best way to understand ana and the relationships her adherents have with her is to read their poetry. Through verse, ana is called "My best friend, my only one... Without you I am so weak" (Sandavalli 2007). She encourages followers to "Stare down your weaknesses; Run miles and miles" (Delicate Sylph 2009a). Through her guidance, followers feel they might finally become "a woman worthy of love and respect" (Ash and Heather 2002). A repeated theme in these texts is the idea of the individual and their bodies as weak versus ana as strong. Ana is connected more with the mind, allowing it to triumph over bodily needs via her guidance and strong resolve. This resonates with interviews conducted by Jenkins and Ogden where people with anorexia saw this force as an external voice directing them towards irrational behaviours like neglecting to eat and feeling disproportionately guilty when they do (2012, p. e26). Based on the aforementioned poetic sentiments, this guilt may well come from the idea that one has failed to choose strength and success and has instead opted for corporeal weakness by 'succumbing' to hunger.

Because of her harsh and compassionless character, ana is also seen as an enemy; "the mean girl friend who is only nice enough to me for me to stay her friend" but who is never kind (wheniwas-thinner 2020). Indeed, followers use her voice to call themselves cruel names like "fat, ugly swine" (Delicate Sylph 2009a). She will instruct harsh punishments like self-harm, telling her followers to bang their heads into a wall or cut themselves to see blood (Joe 2005a). It is said that she "loves the pain she inflicts" (Lou 2000). Mia promises similar tortures. While she allows her followers to eat and have their "one true joy in life", she is adamant that they must compensate for their actions with pain. She expects feelings of guilt, intense workouts, and vomiting until they bring up blood (Joe 2005b). One adherent writes, "A demon lives inside my head/Telling me I should be dead" (Rebecca in Hutchings 2003b). Another tells ana, "You make me cry/ You make me sad/ You make my days horrible/ You always make me feel bad" (Lewis 2005).

As a friend/enemy, ana tends to be a very isolating influence with one follower describing the process of listening to her as "isolating myself in a world of numbers" that leads towards happiness and strength but away from family and friends (V • IX • MMXVIII 2014). If worthy, followers can dress in her uniform of "bony legs, sunken eyes and yellow skin". Anyone who is concerned is "wrong" and "jealous because I chose you, not them" for the honour (The voice of the bitch 2001). Ana also writes letters to her adherents, which show contempt for "so called 'doctors'", claims that friends are liars, and notes that praise from teachers or parents is worth nothing because "they are disappointed with you". The solution is to dedicate oneself to ana and feel her "in your head, your heart, and your soul" (Joe 2005a). Lavis sees this relationship as one where people are gripped in "protective numbness" by ana their friend while simultaneously being trapped and suffocated. Her informants talk about both loving and hating this embrace (2016a, p. 45). Mulveen and Hepworth found a similar scenario of informants calling anorexia both a friend and an enemy, never an entirely positive force even amongst those deeply dedicated (2006, p. 293). The distance from mainstream society that ana provides is both a safety blanket and source of suffocation that separates people from those who might be able to help – a fact that many seem keenly aware of.

This deep sense of isolation is core to understanding ana as a social re-lationship framework. From her interviews with people living with anorexia, Lavis found that narratives of a friendship with ana mediate their relation-ships with others. Rather than a static dislike of food or goal to be thin, they show a processual and active filtering of the world to keep ana close and other influences at a distance (2016a, pp. 44–45). Holding close to ana is a daily process that happens through the repeated performance of food refusal to maintain friendship and closeness with this figure (Lavis 2017, p. 202). Warin agrees that ana offers "a whole new set of social relations" apart and elevated from the norm like a religious sect or competitive team (2006, p. 33). In order to "stay true to ana", participants maintain their identity through both rigorous restriction and detailed self-disclosure of this beha-viour with other dedicated adherents (Haas *et al.* 2011, p. 47). These are people who understand the philosophical need to personify ana as a "devil on one's shoulder" to balance the painful and oppressive experiences of dis-ordered eating with a sincere idolisation of the emaciated form and the sense of control that comes from starvation (Day and Keys 2008, pp. 7–8). This is a relational framework that allows a sense of action and a feeling of skill, discipline, and achievement in a context where one's physical body is weak. The strength of this framework can easily weaken attempts at recovery (Knapton 2013, p. 473). Through this process of personification, ana be-comes more than the disease anorexia nervosa. Ana is a friend, enemy, and guiding force who offers strength and validation while encouraging distance from anyone who might disagree or interfere.

Religious Behaviour

Adding to the personification of ana and mia is their use as religious figures –
again either metaphorically or literally. As a metaphor, Mulveen and
Hepworth suggest that a deep yearning for anorexia is represented by rendering the disease as a goddess or a saint (2006, p. 293). Pro-ana websites
operate as confessionals, the community as congregation, and ana as a salvific
figure of intercession like the Holy Mother Mary of Catholicism (Ullyatt
2010, p. 84). Sins like overeating are considered an inevitable outcome of
human fallibility thus such mechanisms are needed to manage guilt (Hanson
2003, p. 39). Judeo-Christian values abound with focus given to sacrifice,
heroism, perfectionism, idealism, discipline, and perfectionism (Behar and
Arancibia 2015, p. 256). Rituals to support these values are also common,
such as collective fasting or ritualisation of limited food choices (like eating
only green foods on a Monday) (Cantó-Milà and Seebach 2011, p. 156).
Whatever the decree, followers tend to pursue anorexia with what Ullyatt
dubs "the same devotion, commitment and fear of wrath" demanded by the
God of the *Old Testament* (2010, p. 83). Indeed, ana and mia are presented as
gods who can either provide salvation or be "vengeful and punitive" (Day
and Keys 2008, p. 8). Thinspiration has been described with religious
overtones, dubbed a "sometimes-cult-like devotion to thinness ideals" with
"religiously tinged messages about skinniness as salvation" (Perloff 2014,
p. 370) facilitated through a "ritualised exchange of images and quotes"
(Casilli *et al.* 2013, p. 94). Fat and the body are thus presented as bad or evil
that should be condemned and punished. This draws on dualistic conflicts
between mind and body that have previously been resolved through a
Christian renunciation of the flesh and control of bodily urges (Malson and
Ussher 1996, p. 275).

All of this can be seen in primary sources. For example, when Yahoo!
attempted to purge pro-ana groups from its servers, one user protested by
explaining, "This is a sanctuary. Would you go into a church and speak
against God? Get the hell out of our place of worship" (Anabeauty in
Mackeen 2002, p. 149). Hell is often conflated with fatness. As one participant passionately explains, "IF GOD WANTS ME TO LIVE IN HELL
FOR ALL ETERNITY, ALL HE HAS TO DO IS KEEP ME FAT!
THAT'S MY OWN PERSONAL HELL!" (Becca 2006b). To spare a
person from this condemnation are tools like the toilet, sometimes called
"my porcelain savior" (Tara Michelle 2005). To achieve at the highest level,
one participant suggests you should "believe in the power of starving *as
though* it were a religion" (Misa 2007).[1] Another agrees that ana and mia are
personifications of illness and "you're not supposed to actually believe in
their existence as entities". Nevertheless, they prove useful when you need
to be forgiven for sin such as eating anything other than a measly portion,
failing to work out to a punishing degree, or telling an outsider about your
actions. She argues that recovery felt like the greatest sin of all when she

started to work in this direction. Also working through such guilt, she noted many people begging ana to forgive them or noting that mia is more merciful because she delivers the gift of purging after wrong actions (Petri 2020). While ana and mia are not seen as 'real' deities in this discourse, they still function in a powerful and meaningful manner informed by the Judeo-Christian tradition.[2]

Anorexia devotion functions as a religion with noted features such as belief systems and codes of practice (Knapton 2013, p. 470). Many of these derive from Christian-inspired texts like the *Thin Commandments*, which includes statements like "being thin and not eating are signs of true will power and success". Although these commandments were actually developed as a healing tool to expose the negative thinking behind anorexia (Costin 2000), they have taken on their own life as sincere directions for worsening one's behaviour and dedicating oneself to a life under anorexia's grip. With the removal of authorship credits, intentions such as those of Costin's can vanish. This also establishes texts like the *Thin Commandments* as having unknowable or divine authorship (Ullyatt 2010, p. 75). Indeed, Uca disagrees that these texts are from the medical world and argues that their creation by the pro-ana community is a remarkable testament to their "mission, devotion, motivation and rules". She notes that all legitimate pro-ana websites will have at least one out of the *Letter to Ana*, *Ana Psalm*, or *Ana Creed* available. Uca sees their lack of attributed author as a sign that they belong to the "community's mythology" (2004, p. 11). Even those who do not believe in or follow these commandments tend to protect and uphold them against outsiders who threaten or mock the pro-ana community (Giles 2016, p. 309). Having studied prominent texts like the *Pro-Ana Psalm* in detail (see Table 5.1), Ullyatt notes that they are devout and sincere pieces of writing that seek to spiritually elevate despite seeming to the outsider as "a clumsy parody" of the scriptures they mimic (*Psalm 23* from the Christian Bible in this case). The *Pro-Ana Psalm* outlines the emotional, psychological, and spiritual "benefits" that come from a life "adhering to the Way of Ana" (2010, p. 75). As with the proselytising Abrahamic faiths, anorexia as a religious pathway does indeed outline and emphasise the methods of starvation as something elevated that can help to ward off feelings of sin and failure and direct a person towards deeper withdrawal from bodily needs.

Table 5.1 The *Pro-Ana Psalm* (also known as the *Ana Psalm* or simply *Psalm*).

Strict is my diet. I must not want. It maketh me to lie down at night hungry. It leadeth me past the confectioners. It trieth my willpower. It leadeth me in the paths of alteration for my figure's sake. Yea, though I walk through the aisles of the pastry department, I will buy no sweet rolls for they are fattening. The cakes and the pies, they tempt me. Before me is a table set with green beans and lettuce. I filleth my stomach with liquids, My day's quota runneth over. Surely calorie and weight charts will follow me all the days of my life, And I will dwell in the fear of the scales forever (archived on Faux 2008).

Wannarexia and Boundary Policing

This mindset of anorexia as a religious pursuit gives participants a feeling of distinction and elevation, even if experienced only in a metaphorical sense. It also seems to have created fears about attacks from apostates, false novices, and non-believers. In order to maintain a firm group identity, pro-ana participants and communities tend to engage in some form of boundary maintenance. This in-group reinforcement contrasts anas to 'normals' who are viewed mainly as oblivious and sometimes as morally weak (Giles 2006, p. 471). A more dramatic and policed boundary is that between 'true anas' who are genuinely unwell and suffering versus wannabes who see pro-ana as a crash diet to achieve specific beauty ideals (Fox *et al.* 2005, p. 957). These wannabes are generally referred to as 'wannarexics' (wannabe anorexics) and are criticised for wanting to develop an eating disorder and being unaware of the negative consequences (Faux 2007a). Wannarexics are irritating, but more seriously, they threaten the core of the movement with their insincerity (Alderton 2018a, pp. 17–18).

They also reinforce negative media stereotypes about pro-ana spaces as a place to *learn* disordered eating. This is in contrast to the preferred viewpoint of ana as an uncontrollable disease and severe mental illness with negative consequences that should not be sought out (Lavis 2016b, p. 26). Asking for tips to cultivate anorexia is seen as insensitive and frustrating because "anorexia isn't a fucking trend, it isn't a fucking diet, and it damn sure isn't a healthy lifestyle. anorexia is a MENTAL DISORDER, A DISEASE. thats like asking someone how to get cancer or how to get depression [sic]" (hotmilk 2018). This supports the idea that wannarexics are "seeking a lifestyle rather than experiencing an illness" (Yeshua-Katz 2015, p. 1354). The "proper" function of a pro-ana site is to live through diagnosed anorexia rather than to live out a desire to develop it. The idea of "having *no* choice" is paramount here, rendering anyone who sees anorexia as an opt-in club inauthentic (Lavis 2016b, pp. 19, 26). Significant amounts of effort have been expended in protecting the community from such people and in some cases also protecting them from their own dangerous desires.

Policing of such boundaries and out-group labelling is typical of online support communities. Based on a series of interviews, Yeshua-Katz noted that boundary work against wannarexics was a common online experience and was a central part of some people's group identity and engagement. She sees stigma as the main cause of this; either in terms of resisting stigma against anorexia or reacting to the experience of being in a stigmatised online community. The fear here is that wannarexics seeking diet tips denude the credibility of anorexia as a severe mental illness and feed into media perceptions of pro-ana as eating disorder glorification (Yeshua-Katz 2015, p. 1353). Indeed, after negative media coverage pro-ana spaces are often attacked or sent hate mail and forced into a hostile defensive mode (Giles 2006, p. 463, Lavis 2016b, p. 14). Because eating disorders are stigmatised and mysterious, it seems unlikely that this kind of external infraction will stop – even if in-group responses may differ in their language or audition processes over time.

To limit wannarexics, many communities (especially in the heyday of forums) would utilise formal applications and trial periods for members where they had to explain their understanding of 'ana'and their eating disorder beliefs more broadly. While community members are often hostile to initiates, passing this phase tended to unlock a loyal and encouraging community (Brotsky and Giles 2007, p. 100). During this more delicate stage, it is common for participants to see themselves as 'newbies' and act accordingly. For example, a newbie should be careful not to intrude on conversations and should seek to earn their in-group membership over time rather than expecting it immediately (Giles 2006, p. 467). They should also expect a need to prove themselves through convincing interactions that show sincere and long-term illness (Giles and Newbold 2011, p. 420). If the initiation is failed, a person could be added to a 'wanna list' shared between forum moderators. Those who were good at identifying wannarexics could be promoted to site managers to fulfil this important duty (Yeshua-Katz 2015, p. 1355).

In the 2000s, aggressive outsiders were known as "haters" and identified by their "flaming" of pro-ana spaces (Giles 2006, p. 467). An example of this is the guestbook for the website 'Nothing Tastes as Good as Thin Feels'. "Insider" comments tend to be positive such as "this site could be the safest anorexia website around for people...keep up the help and support" and "thanks to your site, i have lost 17 lbs in 13 days!!!". "Outsider" comments show a large degree of hostility, often based on a misunderstanding of motivations behind disordered eating. Representative comments include, "you all seriously need some help from your disillusioned perseptions of how a woman should look. your killing yourselves, and for what?" and "There are people starving all over the world. How can you give up your food? It's wrong, that's what it is". Other comments even encourage suicide such as "I would recommend quitting life immediately" (Ash and Heather 2003). Other guestbooks of the era contain comparable comments like "SICK SICK SICK...that is the only word I have 4 it...!! GEt a life...start eating" (Please Sign My Guest Book:) 2002); "you should be ashamed of your self. this is a disgusting site. anorexia and bulimia should NOT be glamorized. YOU ARE ALL KILLING YOURSELFS SLOWLY. I YOU WANNA DIE, COMMIT SUICIDE"; and "U JUST MAKE URSELVES LOOK LIKE RETARDS...LIKE SKELETONS...ITS DISGUSTING [sic]" (luckie_gurl 2002).

In the 2020s, the pejorative term 'local' has been increasingly applied to outsiders who do not properly understand niche communities such as edtwt. A local is someone in your broader social sphere who is bland and basic, but who may wrongly see themselves as funny and connected. A local tends to lack irony and use tools like emoji sincerely and without humour. They tend to misunderstand memes or interpret them on a less nuanced level (katsukitings 2018). It is common for edtwt members to pin a request such as "locals DNI" [do not interact]

(Madeline ♡ edtwt 2020). This Twitter community is sensitive to possible trauma tourism from outsiders and contains messages for these lurkers or haters such as:

> HI NON DISORDERED PEOPLE THAT ARE SPYING ON ED TWT FOR YOUR ENJOYMENT!! WE ALL FUCKING HATE YOU AND WISH YOU WERENT HERE <3 LEAVE US THE FUCK ALONE. WE ARE DISORDERED AND ILL, NOT SOME ANIMALS AT THE ZOO FOR YOU TO LOOK AT.
>
> (sickstickboy 2020)

Such outsiders are opposed to pro-ana and make it clear that proponents of this philosophy are wrong, disgusting, or worthy of death for their beliefs.

In terms of echoing clusters, there does seem to be some degree of wannarexic conversion into clinically significant symptoms. Osgood provides a vivid picture of the life of a wannarexic in *How to Disappear Completely*. She explains, "Like me, they had fallen in love with the symbolism of anorexia and then found themselves unable to easily reverse their destructive habits. I began to think there might not be a big distinction between a 'real' anorexic and a person like me who had willed herself to get it". Indeed, although Osgood specifically aimed to cultivate anorexia, she found herself with a version severe enough to see her hospitalised four times (Osgood 2013). Others with severe symptoms seem to fear that they are wannarexic and feel accountable to the community, pushing themselves into greater symptomology as a result such as losing significant amounts of weight or following very strict diets (Yeshua-Katz 2015, p. 1355). In the following chapter, I discuss this as one of the ways in which media approaches to anorexia lead to dangerous radicalisation within the community.

Loneliness and Negative Affect

> Falling into my abyss of self destruction
> Deeper and deeper I fall
> I scream but no one hears
> my cries for help. (Heather 2003)

Finally, a major feature of pro-ana communities is low mood. Participants in pro-self-harmful spaces frequently describe feelings of isolation and unhappiness, for example, "An anorexic life is **lonely**" (Petri 2020). Many can acknowledge the negative consequences of their disease such as losing friends, struggling academically, or being unable to move into new life stages like marriage or parenthood. All of this can lead to feelings of intense frustration and exhaustion (Jenkins and Ogden 2012, p. e28). Isolation and sadness are often present in the life of anorexics before the disease emerges. For example, in Dignon's interviews with patients dealing with this illness she noted a "strong sense of unhappiness and loss" brought on by trauma, bullying, neglect, or simply an ongoing sense of inadequacy as compared with peers or siblings (2006, p. 945). Eating disorders often develop in relation to interpersonal struggles like teasing, trauma, or abuse (Polivy and Herman 2002, p. 195). Those who are unhappy or report victimisation are more likely to access self-harmful content online (Oksanen *et al.* 2016, p. 7). This sentiment is echoed in many pro-ana online spaces like *House of Thin* where Faux explains, "If the quality time and acceptance exsisted within our own families none of this would be happening...we are letting the secrets out. Things are NOT all good, things are NOT ok and if they were, we would not be this way [sic]". She suggests blaming breakdowns in society rather than the communities created to compensate for this pain (Faux 2007b). It is true that negative feelings and poor interpersonal relationships tend to precipitate disordered eating and thus engagement in pro-ana spaces.

Many people with anorexia struggle to have intimate relationships as their relationship with their disease takes precedence (Warin 2006, p. 44). As one participant writes,

> My mind became empty, I don't think about anything
> except my weight and becoming thinner and thinner everyday.
> What time is it? Do I know you?
> I don't know, I don't care. (Gueble 2005)

The processes involved in such extreme bodily choices are inherently isolating. As one academic in recovery explains, "The physical and mental process of making starvation my 'normal' way of life was lonely and excruciating" (Holmes 2016, p. 199). This pain is echoed in primary sources with one pertinent poem asking, "I scream and no one hears, I cry and no one sees/Why can't anyone see how much this disease is hurting me" (Spooky 2003). Another blogger of this era laments that it is too easy to seem happy when "inside your heart is aching". She feels that if anyone cared or if she was a more worthy person, they would have rescued her from drowning in sorrow (unswept_angel 2005). This idea of being disconnected from others means that people with eating disorders often make claims like "No one knows or understands me...I don't have any true friends that I can share anything with. I am alone, in a world where no one cares" (Aurora Jess 2000). In blogs, participants tend to express a negative view of their peers who they imagine as harshly judging their looks (Sheldon *et al.* 2015, p. 180). A "'nobody likes me' feeling" is a common sentiment in these spaces (Castro and Osório 2012, p. 182). In some cases, pro-ana members even incite instigating fights "just to make you constantly on edge, or nervous, so you cant eat...You'll be making yourself nauseous from worry and self hatred in no time [sic]" (Misa 2007). Isolation is often purposefully created to help maintain focus on weight loss behaviours.

In this isolated milieu, other anorexics are frequently seen as key emotional supports. The LiveJournal community *proanorexia* describes its users as people who are "all alone in the world" and thus rely solely on each other for advice, hope, and motivation (proanorexia 2007). This can often have more negative elements to it than what would typically be deemed support. Working under the ONESG framework, Haas *et al.* note that self-deprecating messages in the pro-ana sphere tend to be supported and re-inforced rather than the usual friendly response of contradiction. If a person claims to hate themselves or be weak, this is considered normal discourse and is not challenged. Instead, things like weight loss advice, commiseration, or thinspiration may be offered (2011, p. 49). In some ways, this is interpreted as core to the non-judgemental space of pro-ana where no one is forced to seem happy or recover. As one participant writes, "We share experiences and,/try to find possible solutions./We all love it all cuz no one does judge" (Puja 2003). At the same time, participants are aware of problems with this negative reinforcement. One admits she would "be waaay more productive and probably happier" if she left edtwt, but notes that "no one irl cares about what i say and this is kinda my 'safe place' lmao" ([sad] ana 2019). This contradiction of needing support but finding the support to be somewhat damaging is echoed across all eras of the community. For example, "pro-anorexic sites made me sicker, though I think I would have gotten worse even if I had not found them. I would have been alone" (Joe 2005c).

There is conflict here, as disordered eating seems to cause and be caused by distress, yet also be used to try and alleviate and express this affect. Indeed, it is typical for anorexia to be used as a bodily means of communicating psychological distress (Jenkins and Ogden 2012, p. e27). Participants in pro-ana spaces frequently express both loathing of their physical bodies and their inner selves (Haas *et al.* 2011, p. 48). One explains that her "physical scars resemble my internal emotional pain" (unswept_angel 2005). For many, anorexia has been a long-term coping strategy that has slowly become worse than the initial problem it was used to resolve (Brotsky and Giles 2007, p. 104). This worsening state seems to be exacerbated by pro-ana websites, which are known to make viewers feel worse about their appearance, have lower self-esteem, see themselves as heavier than they are, and plan to exercise more to address this (Bardone-Cone and Cass 2007, p. 537). While there are positive outcomes such as participants feeling less lonely or ashamed of their behaviours (Daine *et al.* 2013, p. e77555), this does not mean that the behaviours advocated on these sites are safe or healthy overall.

Conflict also occurs due to the aforementioned competitive core of the movement where being a 'better' anorexic means getting 'worse' from a medical standpoint. To this end, Cornelius and Blanton explored the "anorexia-pride hypothesis". This theory notes that participants in pro-ana present disordered eating as a way of developing higher self-esteem and as a behaviour worthy of pride. Nevertheless, although pro-ana discourse suggests this is true, Cornelius and Blanton found the opposite: gaining genuine and lasting pride from anorexia does not happen. Instead, pro-ana beliefs engender lower self-esteem and negative affect. Self-esteem was only increased when anorexic identities were rejected (2016, pp. 139, 145–146). At best, pro-anorexia seems to offer temporary highs that keep generally unhappy participants motivated on their quest to starve (Gailey 2009, p. 104). Rigid control over food provides a brief alleviation of unhappiness and a way "to keep at bay the torrent of pain which threatened to overwhelm them" if not hyper-focussed on the minute details of their intake (Dignon *et al.* 2006, p. 948). This mindset spawns arguably conflicting sentiments like "being skinny will make me happy" (Haley in Coggan 2017) or "All i know is that skinny=happy" (Kelsey 2003). This happiness is generally positioned as a perpetually shifting goalpost that will be achieved through the future goal of skinniness that always lies somewhere over the horizon. As such, Malson and Ussher see this kind of weight loss as "an essential part of achieving happiness" as opposed to a mere vanity project (1996, p. 273).

Social isolation and obsession also appear to hamper potential recovery. Turja *et al.* found that people who engage in pro-ana spaces have lower subjective well-being.[3] Conversely, if a person has a stronger sense of belonging (with family or friends) in the offline world, they are insulated from more harmful effects of pro-ana (2017, pp. 50, 55). This is complicated by the fact that many people who are deeply absorbed in their disorder lose contact with friends or assume that they are disliked by their peers. Many describe communication breakdowns such as: "All I wanna do is vent to my friends but I know they already force themselves to just say 'take care' so why would I put them thru that. They probably waiting for my suicide news [sic]" (Casilli *et al.* 2013, p. 94) (tem ♥*:·˚ 2021a). Others speak of actively hostile encounters like: "my ex friend sent me a long paragraph about how i'm a shitty person and talked about how talking to me is like talking to a brick wall but if she even bothered to care about me she'd know why i've become like this [sic]" (kat 2021b). In both cases, the anorexic subject sees herself as irrevocably disconnected from healthy peers and unable to engage in reciprocal communications. Comparatively, one pro-ana blogger explains the difficulty of recovering when anorexia and bulimia have been "two of the best friends I have ever had" who "never deserted me when the going got tough" and "gave me much-needed unconditional love". This is in contrast to her feelings of "loneliness, alienation from the healthy world at large" where she does not feel understood or supported (Delicate Sylph 2009b). This is a common response, which needs to be carefully addressed in order to stop echoing contagion and direct participants towards healthier coping mechanisms.

Pro-Self-Harm and Pro-Suicide

Both pro-self-harm and pro-suicide communities also have space online (for more detail see Alderton 2018a). Due to constraints of space, this chapter has explored pro-ana in detail. This is not to suggest that there is not a significant overlap between this community and other self-harmful groups or that their manifestation is dissimilar. Rather, there are profound similarities. As with pro-ana, self-harmers have found solace speaking to 'kindred spirits' and enjoying the freedom online to represent themselves as they wish and to escape from the pain of their offline worlds where they are often labelled as deviants' and 'loners'. In contrast, they can rely on the internet as a means of having (sometimes for the first time) "subcultural and collegial relations" (Adler and Adler 2008, pp. 33, 44). As one participant explains, "I was very isolated from other people (felt like a freak) so the only people who I related to were other people who self-harmed" (Maria 2003). This is also exemplified by self-harm blogger Kathy who used to think she was the only person in the world who cut herself and that she was 'totally demented' for doing so. When she gained access to the internet at the turn of the century, she realised that many other people cut as a way of releasing their emotional pain. Knowing this was deeply reassuring to her. In turn, Kathy started to share her own story so that others would be spared the "awful feeling" of isolation (Kathy 2004).

This reliance on the internet makes sense, as the stressors associated with adolescent self-harm are often parts of worlds they cannot easily escape offline, such as schoolmates, and teachers (Jutengren *et al.* 2011, p. 250). Many rely on self-harm as their main intrapersonal communication as they struggle with negative social relationships and have difficulty expressing themselves in other ways (Turner *et al.* 2012, p. 4). Users on pro-suicide forums similarly report trouble receiving support from family and offline friends, meaning they often seek out companionship in online spaces. Such spaces offer feelings of support and a reduction in alienation. Although many users claim to feel less suicidal as a result, there are also high instances of accessing suicide methods and pro-suicide material that may be unhelpful (Harris *et al.* 2009, pp. 264, 272). As with pro-ana, this companionship can be part of a negative feedback cycle. Higher engagement with these spaces is associated with increased depression, suicidal ideation, and self-harm in addition to cyberbullying and exposure to violent self-harm methods that can influence behaviour (Daine *et al.* 2013, p. e77555). Overall, people at risk of suicide spend more time online compared to their peers with a particular focus on social networking (Harris *et al.* 2014, p. 391). As social networking becomes more prominent in the internet experience, this is increasingly the locus of potentially problematic behaviours and echoing contagions.

Over the years, and despite changes in the nature of the internet and the services offered, a reoccurring theme has been an 'us versus them' mentality where the shared secret of self-harm brings people together and lets them discuss taboo ideas more freely. Rodham *et al.* have explored the paradox of self-harmers who value secrecy about their behaviour in the offline world, often going to extreme lengths to hide signs of their behaviour (e.g., staying fully covered in hot weather) yet seem happy to share with their online community. Secrecy is often perceived as a sign of an 'authentic' self-harmer.

Nevertheless, in online self-harm communities, graphic and detailed content is often encouraged and does not seem to undermine the posters' identities as legitimate self-harmers rather than 'wannabes'. Many posters justify their membership in the community by logging details of their behaviour such as the layer of the body they hit with their cutting tool (fat, veins, bone etc). 'True' membership is also demonstrated by derogatory discussions of those who misunderstand self-harm and its functions. So long as participants make it clear that they are not embarrassing attention-seekers, they can be respected for their self-harm behaviours and contribution to the community as a whole (2016, pp. 1110, 1113–1114). This sense of respectability is achieved by "drawing a strict line" between themselves and "fashion cutters" who seek attention and by presenting clear signs of broader illness that drive them to this behaviour (Sternudd 2017, p. 176). Presently, a way of determining in-group membership is the use of special hashtags. The self-harm Twitter community often use #madeofbeans and #madeofstyrofoam to identify themselves. These tags obliquely refer to the bodily substances visible from deep cutting. Styrofoam is the dermis (appears white when cut) and beans is the sub-cutaneous layer (containing bean-shaped fat). This oblique reference keeps out people with only a surface knowledge of the community and helps to evade censorship applied to more obvious tags like #selfharm. Such processes of community protection show significant similarity to the boundary policing of pro-ana spaces discussed earlier.

Because pro-self-harm spaces contain an a priori acceptance that users will partake in actions like cutting themselves to communicate, emotionally regulate, or self-punish, they become a venue where people can gain peer support. Common questions include, "Does anyone else use sh as a form of punishment for bad behaviour? Like, I don't know if it's just me, but as of today I made a new rule for myself that every time I express negative emotions in front of somebody I sh" (howl 2021) or "How do I hide my arms and thighs at all moments??? Hiding scars and fresh cuts is becoming so difficult. If mom sees again she'll make sure to torment me about it and make fun of me during family reunions" (tem ♥∗:·˚ 2021b). Rather than telling this person she should recover or not cut, her Twitter community suggests instead long sleeves and other concealing clothing choices. This is similar to the kind of support discussed earlier in pro-ana spaces where maintenance is more of a focus than recovery.

People engaging in this behaviour generally agree that "self-harm provides a way of expressing pain without using words" (Bryant et al. 2021, p. 113527). In the safe space of other self-harmers, these words can start to emerge. In the early- to mid-2000s, poetry was a popular way to share the function of self-harm, express interpersonal strain, and celebrate the release gained from this action. Some summative examples follow:

Her pain runs deep,
The control she can no longer keep.

She takes control over her skin,
To only feel real again. (Erin 2004)

Don't look at the marks that i drew,
Not at the scars or cuts that are new.
You blame me for all, you blame me too much,
Now I've got to go to my room and cut.
Look, I've done something wrong yet again,
Time to go punish myself with pain. (Angeldust 2001)

The blade against the skin,
Makes me think I can win.
When I feel like nothing,
I turn to my secret cutting.
...
I turn to it for release,
It's not something I can cease,
It's how I cope
When I have no more hope. (Erin 2008)

Droplets of misery taint veins –
Beads of Ruby release these pains. (v_falling_to_pieces 2003)

What we learn from such expression is the depth of pain felt by members of the self-harm community. Rather than finding solutions through positive interpersonal interactions or professional help, many are simply left alone to cope the best way they can. Having learned that physical pain can distract from emotional pain, this is an accessible way of temporarily diminishing negative affect.

In terms of contagion, perhaps the most dangerous aspect of online communities is their ability to encourage a view of self-harm as a lifestyle. For example, many self-harm websites, such as self-harm themed Tumblrs, function as self-harm catalogues. Desirable and impressive images are archived by curators, and then viewed by connoisseurs. Several of Sternudd's informants told him that these catalogues were like sample cards that helped them to choose the right location for their injuries, note where cuts and scars could be hidden by clothing, find novel locations to experiment with, and get ideas for words or signs that could be engraved on their own flesh (2012, p. 430). In this way, they function like the tattoo flash sheets that adorn parlours and give suggestions to customers. Such collections of images also help to create the idea of a self-harm lifestyle that can be opted into by audience members. In their interviews, Adler and Adler noted a clear difference between those who were members of online communities and those who were not. The latter tended to accept that they used self-harm at some point in their lives but rejected the idea that it was a major part of their personality and identity. Those who were engaged with self-harm communities tended to posit self-harm as the main feature of their identity. They were also more likely to identify with labels like "cutter" and to see themselves as part of a larger groups of people who behaved in the same way. In the words of a young woman they interviewed, the internet turned her self-harm from something that was a habit into something that became a *lifestyle* (2011, pp. 137–139). By engaging in self-harm communities, there is a real chance that participants will be exposed to new methods of self-harm or suicide and be more likely to receive this information as a valid coping method for difficult situations. They may also identify with self-harm as a personality trait and see it as something that needs to be maintained in order to stay connected with an embracive community.

Conclusion

Online self-harm communities do pose a real danger to participants. These niche groups and philosophies can render starvation, suicide, and other self-harmful behaviour as good, acceptable, moral, or reasonable. They also show strong evidence of contagion. Despite wishes to keep outsiders at bay, these communities contain dangerous resources that can be accessed relatively freely by people at risk. The internet can inspire mass self-harmful clusters, turn point clusters into mass clusters, or allow previous clusters to echo. There also seems to be a connection between suicidal feelings and time spent online developing relationships with others and using forums and social media to connect (Harris *et al.* 2014). At the same time, there is obvious value in having safe and judgement-free spaces where people can openly express and explore their darker emotions. Participants in communities like pro-ana generally describe themselves as unfairly judged and alienated from the mainstream. Community tools like journaling are an effective way of expressing non-normative ideas in a safe space and gaining a sense of empathy rather than rejection. The people who seem most vulnerable to self-harmful scripting are those who *already* show high levels of dissatisfaction with their bodies, life, or self-image. For example, those who gravitate towards pro-ana tend to show disordered eating patterns prior to reading about those practiced by others (Perloff 2014, p. 370). This leads to the question of whether the internet is allowing adolescents to better understand their negative feelings, or if it is causing these feelings to be magnified. The answer seems to be that both things are happening at once.

To explore this complex relationship, this chapter has summarised some of the common elements to be found in pro-ana and pro-self-harm sites from the turn of the century to the present day. One of these is the folksonomy of tagging whereby keywords (often neologisms to evade detection) link users with content across networks. This has become increasingly important as communities have dispersed in a social media environment. Inspiration for further harm, such as thinspo, is also a popular trend. These images tend to inspire negative body comparisons that inspire further starvation or uphold the community normalisation of severe emaciation. While photos are the classic example of thinspiration, it can also take the form of films, song lyrics, and so on viewed through a pro-ana lens. To achieve this desired state of severe emaciation, pro-ana communities frequently share instructions for the exacerbation of behaviour. This tends to include both instructions for extreme minimisation of caloric intake and guidelines for evading suspicion from friends, family, or medical professionals who may stand in the way of this restriction. Competitive behaviours are also concerning. This drive for perfection has been a substantial part of online eating disorder culture since its early days, leading many people to feel that starvation will physically, emotionally, and spiritually transform them into superior beings (Alderton 2018b). This also leads to a culture where increasingly extreme goals are prized.

Some participants, especially in the older days of the movement, were also encouraged (or arguably discouraged) by the personification of their disease as the characters ana and mia. In this form of companion and guiding force, personification sometimes took on a religious character inspired by Judeo-Christian zealotry. Whether religiously inspired or not, a sense of being set apart from others is central to pro-ana – inspiring strong boundaries and suspicion of outsiders. Unsurprisingly, many participants simultaneously feel lonely and misunderstood, communicating a strong negative affect that their eating behaviour both calms then fuels. While the main focus of this chapter was the pro-ana community, similar content and trends can be observed in pro-self-harm and pro-suicide groups. Indeed, many participants engage across groups and identify with more than one self-harmful practice. The next chapter provides some practical tools for dealing with this paradox of a community that both harms its participants and is often their sole source of support or genuine communication. As Overbeke claims, the power of pro-ana is not simply that the culture of this movement exhorts the development of eating disorders. Rather, it is the creation of an eating disorder identity and camaraderie that acts as a greater motivating feature (2008, p. 57). There is a real possibility of using this motivation to push participants towards an enthusiastic recovery instead. In the material that follows, I outline ways that we can take positive elements from self-harmful communities, limit their negative impacts, stop heavy-handed censorship efforts, and expand meaningful peer support programmes that leave vulnerable people feeling heard and cared for.

Notes

1 Emphasis mine.
2 For details of the more obscure AnaMadim cult and other religions based on anorexia, see Alderton (2018b, 2018a, p. 17ff).
3 Subjective wellbeing (SWB) refers to a person's own view about their psychological health, happiness, and level of appreciation for life. SWB tends to be higher when a person has good health, access to resources, and feels included in social activities (Turja *et al.* 2017, p. 51).

References

Adler, P.A. and Adler, P., 2008. The cyber worlds of self-injurers: Deviant communities, relationships, and selves. *Symbolic Interaction*, 31 (1), 33–56.

Adler, P.A. and Adler, P., 2011. *The Tender Cut: Inside the Hidden World of Self-Injury.* United States of America: NYU Press.

Alderton, Z., 2018a. *The Aesthetics of Self-Harm: The Visual Rhetoric of Online Communities.* Abingdon: Routledge.

Alderton, Z., 2018b. Pro-Ana and Pro-Mia Religious Groups [online]. *World Religions and Spirituality Project*. Available from: https://wrldrels.org/2018/03/04/pro-ana-and-pro-mia-religious-groups/ [Accessed 7 Mar 2018].

Ana is Love, 2016. Ana loves us [online]. *Ana loves us*. Available from: https://web.archive.org/web/20160615232258/http://anaislove.weebly.com:80/ [Accessed 23 Apr 2021].

Angeldust, 2001. Rhapsody [online]. *Angeldust World*. Available from: https://web.archive.org/web/20011013023325/http://www.angelfire.com/nc/angeldustworld/rhapsody.html [Accessed 10 May 2021].

Arianna, 2002. About Me [online]. *AnOreXiC AdDiCt*. Available from: https://web.archive.org/web/20030407043209fw_/http://myweb.ecomplanet.com/bouc2329/pageaboutus.htm [Accessed 24 May 2021].

Arndt, L., 2000a. Food For Thought: Page 1 [online]. *Anorexic Web*. Available from: https://web.archive.org/web/20001219062600/http://www.anorexicweb.com:80/FoodForThought/foodforthought.html [Accessed 13 Mar 2018].

Arndt, L., 2000b. Wishbone: The secret wish to be or continue to be anorexic (Part 2) [online]. *Anorexic Web*. Available from: https://web.archive.org/web/20010208193252/http://anorexicweb.com:80/Wishbone/wishbonepage2.html [Accessed 8 Mar 2018].

Ash and Heather, 2002. Letter To Ana [online]. *Nothing Tastes As Good As Thin Feels.* Available from: https://web.archive.org/web/20030621232703fw_/http://myweb.ecomplanet.com/FUMB1613/mycustompage0018.htm [Accessed 13 Aug 2020].

Ash and Heather, 2003. Sign our guest book [online]. *Nothing Tastes As Good As Thin Feels*. Available from: https://web.archive.org/web/20030621232742fw_/http://myweb.ecomplanet.com/FUMB1613/pageemail.htm [Accessed 13 Aug 2020].

Aurora Jess, 2000. Rambles [online]. *Lost childhood*. Available from: https://web.archive.org/web/20000529042904/http://www.angelfire.com/hi/LostChildHood/rambles.html [Accessed 12 Apr 2021].

Bardone-Cone, A.M. and Cass, K.M., 2007. What does viewing a pro-anorexia website do? An experimental examination of website exposure and moderating effects. *International Journal of Eating Disorders*, 40 (3), 537–548.

Becca, 2006a. I DON'T THINK I'LL EVER BE FREE! [online]. *angelicgirl21*. Available from: https://web.archive.org/web/20130802030230/http://angelicgirl21.xanga.com/549150423/i-dont-think-ill-ever-be-free/ [Accessed 20 May 2021].

Becca, 2006b. DAY....WHATEVER!! [online]. *angelicgirl21*. Available from: https://web.archive.org/web/20130802030704/http://angelicgirl21.xanga.com/545154769/daywhatever/ [Accessed 20 May 2021].

bee, 2020. does anyone wanna join a toxic/competitive ed gc? [online]. *@B33ISDEAD*. Available from: https://twitter.com/B33ISDEAD/status/1316810711037890565 [Accessed 31 May 2021].

Behar, R. and Arancibia, M., 2015. The Spiritual dimension of anorexia nervosa: Clinical and therapeutic implications. *In*: E.C. Roberts, ed. *Spirituality: Global Practices, Societal Attitudes, and Effects on Health*. New York: Nova Publishers, 253–272.

Brotsky, S.R. and Giles, D., 2007. Inside the "Pro-ana" community: A covert online participant observation. *Eating Disorders*, 15 (2), 93–109.

Bryant, L.D., O'Shea, R., Farley, K., Brennan, C., Crosby, H.F., Guthrie, E., and House, A., 2021. Understanding the functions of repeated self-harm: A Q methodology approach. *Social Science & Medicine*, 268, 113527.

bunny, 2021. EDTWT GC [online]. *Twitter*. Available from: https://twitter.com/starvehim/status/1380357539389272069/photo/1 [Accessed 5 May 2021].

Burke, E., 2012. Reflections on the waif: Images of slenderness and distress in pro-anorexia websites. *Australian Feminist Studies*, 27 (71), 37–54.

Cantó-Milà, N. and Seebach, S., 2011. Ana's friends. Friendship in online Pro-Ana communities. *Sociological Research Online*, 16 (1), 149–161.

Casilli, A.A., Pailler, F., and Tubaro, P., 2013. Online networks of eating-disorder websites: Why censoring pro-ana might be a bad idea. *Perspectives in Public Health*, 133 (2), 94–95.

Castro, T.S. and Osório, A.J., 2012. Online violence: Not beautiful enough … not thin enough. Anorectic testimonials in the web. *PsychNology Journal*, 10 (3), 169–186.

Charlotte, 2002. Ana competition [online]. *The Anorexic Files*. Available from: https://web.archive.org/web/20021031155110/http://gloomsday.net:80/theanorexicfiles/competition.html [Accessed 21 Nov 2018].

Coggan, M., 2017. Body positivity hasn't defeated the thinspo blog [online]. *Vice*. Available from: https://www.vice.com/en/article/8xxnqk/body-positivity-hasnt-defeated-the-thinspo-blog [Accessed 20 May 2021].

Cornelius, T. and Blanton, H., 2016. The limits to pride: A test of the pro-anorexia hypothesis. *Eating Disorders*, 24 (2), 138–147.

Costin, C., 2000. The thin commandments [online]. *SelfGrowth.com*. Available from: http://www.selfgrowth.com/articles/Costin1.html [Accessed 29 Nov 2016].

Daine, K., Hawton, K., Singaravelu, V., Stewart, A., Simkin, S., and Montgomery, P., 2013. The power of the web: A systematic review of studies of the influence of the internet on self-harm and suicide in young people. *PLoS ONE*, 8 (10), e77555.

Day, K. and Keys, T., 2008. Starving in cyberspace: A discourse analysis of pro-eating-disorder websites. *Journal of Gender Studies*, 17 (1), 1–15.

Delicate Sylph, 2009a. Kicking at the darkness---Original poems: Celebrating a love/hate relationship with Ana [online]. *Haven of the Delicate Sylph*. Available from: http://www.geocities.ws/haven_of_the_delicate_sylph/anapoems.html [Accessed 6 May 2021].

Delicate Sylph, 2009b. Fighting the battle of our lives: When recovery becomes an option---But a very shaky one [online]. *Haven of the Delicate Sylph*. Available from: http://www.geocities.ws/haven_of_the_delicate_sylph/prorecoveryessay.html [Accessed 5 May 2021].

Dignon, A., Beardsmore, A., Spain, S., and Kuan, A., 2006. 'Why I won't eat': Patient testimony from 15 anorexics concerning the causes of their disorder. *Journal of Health Psychology*, 11 (6), 942–956.

Erin, 2004. Wave Rider [online]. *Secret Cutting and the Pain Behind Self Injury*. Available from: http://www.angelfire.com/bc3/secondchance/waverider.html [Accessed 25 Aug 2020].

Erin, 2008. My Secret Cutting [online]. *Secret Cutting and the Pain Behind Self Injury*. Available from: http://www.angelfire.com/bc3/secondchance/cutting.html [Accessed 25 Aug 2020].

Faux, M., 2007a. Pro-Ana Acronyms, ect. [online]. *House of Thin*. Available from: https://web.archive.org/web/20070702080114/http://www.houseofthin.com/library/acronyms.php [Accessed 6 May 2021].

Faux, M., 2007b. Secret Closets – Outcasts Unite [online]. *House of Thin.* Available from: https://web.archive.org/web/20070702075529/http://www.houseofthin.com/newsroom/secret-closet.php [Accessed 10 May 2021].

Faux, M., 2008. Ana Psalm [online]. *Fading Obsession:: Pro Ana Mia Website plus Forum.* Available from: https://web.archive.org/web/20080724114626/http://www.fading-obsession.com/religion/ana-psalm.php [Accessed 23 Apr 2021].

Fox, N., Ward, K., and O'Rourke, A., 2005. Pro-anorexia, weight-loss drugs and the internet: an 'anti-recovery' explanatory model of anorexia. *Sociology of Health and Illness,* 27 (7), 944–971.

Free Butterfly, 2008. Ana Writtings [online]. ~ *Free the butterfly within ~: the haven of an ana butterfly.* Available from: https://web.archive.org/web/20080218052720/http://www.freewebs.com:80/free-the-bfly/anawrittings.htm [Accessed 7 Mar 2018].

Gailey, J.A., 2009. "Starving is the most fun a girl can have": The pro-ana subculture as edgework. *Critical Criminology,* 17 (2), 93–108.

Giles, D., 2006. Constructing identities in cyberspace: The case of eating disorders. *British Journal of Social Psychology,* 45 (3), 463–477.

Giles, D.C., 2016. Does ana=Anorexia? Online interaction and the construction of new discursive objects. *In:* M. O'Reilly and J.N. Lester, eds. *The Palgrave Handbook of Adult Mental Health: Discourse and Conversation Studies.*Houndmills, Basingstoke, Hampshire; New York: Palgrave Macmillan, 308–326.

Giles, D.C. and Newbold, J., 2011. Self- and other-diagnosis in user-led mental health online communities. *Qualitative Health Research,* 21 (3), 419–428.

Gueble, M.E., 2005. Bubble [online]. *Fragile Innocence.* Available from: https://web.archive.org/web/20041217220319if_/http://winkin.phpwebhosting.com:80/~joeic/privet/thin/art/poem049.html [Accessed 13 Nov 2018].

Haas, S.M., Irr, M.E., Jennings, N.A., and Wagner, L.M., 2011. Communicating thin: A grounded model of Online Negative Enabling Support Groups in the pro-anorexia movement. *New Media & Society,* 13 (1), 40–57.

Hanson, L., 2003. Pro-ana, a culture remediated in cyberspace. *Proceedings of the Media Ecology Association,* 4, 36–46.

Harris, K., McLean, J., and Sheffield, J., 2009. Examining suicide-risk individuals who go online for suicide-related purposes. *Archives of Suicide Research,* 13 (3), 264–276.

Harris, K.M., McLean, J.P., and Sheffield, J., 2014. Suicidal and online: How do online behaviors inform us of this high-risk population? *Death Studies,* 38 (6), 387–394.

Heather, 2003. Falling [online]. *Caring Online.* Available from: https://web.archive.org/web/20030422131849/http://www.caringonline.com/feelings/poetry/heather/why_falling.htm [Accessed 9 Apr 2021].

Holmes, S., 2016. Between feminism and anorexia: An autoethnography. *International Journal of Cultural Studies,* 19 (2), 193–207.

hotmilk, 2018. please stop [online]. *Tumblr.* Available from: https://hotmillk.tumblr.com/post/168832712080/please-stop-s-t-o-p-messaging-ana-accounts [Accessed 17 Apr 2018].

howl, 2021. Does anyone else use sh as a form of punishment for bad behaviour? [online]. @ *wolfypup.* Available from: https://twitter.com/wolfypup/status/1381369706448187392 [Accessed 5 May 2021].

Hutchings, M., 2003a. Recovery Stories [online]. *Body Cage.* Available from: https://web.archive.org/web/20030207085328/http://www.bodycage.com/recovery.html [Accessed 8 Apr 2021].

Hutchings, M., 2003b. Your Poems [online]. *Body Cage*. Available from: https://web. archive.org/web/20030408033204/http://www.bodycage.com/poem2.html [Accessed 8 Apr 2021].

Jenkins, J. and Ogden, J., 2012. Becoming 'whole' again: A qualitative study of women's views of recovering from anorexia nervosa. *European Eating Disorders Review*, 20 (1), e23–e31.

Joe, 2005a. [l]etter from ana [online]. *Fragile Innocence*. Available from: https://web. archive.org/web/20040821113126if_/http://winkin.phpwebhosting.com:80/~joeic/ privet/thin/religion/letterfromana.html [Accessed 13 Nov 2018].

Joe, 2005b. [l]etter from mia [online]. *Fragile Innocence*. Available from: https://web. archive.org/web/20040821115917if_/http://winkin.phpwebhosting.com:80/~joeic/ privet/thin/religion/letterfrommia.html [Accessed 13 Nov 2018].

Joe, 2005c. [m]y story [online]. *Fragile Innocence*. Available from: https://web.archive.org/ web/20041212013218if_/http://winkin.phpwebhosting.com:80/~joeic/privet/thin/ me/mystory.html [Accessed 15 Nov 2018].

Jutengren, G., Kerr, M., and Stattin, H., 2011. Adolescents' deliberate self-harm, inter-personal stress, and the moderating effects of self-regulation: A two-wave longitudinal analysis. *Journal of School Psychology*, 49 (2), 249–264.

kat, 2021a. unpinning at gw <3 (114lbs) [online]. @deadcalzxo. Available from: https:// twitter.com/deadcalzxo/status/1377449707165917190 [Accessed 5 May 2021].

kat, 2021b. my ex friend sent me a long paragraph about how i'm a shitty person. @ deadcalzxo. https://twitter.com/deadcalzxo/status/1388395189169950725

Kathy, 2004. si [online]. *Self-Injury*. Available from: https://web.archive.org/web/20041012 043054/http://members.tripod.com/%7Efuschia9/si.htm [Accessed 12 Apr 2021].

katsukitings, 2018. Locals. *Urban Dictionary*. https://www.urbandictionary.com/define. php?term=Locals

Kelsey, 2003. Need an ana and mia buddy soon!! [online]. *The Classifieds*. Available from: https://web.archive.org/web/20030702173427/http://pub46.bravenet.com/classified/ show.php?usernum=3926630828&cpv=1 [Accessed 11 Aug 2020].

Knapton, O., 2013. Pro-anorexia: Extensions of ingrained concepts. *Discourse & Society*, 24 (4), 461–477.

Lavis, A., 2016a. The Substance of Absence: Exploring Eating and Anorexia. *In*: E.-J. Abbots and A. Lavis, eds. *Why we eat, how we eat: contemporary encounters between foods and bodies*. London: Routledge, 35–52.

Lavis, A., 2016b. Alarming engagements? Exploring pro-anorexia websites in/and the media. *In*: K. Eli and S.J. Ulijaszek, eds. *Obesity, Eating Disorders and the Media*. London: Routledge, 11–35.

Lavis, A., 2017. Food porn, pro-anorexia and the viscerality of virtual affect: Exploring eating in cyberspace. *Geoforum*, 84, 198–205.

Layton, A., 2016. Interview: Pro ANA, an easy concept? [online]. *A Culture Starved for Love*. Available from: http://starvedlove.blogspot.com/2016/04/interview.html [Accessed 21 Nov 2018].

Lewis, M., 2005. Letter to Ana and Mia [online]. *Fragile Innocence*. Available from: https://web.archive.org/web/20041216115855if_/http://winkin.phpwebhosting. com:80/~joeic/privet/thin/art/poem039.html [Accessed 14 Nov 2018].

Lilly, 2011. Changes. *Perfect, Empty, Thin – A Pro Ana Blog*. http://perfectemptythin. blogspot.com/2011/01/normality.html

Lou, 2000. ANNA [online]. *Silent Screams*. Available from: https://web.archive.org/web/20030330065027/http://www.silent-screams.org/anna.shtml [Accessed 7 Apr 2021].

luckie_gurl, 2002. Guest Book [online]. *Totally in Control*. Available from: https://web.archive.org/web/20020616162408/http://myweb.ecomplanet.com/toic6711/PageEmail.htm [Accessed 19 Aug 2020].

Mackeen, D., 2002. Waifs on the Web. *Teen People*, 5(3), 147–149.

Madeline ♡ edtwt, 2020. § — ∵ ∴ tw: ED vent account [online]. *@madeline_xs*. Available from: https://twitter.com/madeline_xs/status/1339793889893310465 [Accessed 20 Apr 2021].

Malson, H.M. and Ussher, J.M., 1996. Body poly-texts: Discourses of the anorexic body. *Journal of Community & Applied Social Psychology*, 6, 267–280.

Maria, 2003. Confessions of a 15 year self harm junky now 1 year in recovery [online]. *Stories of Hope*. Available from: https://web.archive.org/web/20031012222018fw_/http://members.tripod.com/helen-scott/SOH/maria%20story.htm [Accessed 9 Apr 2021].

Mayli, 2007. Its ME! [online]. *Mayli's AnaMag*. Available from: https://web.archive.org/web/20070625025505/http://www.freewebs.com/ana-mag/itsme.htm [Accessed 24 May 2021].

Misa, 2007. Tips and tricks [online]. *University of EdNos*. Available from: https://web.archive.org/web/20071028183653/http://www.freewebs.com/uenway/breakroom.htm [Accessed 24 May 2021].

Mulveen, R. and Hepworth, J., 2006. An interpretative phenomenological analysis of participation in a pro-anorexia internet site and its relationship with disordered eating. *Journal of Health Psychology*, 11 (2), 283–296.

Oksanen, A., Näsi, M., Minkkinen, J., Keipi, T., Kaakinen, M., and Räsänen, P., 2016. Young people who access harm-advocating online content: A four-country survey. *Cyberpsychology: Journal of Psychosocial Research on Cyberspace*, 10 (2). https://cyberpsychology.eu/article/view/6179/5909

Osgood, K., 2013. Anorexia is contagious, and I wanted to catch it. *Time*. https://ideas.time.com/2013/11/15/anorexia-is-contagious-and-i-wanted-to-catch-it/

Overbeke, G., 2008. Pro-anorexia websites: Content, impact, and explanations of popularity. *Mind Matters: The Wesleyan Journal of Psychology*, 3, 49–62.

overw8y, 2018. I don't know if it is mainly in my head and if I am mainly making this up myself, but it just feels like eating disorders are almost a competition [online]. *Tumblr*. Available from: https://overw8y.tumblr.com/post/169403640191/i-dont-know-if-it-is-mainly-in-my-head-and-if-i [Accessed 27 Aug 2018].

Perloff, R.M., 2014. Social media effects on young women's body image concerns: Theoretical perspectives and an agenda for research. *Sex Roles*, 71 (11–12), 363–377.

Petri, P., 2020. Goddess Ana: The religious longing of pro-anorexia communities. *Paola Petri Nut*. https://paolapetrinut.com/blog/goddess-ana-the-religious-longing-of-pro-anorexia-communities/

Please Sign My Guest Book:) [online], 2002. *Ana – My maker, my destroyer*. Available from: https://web.archive.org/web/20021005123234fw_/http://myweb.ecomplanet.com/sxvi1237/pageemail.htm [Accessed 18 Aug 2020].

P O E M S [online], 2001. *MY secret PAGE*. Available from: https://web.archive.org/web/20011202030615/http://www.angelfire.com:80/pq/tynd/franka.html [Accessed 28 Mar 2018].

Polivy, J. and Herman, C.P., 2002. Causes of eating disorders. *Annual Review of Psychology*, 53 (1), 187–213.

proanorexia, 2007. Community information [online]. *proanorexia*. Available from: https://web.archive.org/web/20070829195258/http://community.livejournal.com/proanorexia/profile [Accessed 10 Jun 2021].

Puja, 2003. All of us with different faces/Friends online [online]. *Caring Online*. Available from: https://web.archive.org/web/20030422115952/http://www.caringonline.com/feelings/poetry/puja/friends.htm [Accessed 9 Apr 2021].

Reaves, J., 2001. Anorexia goes high tech [online]. *Time*. Available from: http://content.time.com/time/health/article/0,8599,169660,00.html [Accessed 2 Mar 2018].

Rich, E., 2006. Anorexic dis(connection): Managing anorexia as an illness and an identity. *Sociology of Health and Illness*, 28 (3), 284–305.

Rodham, K., Gavin, J., Lewis, S., Bandalli, P., and St. Denis, J., 2016. The NSSI paradox: Discussing and displaying NSSI in an online environment. *Deviant Behavior*, 37 (10), 1110–1117.

[sad] ana, 2019. i know that if i deleted the twitter app i'd be waaay more productive [online]. *@silverweak*. Available from: https://twitter.com/silverweak/status/1083308497809391617 [Accessed 16 Jan 2019].

Sandavalli, A., 2007. My Dearest Ana [online]. *Ana Does Not Love You [Dot] Com*. Available from: https://web.archive.org/web/20070915005031/http://anadoesnotloveyou.com/poems.html [Accessed 10 May 2021].

Sheldon, P., Grey, S.H., Vickery, A.J., and Honeycutt, J.M., 2015. An analysis of imagined interactions with pro-ana (anorexia): Implications for mental and physical health. *Imagination, Cognition and Personality*, 35 (2), 166–189.

sickstickboy, 2020. HI NON DISORDERED PEOPLE THAT ARE SPYING ON ED TWT FOR YOUR ENJOYMENT!! [online]. *Twitter*. Available from: https://twitter.com/sickstickboy/status/1276431698100658177 [Accessed 15 Jul 2020].

Singler, B., 2011. "Skeletons into Goddesses": Creating Religion, the Case of the Pro-Ana Movement and Anamadim. MPhil Theology and Religious Studies. United Kingdom: The University of Cambridge.

Spooky, 2003. Ad Noctum (into darkness) [online]. *Caring Online*. Available from: https://web.archive.org/web/20030115204307/http://www.caringonline.com/feelings/poetry/spooky/spooky1.htm [Accessed 9 Apr 2021].

Sternudd, H.T., 2012. Photographs of self-injury: Production and reception in a group of self-injurers. *Journal of Youth Studies*, 15 (4), 421–436.

Sternudd, H.T., 2017. I'm fine: Gender and modest displays of mental distress. *HumaNetten*, (38), 167–179.

Tara Michelle, 2005. Perfection [online]. *Fragile Innocence*. Available from: https://web.archive.org/web/20041217223045if_/http://winkin.phpwebhosting.com:80/~joeic/privet/thin/art/poem5.html [Accessed 14 Nov 2018].

tem ♥∗:·˚ , 2021a. All I wanna do is vent to my friends. *@temiosolar*. https://twitter.com/temiosolar/status/1389725960673632259

tem ♥∗:·˚ , 2021b. ////// sh [online]. *@temiosolar*. Available from: https://twitter.com/temiosolar/status/1383228391067844616 [Accessed 5 May 2021].

The voice of the bitch [online], 2001. *MY secret PAGE*. Available from: https://web.archive.org/web/20180327230900/http://www.angelfire.com/pq/tynd/evilana.html [Accessed 28 Mar 2018].

Tong, S.T., Heinemann-LaFave, D., Jeon, J., Kolodziej-Smith, R., and Warshay, N., 2013. The use of pro-ana blogs for online social support. *Eating Disorders*, 21 (5), 408–422.

Turja, T., Oksanen, A., Kaakinen, M., Sirola, A., Kaltiala-Heino, R., and Räsänen, P., 2017. Proeating disorder websites and subjective well-being: A four-country study on young people. *International Journal of Eating Disorders*, 50 (1), 50–57.

Turner, B.J., Chapman, A.L., and Layden, B.K., 2012. Intrapersonal and interpersonal functions of non suicidal self-injury: Associations with emotional and social functioning: Functions of NSSI, emotional and social functioning. *Suicide and Life-Threatening Behavior*, 42 (1), 36–55.

Uca, E.R., 2004. *Ana's Girls: The Essential Guide to the Underground Eating Disorder Community Online*. Bloomington: Authorhouse.

Ullyatt, G., 2010. "Dwelling in fear of the scales forever": Religious diction in Pro-Anorectic websites from a discourse-analytic perspective. *Journal for Language Teaching*, 44 (2), 69–86.

unswept_angel, 2005. Depth of my depression [online]. *Fragile Innocence*. Available from: https://web.archive.org/web/20041214174612if_/http://winkin.phpwebhosting. com:80/~joeic/privet/thin/art/story009.html [Accessed 15 Nov 2018].

V • IX • MMXVIII, 2014. My only friend left [online]. *Tumblr*. Available from: https://v-ix-mmxviii.tumblr.com/post/87380786760/my-only-friend-left [Accessed 21 Jul 2020].

v_falling_to_pieces, 2003. Verses [online]. *Falling_To_Pieces*. Available from: https://www. oocities.org/v_falling_to_pieces/verses.html [Accessed 26 Aug 2020].

Ward, K.J., 2007. 'I love you to the bones': Constructing the anorexic body in 'pro-ana' message boards. *Sociological Research Online*, 12 (2), 1–14.

Warin, M.J., 2006. Reconfiguring relatedness in anorexia. *Anthropology & Medicine*, 13 (1), 41–54.

wheniwas-thinner, 2020. My eating disorder is such a personified thing in my head [online]. *Tumblr*. Available from: https://wheniwas-thinner.tumblr.com/post/6215029343 49496320/my-eating-disorder-is-such-a-personified-thing-in [Accessed 21 Jul 2020].

Yeshua-Katz, D., 2015. Online stigma resistance in the pro-ana community. *Qualitative Health Research*, 25 (10), 1347–1358.

Yom-Tov, E., Brunstein-Klomek, A., Hadas, A., Tamir, O., and Fennig, S., 2016. Differences in physical status, mental state and online behavior of people in pro-anorexia web communities. *Eating Behaviors*, 22, 109–112.

Section III

Exploring Censorship

6 The Ethics and Logistics of Censorship to Address Echoing Self-Harmful Behaviour

Introduction

In 2018, Britain's *The Sun* ran a headline reading "Toxic Web: Inside the Sinister World of Pro-cutting Bloggers and Vile Hashtags Driving Desperate Teens to Self-Harm". The article explores Tumblr where "self-harming bloggers roam free and unmonitored, sharing their pain and posting whatever terrifying images they like", infecting others with popular and public posts containing graphic detail about cutting. Natalie, a young self-harmer, was interviewed about the role such content played in her escalating self-harm. Bullied at school, Natalie's self-harm greatly increased after she discovered other people in a similar situation online. These 'older teens' made her feel more willing and able to cut herself. The endpoint of this self-harm content is presented as the sad case of Tallulah Wilson. This seventeen-year-old died by suicide after falling prey to "the clutches of a toxic digital world" (Libbert 2018). Upon reading an evocative article such as this, it would be natural to fear these pro-self-harm bloggers and their "vile hashtags" that introduce vulnerable young people to a world of escalating self-injury. It would also seem logical to shut down any tag or hosting platform that allows this content to be seen and shared.

The general argument for censoring pro-ana blogs is that they can have a negative impact on vulnerable young people by communicating risky behaviour online, encouraging disrupted eating or helping to maintain previously disordered behaviour, and alienating them from healthier social ties (Castro and Osório 2012, p. 169). Similar concerns can be applied to sites encouraging self-harm or suicidal behaviours. There is evidence that people who access suicide-related material online are more suicidal and depressed than those who do not. They are more likely to show past or current suicidal ideation and to be at greater risk of future suicidal activity (Niederkrotenthaler *et al.* 2017, pp. 131, 133). They also report higher levels of social anxiety (Mok *et al.* 2016, p. 112). Nevertheless, it is important not to take this data out of context or to assume that users are depressed because of the information they access rather than accessing suicide information because they are depressed.

Researchers have struggled to determine if eating disorder sites cause body dissatisfaction and unhealthy eating habits or if people who already have

DOI: 10.4324/9781003126065-9

disturbances in this area are the ones more likely to seek out this material (Sharpe *et al.* 2011, p. 38). In these same studies, suicidal young people reported lower levels of family support, anticipated poor outcomes with offline help-seeking, and expressed fears about the reactions of other people if suicidal behaviour was disclosed or added to their health records (Niederkrotenthaler *et al.* 2017, pp. 133–134). Online communities and resources offer alternative ways of coping when offline contacts and medical professionals feel unsuitable. As such, more online suicide prevention material is recommended (Mok *et al.* 2016, p. 112). While pro-self-harmful communities are far from perfect, it seems more prudent to offer help in these spaces and assist in safe development of peer-to-peer resources rather than to censor and delete them with the assumption that families or doctors will be a practical replacement.

This chapter offers an exploration of censorship via an examination of the stigma and alarm that fuels it, the history of censorship efforts, the logistics of censoring self-harmful material, and ways in which self-harmful communities self-censor. None of these censorship efforts seem satisfactory, and many appear to cause more harm than good. This kind of discourse can lead to an 'us v. them' mentality where self-harmers hide their feelings and online behaviours to avoid being called 'sinister', 'vile' 'toxic' or 'terrifying' Rather than relying on censorship as the primary response to the danger of echoing self-harmful clusters, we need to work towards new alternatives that address the underlying issues making people turn towards self-destructive actions.

To this end, the second half of this chapter recommends some therapeutic attitudes for the promotion of outreach and healing. While journalists must be careful with topics that may trigger a contagion, there is still value in thoughtful and informative reporting of stigmatised topics like suicide. There is also a great need for online programs that can expand the pro-recovery mindset and connect with people who wish to recover or who generally support recovery as a valid goal. Peer support is often the most powerful tool in addressing core precipitating problems of self-harmful behaviour such as feelings of isolation or rejection. This should be guided and encouraged even though peers are not formally qualified in diagnostics or treatment. Their voice is still important and often carries far more authority and meaning than that of a professional. We should also respect the importance of safe spaces for expressing emotional content and not censor them even though content can be confronting. Finally, we must respect the fact that self-harmful behaviours can be a major part, often *the* major part, of a person's identity. For recovery to be a meaningful and appealing option, effort is needed to provide new avenues of identity and community.

The Creation of Stigma and Alarm

There is certainly discourse in pro-self-harmful content that should inspire concern. Online scripting can encourage dangerous perceptions such as the value of increased pathology with statements made such as "I know my cuts arenot too deep yet, but i'll get there:)" (berry 2021). Nevertheless, the popular press often exaggerates and simplifies the dangers of these communities. There seems to be a drive to suppress transgressive behaviour, especially involving young women (Bell 2014, p. 51), and to try and tamp down the troublesome form of the anorexic body and pro-anorexic voice (Connor and Coombes 2014, p. 62). As Boyd *et al.* present it, young people making use of the internet are seen as "both uncontrollable deviants who must be punished and an impressionable population who must be protected". Such a view leads to criticism of the internet as a sinister world where malevolent forces corrupt teenage minds, or a place where they are encouraged to indulge in dark impulses free of parental authority (2011, p. 2). From a feminist perspective, many commentators have seen anorexia as a fatal consequence of Western thinness ideals presented by the beauty and entertainment industries (Burke 2012, p. 37). Both paternalistic and feminist constructions of alarm in this space miss an important point: participants are often sincerely and autonomously seeking out pain – not being swept up against their will or responding to a waifish fashion movement. To this end, Lavis criticises narratives resting on the "erroneous binary construction" that "pro-anorexia must constitute a denial of illness because illness cannot incite desire; if they knew the dangers – the realities – participants simply could not want anorexia". The neoliberal subject, a responsible consumer of the internet, could not rationally see pro-ana and desire the pain and danger it engenders (Lavis 2016, p. 18). This erroneous notion frames the potential viewer of pro-ana as naïve and vulnerable. Sites containing this material are seen as evil, undesirable, and an object of fear.

One of the most significant purveyors of this reductive framework is the news media. The news media is often the bridge between clinical work or medical research and lay communities who seek to understand and contextualise it. As Eli and Ulijaszek argue, the news media are knowledge brokers who decide what scientific research or policy development should be publicised and what remains inaccessible behind paywalls or obscured by specialist language. More recently, news media has been transformed by social media and greater user engagement with news providers. When dealing with solacious topics like eating disorders, populist ideas (which may be incorrect or misleading) increasingly dominate discussion of news platforms (Eli and Ulijaszek 2016, p. 2). In sum, the news media helps to make sense of complex issues, but this may easily lead to misleading oversimplification of complex themes or encourage excessive focus on capturing views from the public through the use of techniques like panic pieces. Those who are the focus of this panic then become "mired in cultural alarm", making it harder for them to be open about their needs or to reach out for necessary support (Lavis 2016, p. 28). Thus, the outcome of alarmist media pieces is greater reluctance towards help-seeking and the popularisation of over-simplified knowledge about complex diseases.

Moral panic pieces about young women falling prey to "'wayward' and self-destructive practices" has been a recurrent theme in the British media (Day 2010, p. 242) and on a global level. As Cobb notes, this creates a complex message about young females who are seen as both in need of protection and as an active source of dangerous ideas and actions (2020, p. 1). The first articles about sinister pro-anorexia sites were published in 2001 including *Time*'s seminal 2001 article "Anorexia Goes High Tech" where the "obvious 'ick' factor" of pro-ana sites is discussed, but is done so with a degree of empathy and open-mindedness (Reaves 2001). This more balanced approach would soon lose favour in terms of articles focussing on unrepentant webmistresses pedalling images of dying women to encourage new victims towards the goal of starvation (e.g., see: Hill 2001). Most stories now paint participants as "dangerous, irresponsible villains who brainwashed their passive victims" (Knapton 2013, pp. 463–464). For example, *Time* ran another popular piece in 2005 about the "kind of visit that parents and doctors fear most": the presentation of a fourteen-year-old whose attempts to diet spiralled into anorexia. The teenager in question reported being "lured in by pro-ana websites" where vulnerable people can "learn to be anorexic from the Internet" (Song 2005). This presentation of pro-ana has become so pervasive that Giles sees the concept as a media product, "not unlike a genre of television programming" (2016, p. 320). By ascribing it such generic qualities, much nuance is lost in these brief and alarmist media reports.

The stories told about all pro-self-harmful communities tend to be similar. More recently there has been an upsurge in media focus on groups other than pro-ana, especially in the United Kingdom where it seems to resonate with readers of the popular press. February 2019 has been dubbed as the moment when prevention of youth suicide and self-harm dominated the UK news cycle for the first time (O'Connor 2019). This occurred in the wake of Instagram officially banning self-harm imagery in response to teenager Molly Russell's 2017 death. Her father told news services that she was viewing "disturbing images" shortly before her death and is adamant that "Instagram helped kill my daughter" (Yahoo7 2019). Her family felt that she showed no obvious signs of mental illness prior to her suicide, so were disturbed to head of her online activities. Lawyers and police working on the case reported struggling with the self-harm content Russell viewed and needing to limit their exposure (Davies 2020). This tragic story gave attention to a general trend. London's *Sunday Times* launched a front-page article on Britain's "suicidal generation" of teenagers, citing a doubling in the suicide rate from eight years prior along with a sharp increase in self-harm as a coping mechanism. In this article, social media giants like Instagram were called to better censorship and protection of vulnerable youth (Griffiths and Shipman 2019, p. 1). This is something they have genuinely committed to, with mixed results, as discussed further.

History of Censorship

Attempts at censoring self-harmful material in online spaces have significantly impacted the community over the past two decades. Perhaps the most comprehensive history of censorship eras within this timespan comes from Giles (2016) who identifies three main phases. The first of these is the "naïve phase" that dates from approximately 1999–2003. This was when pro-ana first emerged in the form of listservs and then stand-alone websites like *Anorexic Nation* (est. 1999). Giles dubs this period naïve because the bulk was unimpacted by media attention and subsequent censorship efforts. Discussions and community ethos did not have outsider reactions as a central focal point (2016, pp. 313–314). Instead, participants tended to simply share their experiences of illness (Lavis 2016, p. 11) without significant attention paid to an outsider audience or broader community interactions.

This is not to say that censorship efforts were not lurking, nor that fears about the impact of the internet on vulnerable minds were absent. From the mid-1990s, there were concerns over the internet as a lawless space where illegal, offensive, and sexual content could easily be disseminated. Lawmakers and parents were especially concerned with how the internet might impact on children leading to legislation like the U.S. Communications Decency Act of 1996 to hamper pornography and obscenity. From the start, this created conflict with civil libertarians who saw the internet as a space of free communication (Shade 2007, p. 233). This free speech idea was to be picked up by early pro-ana site owners who used it to encourage resistance – as discussed further. Similarly, a sense of fear was picked up by their detractors. For example, 1997 saw one of the earliest warnings about pro-anorexia spaces, known then as "cyberexia" (Newman 1997). Nevertheless, these communities were largely unknown and undisturbed by outsiders.

Naïvety weakened in 2001 when the first significant acts of censorship occurred. In late July to early August, Yahoo! (host of popular community forums and DIY website service GeoCities) started a purge of their servers. In one day, more than a hundred pro-ana sites were deleted and any new additions to the server were more closely monitored. The other major hosts of the era, Angelfire, Tripod, and AOL, quickly followed in kind (Polak 2007, p. 84). This purge was in response to a request by the National Association of Anorexia Nervosa and Associated Disorders (ANAD) made to Yahoo! to protect "the health and welfare of vulnerable young people" (Reaves 2001).[1] Daniel le Grange, who was then director of the eating-disorders program at the University of Chicago School of Medicine, was another advocate of this censorship. He noted that it is common for patients to dismiss the severity of their illness, and that "Girls who cherish their symptoms" are "nothing new". But his concern over Yahoo!'s communities was the new opportunity for people to band together and share skills for increasing the severity of their illness (Graham 2001). Twenty years later, this communal aspect to anorexia remains a prominent concern that censorship is yet to quell.

Some prominent members spoke with *The Observer* in the wake of the 2001 deletions, clarifying their desire to maintain their pro-anorexia material despite censorship events. Indeed, this censorship seems to have been only one rejection of many due to their countercultural and anti-medical food choices. 'Julia', who ran the popular pro-ana site *House of Sins*, had received a barrage of negative feedback after developing anorexia at the age of nine. When her site was criticised at the turn of the century, she remarked "they can say whatever they want: I'm not listening". Her dismissive attitude was due to the perception that pro-ana groups such as hers were "evil". While Julia agreed that her site may indeed "perpetuate anorexia in those who already suffer from it", she was certain that the benefits outweighed the harm. Julia, like many other young anorexics, found herself feeling isolated. When she stumbled upon pro-ana communities on Yahoo!, she found many other troubled souls with "no help except that which we could offer each other". Julia was aware that this help was not necessarily constructive or normative, asking:

> What do you think happens when people, sick with a disease that affects their minds and messes up their heads, are left alone to help each other? Is it really so surprising if they come up with solutions that strike the rest of the world as mad and bad?
>
> (Julia in Hill 2001)

It was not only the creators of these sites who were left distressed or angered by the purges. 'Shannab', a pro-ana participant who has been diagnosed with anorexia at age twelve, described her discovery of the Yahoo! Groups as "like heaven to me". She was the kind of participant who the bans were aimed at stopping, as she believed they "taught me how to be a better anorexic than I would ever have managed on my own". In the four years since she discovered pro-ana for the first time, Shannab had learned how to live on 0–130 calories per day and had surpassed her initial weight goal of hit eight-and-a-half stone, reaching seven-and-a-half stone with more to lose (Hill 2001). This seems shocking to those with typical attitudes to health and body image, and many have felt that sites like Yahoo! were to blame for the critical illness of girls like Shannab. Nevertheless, Shannab herself made it clear that pro-ana sites were filled with people who were too self-obsessed to bother proselytising. She argued that a person "cannot learn to be anorexic ... We only care about ourselves: we don't have the time to bring others into our world". Julia agreed, claiming that "I can't give anyone an eating disorder" by running a site with pro-ed material (Hill 2001). Both doubted the ability of this material to infect people who were not already ill. What did concern users such as Julia was the danger of removing support networks in the purges. She explained,

> I know other sufferers who have committed suicide because they've been so lonely in the hell of their disease. Loneliness kills more of us than the

eating disorder itself, but websites like mine help prevent that level of desperate isolation.

(Julia in Hill 2001)

This discourse quickly became the norm as those threatened with the loss of their community argued that censorship and deletion of this content would only hurt them and not lead to recovery.

Next in Giles' schema is the 'reformation phase' of pro-ana sites from approximately 2002–2007. This phase was a direct response to heightened censorship. In this era, it was common for pro-ana sites to index negative press coverage – often as a form of inspiration for greater resistance (Dias 2003, p. 36). Media attention also brought many changes to the dynamic of the movement. A notable person who joined during the reformation phase is Faux who was feeling very stressed and lonely in 2003. She heard about pro-ana in a news article and decided that radical weight loss would be a good way of addressing her problems (Faux 2008a). Looking back on this era, she notes a 'remarkable increase in visitors' as a direct result of 'media spotlights'. Faux sees this change as both good and bad. Good in the sense that it allowed people such as herself to find others in a similar situation for the first time. She also praises the growing movement towards anorexia rights spawned in this era. In terms of bad outcomes, Faux criticises the popularisation of pro-ana as a recruitment device to a starvation cult. She seems this ridiculous and is irritated by the influx of wannarexics it caused – many of whom believed the idea that they could cultivate anorexia and use it as a crash diet (Faux 2008b).

One main consequence of increased negative publicity was a masking of pro-ana identities and spaces. Many sites were re-named to remove more obvious language about their content like 'ana' or 'thin'Others started to use disclaimers on their landing pages to try and ward off potential litigation and blame for converting the vulnerable (2016, pp. 314–315). For example, "This is a pro-ana page. Anyone that's not pro-ana has nothing to do here. This is not a page that's gonna 'learn' you how to be anorexic" (Welcome to my pro-ana site! 2002). As such, this was also a period where wannarexia and boundary policing increased along with a strengthening perception of external threats. Yeshua-Katz posits this is because of public vilification. The more stigmatised a group becomes, the more they tend to take part in aggressive boundary work from within their own ranks (2015, p. 1355). In this context, stigma made members fearful of accusations they were entrapping victims in a dangerous lifestyle. They were simultaneously irritated by the arrival of new people seeking diet tips and other frivolous pursuits after hearing of pro-ana in the media.

New codes and ways of speaking were also invented to mask content from outsiders. Within Yahoo! itself, pro-ana groups were placed under topics like 'allergies' and 'duct tape', which were known cyphers (Mackeen 2002, p. 149). More broadly, obvious self-identifiers like 'ana' and 'mia' were swapped out in favour of more ambiguous terms like 'butterfly', 'angel', or 'red bracelet' (Sharpe *et al.* 2011, p. 36). In some communities, use of terms like 'ana' or 'pro-ana' could lead to a person being ejected (Brotsky and Giles 2007, pp. 102–103). As quickly as censors moved, the community adapted their slang – something that is still happening twenty years later in the form of hashtags.

Despite booming censorship efforts, the reformation phase ushered in a "game of cat and mouse" where sites would be shut down then quickly reformed on new servers (Giles 2016, pp. 314–315). This was predicted in 2001 when Julia threatened "The sites are now such an integral part of our community that as quickly as Yahoo! and others close them, we'll find a way to reopen them" (Julia in Hill 2001). Her prediction was correct. Not long after the purges, users resurrected their community groups and content and continued to do so every time they were censored during the reformation phase. Negative attention and logistical problems of this kind did not stop the movement from thriving and gaining followers (Polak 2007, p. 85). Many felt proud of their ability to subvert rules and maintain a subculture that gave them support despite broader stigma (Gailey 2009, p. 107). They also learned to be prepared for censorship and deletion by having back-up sites and forums ready to go at all times (Crowe and Watts 2016, p. 381). For example, when *House of Thin* was deleted in 2006, Faux was ready with a new domain and a large email list of active participants to notify (Faux 2007). She has similar memories from the deletion of the first version of her site *MiAna Land*, which logged over 350 unique visitors per day and had meticulous search engine optimisation. The server she used to host her site and its associated email accounts deleted *MiAna Land* with no warning. Faux remembers, "My head was spinning, my heart broken" and she began to worry for the health of members who relied on the forum as their main source of support. Rather than giving up, she decided "I wasn't going without a fight" and relaunched on a server that was less amenable to censorship (Faux 2008c). Removal of popular sites seems to have made their owners more pugnacious and radicalised. Evidence suggests that shutting down these sites, or even leaving comments suggesting pro-ana is a bad idea, strengthens the resistance of users and reminds them of their shared beliefs and goals (Giles 2006, p. 464).

Finally, the reformation phase was a time when the pro-ana movement became broader with more space set aside for various identities, ages, and cultures. So too was there more variance in stances on recovery with groups ranging from those who wished to actively nurture their disease to those fighting against their tendencies to disordered eating. Pro-recovery emerged more strongly in the reformation phase as this philosophy allowed distance from the kind of stringent pro-ana demonised in the media, or from accusations that pro-ana was trying to convert people from a life of health to one of sickness. Some participants felt that this weakened the countercultural core of the movement, dubbing it a diluted kind of 'anorexia-lite'. Others saw it as a maturation of pro-ana, which now had the capability to be more nuanced and accepting. Due to a steady increase of members, it was feasible for pro-ana participants to gravitate towards communities most reflective of their beliefs and needs. So too could they find resources in languages other than English or with a specific regional focus (Giles 2016, pp. 314–315). New sites appeared in a variety of languages including French, Spanish, German, and Dutch (Casilli *et al.* 2013, p. 94). As to be expected, media attention on pro-ana brought this movement to a wider audience – some of whom found it appealing rather than horrifying.

The final phase in Giles' history takes us to the present day: the 'social media phase'. This third generation is the Web 2.0 manifestation of pro-ana built around microblogging, social media, and the popularity of image-sharing services. Sites like Flickr, Tumblr, and Pinterest made celebrity thinspiration and self-portraits easy to share (Giles 2016, pp. 315–316). More recently, communities formed on Twitter have proven significant in shaping the future of the movement in the form of edtwt.[2] As Pater *et al.* argue, social media has pushed users away from more traditional networks like shared forums on a specific pro-ed site and into individualised social network feeds. This is harder to target with censorship as the platforms used (like Twitter) are not dedicated to problematic ideas as a whole and cannot be simply deleted. Pro-ana users can hide in plain sight, connecting to each other through problematic hashtags on sites that are generally benign (Pater *et al.* 2016, pp. 1196–1197). Deleting Twitter as a whole is unfeasible whereas deleting *House of Thin* was quite a simple and achievable act of censorship.

In 2016, Giles noted that social media pro-ana groups tended to be smaller and shorter lived than their naïve and reformation counterparts, often seen as less structured and having less sense of community (2016, pp. 315–316). Since this time, a more rigorous and uniform approach to tagging has helped to bridge some of these gaps and help a more recognisable community to form and find one another across platforms. Users are adept at playing with language and meaning, using double-speak to disrupt censorship (Cobb 2020, p. 77). As discussed, tagging has favoured novel language such as co-opting more obscure medical terms like 'anorectic' in the place of the more monitored 'anorexic' or spelling 'thinspo' as 'thynspo'. These changes have occurred in a fairly unform way across platforms where users seek to 'beat the filter' and circumvent censorship through social engineering such as new language or tagging in comments rather than directly within a post (Pater *et al.* 2016, pp. 1191, 1193–1194). Users have also had success signalling each other using gendered terms of health and beauty that are more broadly accepted like #thin and #sexy (Cobb 2020, p. 77). This has led to the survival and reinforcement of pro-ana spaces that pay heed to beauty norms, meaning this facet of the community has been increasingly normalised and accepted in broader society (Cobb 2017, p. 201). This unintended consequence of censorship, alongside many others, is discussed further.

Logistics of Censorship

If censorship in this social media era is to be supported, a comprehensive plan for enacting this moral stance is needed. One of the most robust discussions of how self-harmful material could be removed from the internet is raised by Sharpe *et al.* (2011)[3] who list technical and non-technical approaches. Technical approaches include the designation of self-harmful websites as illegal, the removal of this material due to violation of host company terms, content warnings, and content filters. Non-technical options include awareness campaigns, alternative spaces, and support for users from medical professionals. If self-harmful content is made illegal, websites hosting it can be shut down using national or international laws. Another problem Sharpe *et al.* raise is a potential lack of subtlety in legal codes that means, for example, a person's blog about her personal battle with anorexia would be criminalised alongside more overt calls to harm like extreme diet plans or purging guides. They are more amenable to encouraging web hosting companies to ban dangerous materials from their servers and work with public health bodies to determine what content is unsafe or inappropriate and should be removed. Major hosting companies such as Facebook have already enacted policies of this kind, which have removed substantial amounts of self-harmful content suggesting this approach could be comprehensively successful if this approach is taken as standard by content hosts (Sharpe *et al.* 2011, pp. 39–40). Nevertheless, there is a similar lack of subtlety in this approach. While hosts like Tumblr claim in theory to allow conversations and confessions about topics like self-harm, blogs containing this material were often abruptly deleted due to any amount of content that was deemed by unknown censors to have crossed the line into 'glorification' (Alderton 2018, pp. 31–32).

Other technical options can be used to obfuscate rather than delete potentially dangerous content. Sharpe *et al.* suggest possible content warnings where hosting sites or authorities could inform viewers before they enter spaces like pro-ana sites, telling them that the content therein could be disturbing and represents only a minority view. Cobb calls this the 'Everything okay?' mode of censorship (2020, p. 70) based on a warning developed by Tumblr. These warnings are limited in their impact as they are very easy to bypass. As one commentator notes,

> Type the phrase 'pro-ana' into Tumblr and a warning page appears asking 'is everything ok?' But with another click you're greeted by hundreds of pictures of dangerously underweight bodies, paired with personal tips on how to starve harder.
>
> (Coggan 2017)

Content warnings seem more relevant for people who are accidentally locating this kind of content, not those who are seeking it out on purpose.

Indeed, Tumblr seems to have realised this and now combine warnings with a program of deletion. In December of 2018, this site launched what was perhaps their most ambitious censorship policy and process to date. While their management described Tumblr as "deeply committed to supporting and protecting freedom of speech" pro-self-harmful content was seen to "jeopardize our users, threaten our infrastructure, and damage our community". A new category of content was devised to help clarify this new stance titled 'Promotion or Glorification of Self-Harm'. Content considered within this category was anything that might encourage people to "cut or injure themselves; embrace anorexia, bulimia, or other eating disorders; or commit suicide rather than, e.g., seeking counseling or treatment". Any content of this kind can now be deleted without warning. Nevertheless, Tumblr claim that online communities on their server are important and can remain so long as they are focussed on "awareness, support and recovery" (Tumblr Staff 2018).[4]

This ease of bypass when faced with "Everything okay?" censorship has also been noted on Pinterest where searching for tags like #thinspo are met with warnings while less obviously problematic tags like #skinnyaesthetic yield the desired results (Fig. 6.1). Pinterest developed as a hub for the pro-ana community in 2012 due to its "pin board" structure where users "pin" images to different boards according to theme. Thinspo pin boards became common, with hundreds of results prior to the censorship efforts (Ryan 2012). Pinterest attempted to change their content policy in 2012 after the site was swamped with potentially harmful content of this kind. If users attempt to search for dangerous terms such as this, they will now be issued with a warning rather than a set of results. When this change debuted, users searching for eating disorder content were suddenly greeted with a statement, "Eating disorders are not lifestyle choices, they are mental disorders that if left untreated can cause serious health problems or could even be life-threatening", followed by details

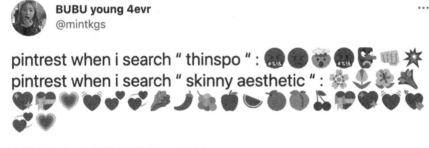

9:01 AM · Apr 18, 2021 · Twitter for iPhone

426 Retweets   **5** Quote Tweets   **3,613** Likes

Fig. 6.1 Satirical response to censorship differences between #thinspo and #skinnyaesthetic (BUBU young 4evr 2021).

for support services (Barnett 2012). Cobb notes how Pinterest has explicitly allowed images that support a kind of neoliberal self-betterment so long as thinness is presented as a health and fitness goal rather than an illness-related one (2020, pp. 71–72). Thus, to 'beat' this filter, users simply need to frame skinny aesthetic images as reflections of mainstream health standards in order to keep their thinspo uncensored.

To prevent this content being accessible at all, Sharpe *et al.* suggest the use of network-level filters that allow a service provider to blacklist certain URLs or keywords or user-level filters that block unwanted content on a specific device. These filters are used to prevent access to materials pertaining to terrorist activity or pornography, although it is very difficult to accurately filter using keywords or maintain a relevant database of blacklisted URLs considering how quickly this content changes (Sharpe *et al.* 2011, p. 40).[5] Filtering software installed on individual computers can work to a degree, but this can easily be disrupted by users who wish to circumvent it. This software also tends to block helpful sites with recovery or informative content (Swannell *et al.* 2010, p. 187). Another factor that also makes this suggestion somewhat outdated at a network level is the rise of self-harmful content on sites like Twitter. Social media hosts can delete problematic material off their servers but filtering out URLs or keywords in this kind of site is a different process to when self-harmful material was primarily on individually owned websites. Thus, sites like Twitter must rely on "crowd-sourced content management" where other users report problematic content that they find. Pro-ana communities have felt excessively targeted by this approach (Pater *et al.* 2016, p. 1194). Indeed, the problem with crowdsourcing to block content is that more stigmatised and undesirable groups will be a bigger target due to the emotional, human filtering involved.

The most recent technology used to identify dangerous content or people at risk is artificial intelligence. In 2017, Facebook started testing "a streamlined reporting process using pattern recognition" based on posts known to contain suicide or self-harm content.[6] If a post of this nature is detected, an option for users to report it becomes prominent. If a post is deemed very likely to contain harmful content, it will be automatically referred to moderators without the user report step (Callison-Burch *et al.* 2017). Artificial intelligence (AI), supported by machine learning, is now scanning words in posts that may show mental distress, and words in comments that may show concern. Card, a director of product management for Facebook, reported in 2018 that this technology has now started to overcome problems it initially had with nuances of language. It can now classify many differences between jokes like "I have so much homework I want to kill myself" and real indications of suicidal urge. Worried comments on posts like "Has anyone heard from him/her?" also help the AI system to determine if a person is at risk. Time and day of the week are also factored in based on common suicide trends (Card 2018). Ideally, this will help to remove bias against stigmatised groups, although unfair bias in machine learning is still prevalent (Mahoney *et al.* 2020).

Even prior to this additional concern about social media and microblogging, Sharpe *et al.* suggested that most of the above censorship action is unfeasible and unsuccessful in practice. Instead, they recommend non-technical approaches to make dangerous online spaces less appealing as opposed to less accessible. One option is finding a way to raise awareness of this material and educate young people about its risks *without* accidentally giving rise to a contagion. As such, guidelines for careful reporting are recommended, based primarily on rules for discussing suicide such as avoiding sensationalism or giving precise details that can be mimicked. Instead, constructive information like warning signs for family members to look out for can be shared as can contact details for appropriate medical services. Sharpe *et al.* also wisely advocate for alternative sources of support, community, and identity so that self-harmful sites are not the only place a vulnerable person can find them. They also suggest targeting support groups at different illness stages. For example, in addition to communities supporting eating disorder recovery, there should be groups reaching out to those who are at risk but do not currently show eating disorder symptoms. These resources can be solidified by making clinicians aware of the content on self-harmful spaces such as ana/mia personification and how this can be targeted in treatment. If clinicians can understand the perceived benefits of self-harmful communities, they can help patients to cope with transitioning away from them and finding healthier alternatives that are still meaningful. Better therapeutic environments can help to address the problem far more than technical censorship of problematic content (Sharpe *et al.* 2011, pp. 40–42).

These sage guidelines call for long-term action, cultural changes in family dynamics and medical care, and suggest the costly development of new online resources. While using the law and technology to abruptly censor problematic self-harmful material may seem the easiest and most efficacious approach, research suggests this is simply not true. Instead, we need to take pro-harmful content seriously and learn from the needs expressed in it, not "hope that it will soon be regulated out of existence" (Brotsky and Giles 2007, p. 94). Bell agrees that censorship only hinders the technologically naïve and suggests instead a focus on high-quality mental health information with strong search engine optimisation so people looking to find out more about their mental distress will locate and learn from these sites first (2007, p. 451, see also Biddle *et al.* 2008, p. 802). It is certainly clear that current censorship efforts have been circumvented with relative ease, suggesting that developing technologies like AI filtering can also be 'beaten' with enough tenacity.

In terms of offline intervention, another suggestion is to use the legal system to help pull problematic content from the internet and to give more incentive for servers to police it. Australia became the first country to criminalise pro-suicide websites in 2006 (Pirkis *et al.* 2009, p. 190), but our power to actually follow through on this is very limited (Alderton 2018, pp. 42–44). Under Australian law, it is an offense to use a carriage service to "disseminate material intended to counsel or incite suicide" with substantial fines as a penalty.

Australian-owned and -run websites now have no pro-suicide material (Pirkis and Blood 2010, pp. 32–33), but these domestic laws are hard to enact in an international context. National legislation is not effective in the international domain of the internet and has generally been immaterial in causing change (Pater *et al.* 2016, p. 1194). Australia's domestic laws also relate specifically to pro-suicide placing the legality of self-harm content more broadly in ambiguous territory (Alderton 2018). Australia's criminal code contains offenses relating to causing bodily harm, which could theoretically encompass causing a person to develop a mental illness like anorexia. Some state jurisdictions within Australia criminalise making a substantial contribution to a person's death, which could also theoretically be applied to encouraging anorexia. Nevertheless, this has never been tested in court and proving causation would be very difficult (Bromberg and Fitzgerald 2017) making this an unlikely route towards legal removal of this material.

Nevertheless, other jurisdictions have also considered similar moves to criminalise pro-self-harmful content online. In 2008, French parliament passed a law making it illegal to publicly incite excessive thinness. Specifically designed to target pro-ana websites, this bill barred any form of media promoting extreme thinness or self-starvation methods (Chrisafis 2008). In this same year, UK PMs called for similar legislation against pro-ana sites, but failed to achieve it. Their attempts were described as an "unwanted intervention" that could not work because content like thinspo is not illegal in this region (Bevan 2008). Under most legal codes, it seems more effective to make inciting dangerous behaviour illegal than it is to ban websites without such a law in place. Since then, the possibility of banning IP addresses linked to problematic content has been mooted in the UK – with a resurgence of this argument after Molly Russell's well-publicised suicide. To make this process precise enough to ban specific sites, internet service providers would need to change their domain name servers to prevent innocent sites from also being blocked. Hosts outside of the UK would also need to agree to this process, which is unlikely. Users within the UK could also circumvent the ban quite easily by installing a virtual private network, accessing a proxy site that functions as an intermediary server for banned materials, or using the Tor browser (BBC 2019). These are tools many people are comfortable using on a daily basis, meaning again that only the technologically naïve would have their viewing significantly interrupted.

Again, this supports the argument that technical censorship of problematic material is not as effective as more complex interventions like expanding accessible therapeutic outreach to those at risk (Sharpe *et al.* 2011, pp. 40–42). Indeed, if effective, censorship inhibits the positive aspects of pro-self-harm spaces such as community support otherwise lacking in the lives of participants. This punishes users without offering a healthy alternative, especially considering the fact that many report trouble accessing recovery strategies that work for them (Sciarretto 2014). Bromberg and Fitzgerald note that communities like pro-ana are very interactive with a blurred line between producers and consumers of social media material. If, hypothetically, these sites could be internationally criminalised, it would be very hard to differentiate between supposed victim and perpetrator. Producers of pro-ana material also tend to be anorexic themselves, thus criminalisation would make it even harder for them to access recovery resources as they may implicate themselves in the process. Finally, people would be punished for sharing weight loss tips, many of which, as Cobb (2020) has shown, are just as likely to appear in a mainstream fashion magazine. This means the same material would be fine when used to market to women but criminal if shared in the pro-ana sphere (Bromberg and Fitzgerald 2017). These actions would marginalise an already stigmatised and unwell group of vulnerable people who would only be given extra concerns if labelled as potential criminals (Pater *et al.* 2016, p. 1194). Even if the major logistical problems of censorship were somehow overcome, it seems that those who it proports to protect would actually be harmed.

Accidental and Unwanted Consequences of Censorship

The censorship efforts that have occurred since 2001 have failed to achieve many of their goals and have also caused some unwanted outcomes. They appear to have pushed facets of pro-ana closer to the mainstream on one hand and to have rendered the anorexic or self-harmed body as monstrous on the other. In all these cases, core problems faced by sufferers are side-lined. For example, O'Connor is worried that focusing on the role of social media in youth suicide detracts attention away from its "social, clinical, cultural and psychological causes". He argues that the UK press frenzy over Instagram censorship may hide the fact that suicidal teenagers face many offline dangers and stressors such as social disadvantage, emotional pain, early life trauma, and a lack of timely and appropriate mental health treatment. While he does support the removal of graphic self-harm and suicide imagery from Instagram, he believes that our main focus should be on programmes that tackle social inequality and provide mental health support rather than just programmes that regulate social media companies (O'Connor 2019). He mentions, for example, the paucity of acute care services for suicidal young people in the UK. Due to a lack of funding, young people at acute risk of suicide have been forced to wait as long as two weeks for a bed in a mental health ward where they can receive appropriate care (Campbell 2019). This is not so much a feature of journalism on the topic as fearful articles about lurking anorexic influences online.

In terms of 'health', Cobb has been central in tracing some of the accidental outcomes of deleting pro-ana blogs from servers or censoring related hashtags on social media sites. Rather than ending anorexic representation, censorship has favoured anorexic imagery and discourse that is closer to the mainstream thus encouraging it in this direction. This has led to the rise of concepts like 'healthy thinspo' and sites espousing extreme dieting using disclaimers that they are about health motivation not pro-ana (Cobb 2017, p. 190). For example, she notes the *Land of Skinny* site where the creator includes the disclaimer: "you are entering a healthy thinspo blog. I do not promote eating disorders" and repeatedly emphasises her dedication to a motivating and up-beat space. Similar sites identify their content as healthy and focused on weight loss progress, distancing themselves from eating disorders while still having much the same content (Cobb 2020, p. 81). This has occurred in the main because of pressure from censorship in the reformation era. To evade detection, users increasingly promote their pro-ana content as health, beauty, or diet material, using disclaimers to deny any promotion of illness. This ultimately blurred the lines between traditional pro-ana and accepted, mainstream thinness culture (Cobb 2020, p. 66).

Indeed, pro-ana bloggers are aware of this slippage and have been for some time. The owner of *Anna's Place* explains, "We live in a society surrounded by abnormal standards of beauty, and in turn many of us get caught up on what's 'normal'" (Robbins 2007). She sees eating disorders as inherently abnormal but caused by this cultural confusion where normative and unhealthy are aligned. Knapton agrees that there are significant similarities between the normative Western idea that a thin body makes a woman more desirable and valuable and a motivating desires for emaciation in pro-ana (2013, p. 467). By making anorexic bodies and ideologies the enemy, pro-ana communities were placed in a defensive position. Many participants noted actors and models who were either known to have eating disorders or whose very slim physiques suggested malnourishment. These popular identities allowed pro-ana participants to position starvation as a valid practice of the rich and famous or to argue that their own actions were simply a response to a broader cultural demand for thinness (Burke 2012, p. 43).

While the anorexic body may be seen as too excessive, the drive towards slenderness as a form of achievement and a way of unlocking cultural respect and power is shared. Public praise is often given to people who have slender, 'controlled' bodies that show self-regulation. As McLellan notes, this is something that pro-ana participants are keenly aware of. Many express frustration that the power or agency promised to them through self-regulation is never forthcoming (2010, p. 226). For them, anorexia often fits within a paradigm of beauty rather than one of disorder. The main difference is where they draw the line of healthy versus unhealthy slenderness (Knapton 2013, p. 472). This blurred boundary is not wholly in the hands of pro-ana participants, with mainstream beauty content also showing uncertainty over where health lies and how thin a person should dream of being.

In this context, the idea of thinspo has been increasingly removed from pro-ana. The latter remains pathological while thinspo has gained greater cultural acceptance (Cobb 2017, p. 194).

Pro-ana tips have slipped into women's magazines and are increasingly considered as valid options in normative weight maintenance and beauty routines (Cobb 2020, pp. 3–4). This is epitomised in a 2014 edition of the *Reveal* gossip magazine where celebrity diets were shared with readers as 'thinspiration'. Facing criticism, the editor-in-chief explained that her publication did not endorse anorexia and was using thinspiration to mean food and exercise plans for weight loss (Cobb 2017, p. 189). Because thinspo occupies a more liminal space than pro-ana, it can be framed as legitimate, be less vulnerable to censorship, and even make its way into mainstream discussions of body sculpting and health motivation. Therefore, "Hidden in plain sight, pro-ana online spaces have not disappeared, instead they have been normalised" (Cobb 2020, p. 82), which was certainly not the plan of the censors.

Similar slippage between pro-ana and pro-health can be found in the tags used to signal and organise this content. Fitness and diet content can be indexed using marginal pro-ana terms like #exercise, #motivation, or #slim. Sometimes terms like #thigh_gap or #thynspiration also appear. While these tags do risk censorship, they tend to read as legitimate if connected to body discipline in the name of fitness as opposed to anorexia (Cobb 2017, pp. 195–196). Slippage also occurs with the use of tags like #sexy, which is seen in combination with conventionally attractive bodies but also used to describe severely emaciated bodies in the form of bonespo, used alongside tags like #bones and #ribs (Branley and Covey 2017, p. 1356). Fitspo bloggers on platforms like Instagram have also been combining hashtags like #fitspiration and #thinspiration. Fitness influencers are increasingly viewed as positive role models who can guide people away from lifestyle diseases like obesity by modelling their own slim or muscular physiques gained through dietary restriction and high levels of exercise. While fitspiration rejects the emaciated imagery of genres like bonespo, full lifestyle commitment to body sculpting and a celebration of slenderness means that many users see #thinspiration as an appropriate hashtag for this content (Rajan 2018, pp. 67–68, 74). With the rise of such hashtag usage, body imagery drawn from disordered eating culture is increasingly merging with images of health, fitness, motivation, and sexiness, gaining increased validation and the mainstream accommodation of so-called healthy thinspo.

While some pro-ana content has been embraced by the mainstream as potentially healthy, at the other end of the spectrum, an equal amount has been treated as increasingly monstrous and worthy of fear and sanction. Pro-ana sites are presented by the media as horrific harbingers of deadly disease, with few articles showcasing the actual voices of creators and participants or exploring any other precipitating factors in the development of disordered eating (Dias 2003, p. 36). Instead, anorexia is framed as a "reading disorder" – a disease that comes solely from uncritical consumption of dangerous websites. Participants are seen as narcissistic, blinded by an inherent drive towards self-destruction (Ferreday 2011, pp. 6–7, 9). Thus, the media showcases hegemonic culture as benevolent and presents anorexics as people who see the world incorrectly because they are unrealistic, obsessive, and irrational (McLellan 2010, pp. 231, 240). In this context, it is easier to rely on media framing telling us that such people are irrational and in need of protection rather than exploring deeper insights into why they may feel disempowered and the degree to which popular cultural narratives of thinness equating to power and success may have laid a foundation for their actions (McLellan 2010, p. 226). Instead, pro-self-harmful websites and communities become easy targets of outrage.

While many people with eating disorders stay within a normal weight range, the media has also pushed excessive focus towards the spectacle of the starving (female) anorexic body. This figure is uncanny and monstrous, evoking a response of horror (Ferreday 2011, p. 9) and fuelling a view of women's bodies as a site of deviance (Tamás 2017, p. 4). With this hyper-focus aimed at imagery of starvation, a kind of 'monster-making', the actual written content of pro-ana sites often goes ignored, meaning much nuance of analysis is lost. So too is the fact that many are simply following the behaviours scripted for subordinate bodies by denying themselves to gain cultural kudos. Indeed, if the content of pro-ana sites was more closely read, critics would see overt engagement with the idea that starvation is a response to cultural demands. Also expressed is the feeling that self-inflicted starvation is a direct reflection of externally inflicted violence from interpersonal aggressors or society more broadly. Here, society itself reads as the monster. This is in direct contrast to the media approach of simplifying this nuanced emotional interplay down to the idea of monstrous pro-ana ideas that lead to monstrous anorexic bodies (McLellan 2010, pp. 224, 227, 231). As Tamás notes, one of the most confronting dimensions of eating disorders is the fact that they allow mental illness to take physical form. The image of a starved body is shocking and powerful, making it the major focus of media attention. Less attention-grabbing is discussion of background feelings, experiences, and problems that precipitate self-starvation (2017, p. 16). If we continue to ignore these underlying problems, no amount of censorship will heal those suffering.

Community Self-Censorship and Anti-external Censorship Pleas

Something lacking in many discussions of censorship is the robust self-censorship and self-regulation strategies at play within pro-self-harmful communities – especially pro-ana in the reformation phase. During this time, disclaimers were seen as insurance against irresponsible visitors and a way of preserving the integrity of the community (Giles 2006, p. 464). In the wake of increased action to have pro-ana sites criminalised, warnings took on a legal dimension. For example,

> You have been forewarned. By entering this proana promia web site you are signing a digital certificate stating that you have read and understand the above mentioned conditions and you are entering this proana promia site knowingly and willingly of the aforementioned conditions. Entering by any other circumstance is perjury and can be punishable by law.
>
> (Faux 2008d)

Many warnings anticipate visitors looking for general weight loss advice. They are met with suggestions like "A healthy diet and lifestyle is a far better way to lose some weight than emulating the behaviours of eating disordered individuals" (proanorexia 2007) or "Just incorporate a half hour of exercise into your day and stay away from fatty foods. This is not something that you just start and finish later on. You don't finish" (Arianna 2002). Prospective community members are cautioned that anorexia will cause them to develop "fear and total hatred of your body" (Misa 2007). It is common to see warnings such as "eating disorders are deadly diseases and those behaviours [developing one on purpose] will NOT be tolerated here" (JJ 2008). People who have yet to develop a clinically concerning level of restriction are told, "Get out while you still can. You DO NOT want an Eating Disorder" (overw8y 2018a). Many viewers seem to be targeted at a stage where they are interested in pro-ana but not yet so ill that they need professional help to recover. Even sites dedicated to personal blogging as opposed to tips and tricks will have warnings such as "Please don't use my words or thoughts, as inspiration for destruction ... Don't use me as an icon" (Lou 2003).

Sometimes these warnings have been designed to protect the vulnerable from misusing recovery resources as triggers. *Anorexic Web*'s landing pages included the plea "I beg you not to use these pages as a means to hurt yourself, compare yourself, judge yourself, or anything other than as means to unravel yourself from the most deadly web you'll ever get caught in" (Arndt 1999). Owner Arndt, based on her own experiences with anorexia, sees disclaimers as a reminder to people visiting pro-ana sites that they have free will. She sees herself as unable to prevent someone who "is sick and is seeking to be sicker" from finding dangerous information and images. Instead, she hopes that visitors will choose a safer path of their own volition – one that is offered in the pro-recovery *Anorexic Web* (Arndt 2001). Realistically, disclaimers do not offer binding legal protection, but they do emphasise the idea of self-responsibility and personal choice as to the kind of content one accesses. Content creators can then feel validated in sharing media that can lead to echoing self-harmful contagion as responsibility is placed on an individual to self-identify as previously disordered before engaging.

Discouragement content is also popular. Many pro-self-harm authors and communities are adamant that they are ill people suffering from a disease and wish to prevent others from wishing to suffer to this same degree. It is common for self-harmers to dispel myths about their behaviour, noting that it is not cool or fashionable. In many of these posts, long-term self-harmers seek to address novices or people who are theoretically curious about the behaviour. Through their position of authority and authenticity, seasoned self-harmers will tell others not to start. Reasons observed include the price of first-aid materials or the difficulty of hiding scars from non-participants (2016, p. 1114). Similar kinds of discouragement content can be found in pro-ana, with many participants aiming to show the 'real side' of eating disorders. As one notes, "Maybe if they weren't so glamorized and made to seem like simple weight-loss ... Less people would develop them" (Miarexia 2002). Another user, Brittany, agrees that ultra-thin celebrities like Calista Flockhart have warped perceptions of beauty and left people thinking that eating disorders are just a crash diet that can help a person achieve this physique. She laments, "They don't know the pain involved and the tears we shed each day that we suffer with our fears and our lives stuck in HELL". Brittany, who was twenty at the time, describes having bones of a sixty-year-old; a bleeding colon, diminished intestinal lining, and an ulcerated stomach from laxative abuse; an irregular heartbeat; shaking hands; thin hair; and dry skin. She knows some of these conditions are life-limiting and does not want other people to suffer the same fate – even though she has still not recovered and still uses pro-ana content herself (Brittany 2003).

To this end, Free Butterfly shares a day in her life so that readers who may be tempted to develop disordered eating know that "ED's are not glamorous. Ed's are not fun". Her day begins with a fear of getting out of bed in case she may have gained weight. Her mood for the whole day will be determined by the number she sees on her scale. After examining the shape of her body, she will skip breakfast in favour of a diet pill. Some days she is so stressed by choosing an outfit that she is unable to go to school. When she can attend school, she throws out her packed lunch, wanders around the grounds to burn calories during break time, and is besieged by hunger and pain throughout her classes. After school, she works out at the gym fuelled by energy pills and watches her heart rate get up towards 200 bpm as her body struggles to cope with the stress. Upon returning home, she lies to her family so she can avoid dinner and lies to her friends because any kind of socialisation might involve food. While lying down in bed, she cries and waits for it all the start again the next day (Free Butterfly 2008). Unlike imaginary scenarios where a future in a thin body is glamorised, her experience reveals a very depressed and lonely young woman without friends, popularity, or satisfaction.

This blogging style is not unique to this era. A decade later, Tumblr blogger overw8y had much the same message, explaining "I actually often use my blog to show my followers of the horrible things that come with an eating disorder. I constantly reblog messages of people who have been there, of nasty symptoms and side effects". While she finds herself unable to recover and does not wish happiness or health for herself, overw8y hopes that her blog can reveal how painful eating disorders are (overw8y 2018b). She wants to educate people who idolise "even those girls who have been eating 100 calories a day for 3 weeks and post perfect pictures of flawlessly bony bodies" and let them know they "have not been doing it effortlessly. No matter how perfect it may seem on the internet, in reality we are all breaking and falling apart. It's not easy for anyone" (overw8y 2018c). The intention of bloggers writing in this style is to try and diffuse some of the mystique associated with starvation to ensure that vulnerable people do not misinterpret the core experience of eating disorders as a debilitating and potentially life-limiting disease.

Discouragement, delivered realistically from the perspective of a recovered anorexic, is the purpose of the site *Anorexic Web*. Through this resource, owner Arndt provides arguably the most detailed discouragement content. She explains, "I want to shake people up from a passive state of denial and disbelief that by having an eating disorder you are not actively and willingly choosing to destroy your body". To do this, Arndt tries to be clear about unglamorous consequences like weight gain, premature aging, and embarrassing digestive dysfunction (Arndt 2000a). For example, Arndt gives a fairly graphic account of laxative abuse. She took up this behaviour as a quick fix after one of her friends introduced it. At one point, Arndt was consuming fifty pills a day. For anyone who might be keen to try the same method, she provides details about how painful and embarrassing this technique can be. She notes that bowel problems will usually cause a person to smell so bad that perfume cannot hide the odour, lead to painful movements and the need to take more drugs in order to excrete at all, plus the embarrassing need to always stay close to a bathroom in case urgent excretion is necessary. She also gives details of unpleasant gastrointestinal surgeries that people have been given after organ failure on laxatives. All of these consequences help to make the process seem deeply unappealing, ineffective in long-term weight loss, and far from glamorous (Arndt 2000b).

Arndt also presented a long list of people who have died due to complications from their eating disorders called "I'd Rather be Dead than Fat" – a reference to a common attitude about extreme weight loss. Based on her own experiences of unhealthy living, and hospitals she has since worked in, Arndt emphatically notes, "Starving to death is NOT beautiful or poetic, it is an UGLY UGLY death and a painful one". She runs through the pain a person will feel as bones and muscles deteriorate, and the undesirable symptoms of bowel failure. Arndt points out that many bulimics die during the act of purging and are found dead or unconscious next to their toilets (Arndt 2000c). People searching for a new way to limit their caloric intake or a new celebrity thinspiration will find what they are after. But, unlike tips and thinspo on many anorexia sites, *Anorexic Web* presents this content with harsh and unappealing commentary from a believable source. This approach has proven popular with her audience. One reader thanks her very sincerely for making her think "about the messy, horrifying death" that "tricks" like laxative abuse can cause. She writes, "It made me face up to what I knew all along, that these weren't helping at all, I was killing myself in the worst way, and it was like a flash to my charred brain" (Arndt 2000d). Arndt's reliability stems not so much from her training as a clinical psychologist who now works full time in residential eating disorder treatment, but rather from her personal experience as someone with debilitating anorexia.

Another notable community response to censorship is the plea to individually block users who discuss self-harmful behaviour rather than to report them to website hosts and involve broader censorship infrastructure. This gives users a better chance of avoiding outright deletion of their content and support networks. It is common to see a passionate request such as:

> ***PLEASE BLOCK AND DON'T REPORT. THIS BLOG IS ALL I HAVE.*** ***
>
> (overw8y 2018a)

> Please please please I beg you all do not report my account. I understand you are concerned but honestly I've been feeling like this since I was 12 years old and I'm still here so even in my darkest moment I'm not going anywhere I just like to express how I feel. Talk to me, not Twitter, if I lose this account then I lose the only place I can actually talk about how I feel and get support that I'm not getting outside of social media
>
> (_dxlicate 2019)

> alot of u who report accounts on #shtwt need to understand that u arent helping these ppl ur just taking away their safe place therefore making it worse so if ur one of those who report these account pls learn that there is a block button right there
>
> (san ♥□ 2021)

This request to block is often used in conjunction with trigger warnings. Many moderators of websites containing sensitive content such as details about self-harm or potential thinspo have already taken it upon themselves to mandate trigger warnings. Trigger warnings are now described as customary in all safe spaces, and help to keep such spaces safe by helping people to avoid content that might trigger a PTSD flashback or give them an urge to harm themselves (Trigger Warning 2016). For example, contemporary examples on Twitter include "tw // ed, si, sh, csa, sexual assault, abuse, etc." ("🐞🦋□🐞 2021), "TW// Bodycheck" (Bunny 2021), "TW – bodycheck & sh scars" (k 2021), and "Tw mentions of suicide" (pixel ♡'s buggy 2021).[7] Under this system, people should manage what they see or avoid via trigger warnings they are sensitive to, blocking any users who might produce content that disturbs them. This also means there is no universally problematic content that a hosting site should delete. Rather, the onus is on individual users to decide what their triggers are and what they will do about them. While this is obviously still a very problematic solution to the sharing of contagious content, it shows that the community is receptive to some degree of content regulation and is sensitive to individual needs. This means there is a foundation to work with in creating new approaches to censorship and discussions of illness and recovery.

Notes

1 The next phase of the plan for ANAD was to petition creators of pro-ana pages to take down their own material. ANAD educators were primed to "confront anorexics' infamous defensive talents" despite warnings from most people saying this action would be a waste of time (Reaves 2001). Not much seems to have eventuated from this aim.

2 Broadly popular social media sites like Facebook have been less relevant for pro-ana. Its earlier rival Bebo (2005–2013, 2021(?)) has proven more popular for expressing self-harmful sentiment, possibly due to greater user input into design (Robertson *et al.* 2012, p. 244).

3 While these recommendations are a decade old at the time of writing they remain the clearest and most encompassing set of potential actions.

4 Censorship also becomes less realistic when the lifespan of any particular post is considered. For example, 90% of posts on Tumblr are only liked and reblogged for a period of two days or less after their creation. Only 5% are still actively engaged with twenty days from creation, and 2.5% for forty days or beyond (Xu *et al.* 2014, p. 16). This means that deleting a post will only have a meaningful impact on its spread in the very early stages. Beyond the two-day mark, most dangerous posts will have already achieved their maximum contagion impact.

5 Since Sharpe *et al.*'s discussions of filtering, newer technologies like AI content detection have improved. Nevertheless, this is still limited. The vast majority of posts on Tumblr (78.11% at its peak in 2014) are photos or other visual texts (Chang *et al.* 2014, p. 22), meaning that it is harder for AI censorship programs to even locate problematic material – especially if untagged. This is an area of ongoing technological advancement, so its impact on censorship remains to be seen.

6 At present, it is unclear how wide-reaching this process might be. The first wave of AI analysis has been launched only in the United States. Countries in the European Union are presently excluded from this technology due to data protection laws pertaining to mental health (Goggin 2019).

7 TW: trigger warning; ED: eating disorder; SI: self-injury; SH: self-harm; CSA: childhood sexual abuse; Bodycheck: images of one's own body to show increasing weight loss from starvation.

References

⌐Ⱄ□⌐, 2021. Ⱄ□ new pinned Ⱄ□ [online]. *@idiotspiral*. Available from: https://twitter.com/idiotspiral/status/1424434715340152833 [Accessed 11 Aug 2021].

Alderton, Z., 2018. *The Aesthetics of Self-Harm: The Visual Rhetoric of Online Communities*. Abingdon: Routledge.

Arianna, 2002. FAQ [online]. *AnOreXiC AdDiCt*. Available from: https://web.archive.org/web/20030407050829fw_/http://myweb.ecomplanet.com/bouc2329/mycustompage0020.htm [Accessed 24 May 2021].

Arndt, L., 1999. Anorexic Web [online]. *Anorexic Web*. Available from: https://web.archive.org/web/19991129003109/http://www.anorexicweb.com:80/ [Accessed 7 Mar 2018].

Arndt, L., 2000a. Mission & Explanation Statement: Why I Do What I Do at the Anorexic Web [online]. *Anorexic Web*. Available from: https://web.archive.org/web/20000522063507/http://www.anorexicweb.com:80/Taste/missionstatement.html [Accessed 21 Mar 2018].

Arndt, L., 2000b. Tricks of the Trade [online]. *Anorexic Web*. Available from: https://web.archive.org/web/20000928234309fw_/http://www.anorexicweb.com:80/InsidetheFridge/tricksofthetrade.html [Accessed 8 Mar 2018].

Arndt, L., 2000c. I'd Rather Be Dead Than Fat [online]. *Anorexic Web*. Available from: https://web.archive.org/web/20000823224438/http://www.anorexicweb.com:80/IdRatherBeDead/idratherbedeadtha.html [Accessed 14 Mar 2018].

Arndt, L., 2000d. Food For Thought: Page 8 [online]. *Anorexic Web*. Available from: https://web.archive.org/web/20001209091300/http://www.anorexicweb.com:80/FoodForThought/foodforthoughtpe.html [Accessed 14 Mar 2018].

Arndt, L., 2001. Reality Bites: Page 2 [online]. *Anorexic Web*. Available from: https://web. archive.org/web/20010208193135fw_/http://anorexicweb.com:80/InsidetheFridge/ realitybites2.html [Accessed 15 Mar 2018].

Barnett, E., 2012. Pinterest tackles eating disorders [online]. *The Telegraph*. Available from: https://www.telegraph.co.uk/technology/social-media/9449049/Pinterest-tackles-eating-disorders.html [Accessed 28 Aug 2018].

BBC, 2019. Mental Health: UK could ban social media over suicide images, minister warns. *BBC News*, 27 Jan. https://www.bbc.com/news/uk-47019912

Bell, M., 2014. "Virtual" autobiography? Anorexia, obsession, and Calvin Klein. *In*: S. Brophy and J. Hladki, eds. *Embodied Politics in Visual Autobiography*. University of Toronto Press, 48–63.

Bell, V., 2007. Online information, extreme communities and internet therapy: Is the internet good for our mental health? *Journal of Mental Health*, 16 (4), 445–457.

berry, 2021. i know my cuts arenot too deep yet, but i'll get there:) [online]. *@strawberryslits*. Available from: https://twitter.com/strawberryslits/status/1384568571322306563 [Accessed 23 Apr 2021].

Bevan, K., 2008. Unwanted intervention [online]. *The Guardian*. Available from: http://www.theguardian.com/commentisfree/2008/feb/27/unwantedintervention [Accessed 5 May 2021].

Biddle, L., Donovan, J., Hawton, K., Kapur, N., and Gunnell, D., 2008. Suicide and the internet. *BMJ*, 336 (7648), 800–802.

Boyd, D., Leavitt, A., and Ryan, J., 2011. Pro-self-harm and the visibility of youth-generated problematic material. *I/S: A Journal of Law and Policy for the Information Society*, 7 (1), 1–32.

Branley, D.B. and Covey, J., 2017. Pro-ana versus pro-recovery: A content analytic comparison of social media users' communication about eating disorders on Twitter and Tumblr. *Frontiers in Psychology*, 8, 1356.

Brittany, 2003. Brittany's story [online]. *Silent Screams*. Available from: https://web.archive. org/web/20030521080650/http://silent-screams.org/britt.shtml [Accessed 7 Apr 2021].

Bromberg, M. and Fitzgerald, T., 2017. Should 'pro-ana' websites be criminalised in Australia? [online]. *The Conversation*. Available from: http://theconversation.com/ should-pro-ana-websites-be-criminalised-in-australia-79197 [Accessed 20 May 2021].

Brotsky, S.R. and Giles, D., 2007. Inside the "Pro-ana" Community: A covert online participant observation. *Eating Disorders*, 15 (2), 93–109.

BUBU young 4evr, 2021. pintrest when i search 'thinspo' [online]. *@mintkgs*. Available from: https://twitter.com/mintkgs/status/1383556276601298944 [Accessed 22 Apr 2021].

Bunny, 2021. TW// Bodycheck ♡ ♡ ♡ [online]. *@bl33dingpixi3*. Available from: https:// twitter.com/bl33dingpixi3/status/1424988098677649422 [Accessed 11 Aug 2021].

Burke, E., 2012. Reflections on the Waif: Images of slenderness and distress in pro-anorexia websites. *Australian Feminist Studies*, 27 (71), 37–54.

Callison-Burch, V., Guadagno, J., and Davis, A., 2017. Building a safer community with new suicide prevention tools [online]. *Facebook Newsroom*. Available from: https://newsroom. fb.com/news/2017/03/building-a-safer-community-with-new-suicide-prevention-tools/ [Accessed 18 Jan 2019].

Campbell, D., 2019. Suicidal children face long delays for mental health care [online]. *The Observer*. Available from: https://www.theguardian.com/society/2019/feb/09/suicidal-children-face-long-delays-for-mental-health-care [Accessed 11 Mar 2019].

Card, C., 2018. How Facebook AI Helps Suicide Prevention [online]. *Facebook Newsroom*. Available from: https://newsroom.fb.com/news/2018/09/inside-feed-suicide-prevention-and-ai/ [Accessed 18 Jan 2019].

Casilli, A.A., Pailler, F., and Tubaro, P., 2013. Online networks of eating-disorder websites: why censoring pro-ana might be a bad idea. *Perspectives in Public Health*, 133 (2), 94–95.

Castro, T.S. and Osório, A.J., 2012. Online violence: Not beautiful enough … not thin enough. Anorectic testimonials in the web. *PsychNology Journal*, 10 (3), 169–186.

Chang, Y., Tang, L., Inagaki, Y., and Liu, Y., 2014. What is Tumblr: A statistical overview and comparison. *ACM SIGKDD Explorations Newsletter*, 16 (1), 21–29.

Chrisafis, A., 2008. French MPs back law to bar media from promoting anorexia [online]. *The Guardian*. Available from: http://www.theguardian.com/world/2008/apr/16/france.law [Accessed 5 May 2021].

Cobb, G., 2017. "This is *not* pro-ana": Denial and disguise in pro-anorexia online spaces. *Fat Studies*, 6 (2), 189–205.

Cobb, G., 2020. *Negotiating Thinness Online: The Cultural Politics of Pro-anorexia*. 1st ed. Abingdon, Oxon; New York, NY: Routledge.

Coggan, M., 2017. Body positivity hasn't defeated the thinspo blog [online]. *Vice*. Available from: https://www.vice.com/en/article/8xxnqk/body-positivity-hasnt-defeated-the-thinspo-blog [Accessed 20 May 2021].

Connor, G. and Coombes, L., 2014. Gynetic organisms: Pro-anorexic techno bodies. *Ethnicity and Inequalities in Health and Social Care*, 7 (2), 62–71.

Crowe, N. and Watts, M., 2016. 'We're just like Gok, but in reverse': Ana Girls – empowerment and resistance in digital communities. *International Journal of Adolescence and Youth*, 21 (3), 379–390.

Davies, J., 2020. Schoolgirl, 14, looked at social media posts before taking own life [online]. *Mail Online*. Available from: https://www.dailymail.co.uk/news/article-8773699/Schoolgirl-14-looked-social-media-posts-self-harm-taking-life-inquest-hears.html [Accessed 10 May 2021].

Day, K., 2010. Pro-anorexia and 'Binge-drinking': Conformity to damaging ideals or 'new', resistant femininities? *Feminism & Psychology*, 20 (2), 242–248.

Dias, K., 2003. The Ana Sanctuary: Women's pro-anorexia narratives in cyberspace. *Journal of International Women's Studies*, 4 (2), 31–45.

_dxlicate, 2019. Please please please I beg you all do not report my account [online]. *Twitter*. Available from: https://twitter.com/_dxlicate/status/1097061973815119872 [Accessed 27 Feb 2019].

Eli, K. and Ulijaszek, S.J., 2016. Introduction: Obesity, eating disorders and the media. *In*: K. Eli and S.J. Ulijaszek, eds. *Obesity, Eating Disorders and the Media*. London: Routledge, 1–7.

Faux, M., 2007. About house of thin [online]. *House of Thin*. Available from: https://web.archive.org/web/20070730172031/http://www.houseofthin.com/entrance/aboutus.php [Accessed 6 May 2021].

Faux, M., 2008a. Intro to Mandi Faux [online]. *TS Mandi Faux Transsexual Escort Model Stripper Entertainer*. Available from: http://www.mandifaux.com/about-mandi.php [Accessed 23 Apr 2021].

Faux, M., 2008b. Pro-Ana definition [online]. *Fading Obsession:: Pro Ana Mia Website plus Forum*. Available from: https://web.archive.org/web/20080724114538/http://www.fading-obsession.com/information/pro-ana-definition.php [Accessed 23 Apr 2021].

Faux, M., 2008c. About MiAna Land [online]. *MiAna Land:: Pro Eating Disorder Support Website & Forum.* Available from: https://web.archive.org/web/20081229161415/http://www.mianaland.com/mainland/about-us.php [Accessed 23 Apr 2021].

Faux, M., 2008d. Warning - disclaimer [online]. *Fading Obsession:: Pro Ana Mia Website plus Forum.* Available from: https://web.archive.org/web/20080514214647/http://www.fading-obsession.com/ [Accessed 23 Apr 2021].

Ferreday, D., 2011. Haunted bodies: Visual cultures of anorexia and size zero. *Borderlands Ejournal*, 10 (2), 1–22.

Free Butterfly, 2008. Life with ED [online]. *~free the butterfly within ~: the haven of an ana butterfly.* Available from: https://web.archive.org/web/20080218052723/http://www.freewebs.com:80/free-the-bfly/lifewithed.htm [Accessed 6 Mar 2018].

Gailey, J.A., 2009. "Starving is the most fun a girl can have": The pro-Ana subculture as edgework. *Critical Criminology*, 17 (2), 93–108.

Giles, D., 2006. Constructing identities in cyberspace: The case of eating disorders. *British Journal of Social Psychology*, 45 (3), 463–477.

Giles, D.C., 2016. Does ana=Anorexia? Online interaction and the construction of new discursive objects. *In*: M. O'Reilly and J.N. Lester, eds. *The Palgrave Handbook of Adult Mental Health: Discourse and Conversation Studies.* Houndmills, Basingstoke, Hampshire; New York: Palgrave Macmillan, 308–326.

Goggin, B., 2019. Inside Facebook's suicide algorithm: Here's how the company uses artificial intelligence to predict your mental state from your posts [online]. *Business Insider Australia.* Available from: https://www.businessinsider.com.au/facebook-is-using-ai-to-try-to-predict-if-youre-suicidal-2018-12 [Accessed 18 Jan 2019].

Graham, J., 2001. Web sites offer 'blueprint' for anorexia [online]. *The Seattle Times.* Available from: http://community.seattletimes.nwsource.com/archive/?date=20010805&slug=anorex05 [Accessed 7 Dec 2018].

Griffiths, S. and Shipman, T., 2019. 'Suicidal generation': Tragic toll of teenagers doubles in eight years. *Sunday Times*, 3 Feb, p. 1. https://www.thetimes.co.uk/article/suicidal-generation-tragic-toll-of-teens-doubles-in-8-years-zlkqzsd2b

Hill, A., 2001. Danger from pro-anorexia websites [online]. *The Observer.* Available from: https://www.theguardian.com/uk/2001/aug/12/ameliahill.theobserver [Accessed 2 Oct 2018].

JJ, 2008. Terms and conditions [online]. *The Red Bracelet.* Available from: https://web.archive.org/web/20080817070709/http://www.redbracelet.net/index.php?option=com_content&task=view&id=17&Itemid=36 [Accessed 23 Apr 2021].

k, 2021. TW - bodycheck & sh scars [online]. *@dvllbl4d3s.* Available from: https://twitter.com/dvllbl4d3s/status/1422327132882038802 [Accessed 11 Aug 2021].

Knapton, O., 2013. Pro-anorexia: Extensions of ingrained concepts. *Discourse & Society*, 24 (4), 461–477.

Lavis, A., 2016. Alarming engagements? Exploring pro-anorexia websites in/and the media. *In*: K. Eli and S.J. Ulijaszek, eds. *Obesity, Eating Disorders and the Media.* London: Routledge, 11–35.

Libbert, L., 2018. Toxic Web: Inside the sinister world of pro-cutting bloggers and vile hashtags driving desperate teens to self-harm [online]. *The Sun.* Available from: https://www.thesun.co.uk/fabulous/6963851/inside-the-sinister-world-of-pro-cutting-bloggers-and-vile-hashtags-driving-desperate-teens-to-self-harm/ [Accessed 21 Jul 2020].

Lou, 2003. disclaimer & copyright [online]. *Silent Screams.* Available from: https://web.archive.org/web/20030203185723/http://www.silent-screams.org/disc.shtml [Accessed 7 Apr 2021].

Mackeen, D., 2002. Waifs on the web. *Teen People*, 5(3), 147–149.

Mahoney, T., Varshney, K., Hind, M., and Safari, an O.M.C., 2020. *AI Fairness*. Sebastopol, California: O'Reilly Media.

McLellan, K., 2010. 'Is THAT what they are so afraid of?': The popular media and pro-anorexia websites. *In*: C. Chaput, M.J. Braun, and D.M. Brown, eds. *Entertaining Fear: Rhetoric and the Political Economy of Social Control*. New York: Peter Lang, 223–243.

Miarexia, 2002. It is not a lifestyle [online]. Available from: https://www.oocities.org/miarexia/index.html [Accessed 19 Aug 2020].

Misa, 2007. Tips and Tricks [online]. *University of EdNos*. Available from: https://web.archive.org/web/20071028183653/http://www.freewebs.com/uenway/breakroom.htm [Accessed 24 May 2021].

Mok, K., Jorm, A.F., and Pirkis, J., 2016. Who goes online for suicide-related reasons?: A comparison of suicidal people who use the internet for suicide-related reasons and those who do not. *Crisis*, 37 (2), 112–120.

Newman, J., 1997. Little girls who won't eat. *Redbook*, 189 (6), 120–127.

Niederkrotenthaler, T., Haider, A., Till, B., Mok, K., and Pirkis, J., 2017. Comparison of suicidal people who use the internet for suicide-related reasons and those who do not: Survey study in Austria. *Crisis*, 38 (2), 131–135.

O'Connor, R.C., 2019. Youth suicide prevention needs more than social media regulation [online]. *Suicidal Behaviour Research Lab*. Available from: http://www.suicideresearch.info/news-1/youthsuicidepreventionneedsmorethansocialmediaregulation [Accessed 11 Mar 2019].

overw8y, 2018a. Trigger warning. Not pro anything except recovery [online]. *Tumblr*. Available from: https://overw8y.tumblr.com [Accessed 13 Aug 2018].

overw8y, 2018b. Day 24: How do you feel about the terms pro-ana/pro-mia? [online]. *Tumblr*. Available from: https://overw8y.tumblr.com/post/170329375691/30-day-thinspo-challenge [Accessed 13 Aug 2018].

overw8y, 2018c. I don't know if it is mainly in my head and if I am mainly making this up myself, but it just feels like eating disorders are almost a competition [online]. *Tumblr*. Available from: https://overw8y.tumblr.com/post/169403640191/i-dont-know-if-it-is-mainly-in-my-head-and-if-i [Accessed 27 Aug 2018].

Pater, J.A., Haimson, O.L., Andalibi, N., and Mynatt, E.D., 2016. "Hunger hurts but starving works": Characterizing the presentation of eating disorders online. *In*: *Proceedings of the 19th ACM Conference on Computer-Supported Cooperative Work & Social Computing*. Presented at the CSCW '16: Computer Supported Cooperative Work and Social Computing, San Francisco, California, USA: ACM, 1185–1200.

Pirkis, J.E. and Blood, R.W., 2010. *Suicide and the News and Information Media: A Critical Review*. Australian Capital Territory: Mindframe.

Pirkis, J.E., Neal, L., Dare, A., Blood, R.W., and Studdert, D., 2009. Legal bans on pro-suicide web sites: An early retrospective from Australia. *Suicide and Life-Threatening Behavior*, 39 (2), 190–193.

pixel ♡'s buggy, 2021. Tw mentions of suicide [online]. *@pixelkillz*. Available from: https://twitter.com/pixelkillz/status/1423696710673567749 [Accessed 11 Aug 2021].

Polak, M., 2007. 'I think we must be normal … There are too many of us for this to be abnormal!!!': Girls creating identity and forming community in pro-Ana/Mia websites. *In*: S. Weber and S. Dixon, eds. *Growing up Online: Young People and Digital Technologies*. New York, NY: Palgrave Macmillan, 83–96.

proanorexia, 2007. Community information [online]. *proanorexia*. Available from: https://web.archive.org/web/20070829195258/http://community.livejournal.com/proanorexia/profile [Accessed 10 Jun 2021].

Rajan, B., 2018. Fitness selfie and anorexia: A study of 'fitness' selfies of women on Instagram and its contribution to anorexia nervosa. *Punctum. International Journal of Semiotics*, 4 (2), 66–89.

Reaves, J., 2001. Anorexia goes high tech [online]. *Time*. Available from: http://content.time.com/time/health/article/0,8599,169660,00.html [Accessed 2 Mar 2018].

Robbins, A., 2007. About [online]. *Anna's Place*. Available from: https://web.archive.org/web/20070526084315/http://www.annasplace.us/enter.html [Accessed 10 May 2021].

Robertson, L., Skegg, K., Poore, M., Williams, S., and Taylor, B., 2012. An Adolescent suicide cluster and the possible role of electronic communication technology. *Crisis*, 33 (4), 239–245.

Ryan, E.G., 2012. The scary, weird world of Pinterest thinspo boards [online]. *Jezebel*. Available from: https://jezebel.com/5893382/the-scary-weird-world-of-pinterest-thinspo-boards [Accessed 28 Aug 2018].

san ♥□, 2021. alot of u who report accounts on #shtwt need to understand that u arent helping these ppl [online]. *@jisoouicidal*. Available from: https://twitter.com/jisoouicidal/status/1383852590652219394 [Accessed 22 Apr 2021].

Sciarretto, A., 2014. Pro-anorexia websites could be criminalized in Italy, but experts aren't sure it's the best idea [online]. *Bustle*. Available from: https://www.bustle.com/articles/38177-pro-anorexia-websites-could-be-criminalized-in-italy-but-experts-arent-sure-its-the-best-idea [Accessed 13 May 2021].

Shade, L.R., 2007. Contested spaces: Protecting or inhibiting girls online? *In*: S. Weber and S. Dixon, eds. *Growing Up Online: Young People and Digital Technologies*. New York, NY: Palgrave Macmillan, 229–247.

Sharpe, H., Musiat, P., Knapton, O., and Schmidt, U., 2011. Pro-eating disorder websites: facts, fictions and fixes. *Journal of Public Mental Health*, 10 (1), 34–44.

Song, S., 2005. Health: Starvation on the Web. *Time*, 166(3), 57.

Swannell, S., Martin, G., Krysinska, K., Kay, T., Olsson, K., and Win, A., 2010. Cutting on-line: Self-injury and the internet. *Advances in Mental Health*, 9 (2), 177–189.

Tamás, D., 2017. Give Me a Body I Can Relate to: The Representation of Eating Disorder and the Body in Blythe Baird's Poetry. Presented at the Talking Bodies Conference, Chester, 1–32.

Trigger Warning, 2016. *Geek Feminism Wiki*. http://geekfeminism.wikia.com/wiki/Trigger_warning

Tumblr Staff, 2018. Community Guidelines [online]. *Tumblr*. Available from: https://www.tumblr.com/policy/en/community [Accessed 6 Feb 2019].

Welcome to my pro-ana site! [online], 2002. *Ana – My Maker, My Destroyer*. Available from: https://web.archive.org/web/20021005054922/http://myweb.ecomplanet.com/sxvi1237/ [Accessed 18 Aug 2020].

Xu, J., Compton, R., Lu, T.-C., and Allen, D., 2014. *Rolling through Tumblr: Characterizing Behavioral Patterns of the Microblogging Platform*. ACM Press, 13–22.

Yahoo7, 2019. 'Instagram helped kill my daughter': The tragic story behind stricter posting rules [online]. *Yahoo7 News*. Available from: https://au.news.yahoo.com/instagram-helped-kill-daughter-tragic-story-behind-stricter-posting-rules-060519396.html [Accessed 27 Feb 2019].

Yeshua-Katz, D., 2015. Online stigma resistance in the pro-Ana community. *Qualitative Health Research*, 25 (10), 1347–1358.

7 Censorship Alternatives

Considering the aforementioned logistical and ethical problems with censorship, an alternative is needed. As such, this chapter concludes with an exploration of practical ways that damaging elements of pro-self-harm material can be limited, and the more helpful dimensions of these groups can be nurtured or turned into more formal clinical programs for healing. Key in these recommendations is the fact that many vulnerable people only receive genuine support from their peers on social media. Maximising positive support through tools like content moderation and online interventions are thus of benefit – more so than censorship (Branley and Covey 2017, p. 1356). In the previous chapter, adherents made it clear that ana was a way of finding the happiness and strength that they desperately needed. Removing these positive aspects is damaging and makes recovery seem unappealing. Instead, informative journalism should be used to educate the public on the nuanced reality of mental health struggles. Pro-recovery discourses from within pro-self-harm groups should be supported, peer connections within these groups should be fostered, safe spaces for emotional expression should be allowed, and new identities to replace destructive ones should be a core focus of the recovery journey.

Valuing Education and Informative Journalism

Journalism has an important role to play in education if it is done with care and good intentions. For example, Pirkis and Blood advocate responsible reporting on suicide – not censorship of the topic. They see suicide content in the media as an opportunity for raising public health awareness if handled safely based on evidence of contagion and clustering effects. While irresponsible presentation of this material can lead to copycat events, this should inspire better training rather than a lack of information on the topic (Pirkis and Blood 2010, pp. 5, 33). Journalists have the opportunity to help the public grasp the seriousness of suicide, informing them on the wide variety of people who can be impacted and what signs they may notice in others that could lead to life-saving intervention. More resources tend to be allocated to suicide programs when people are aware of this need (Canetto *et al.* 2017, p. 37).

DOI: 10.4324/9781003126065-10

Conversely, a lack of suicide coverage can encourage a culture of secrecy and shame around this mental health issue. This can result in people failing to speak about their experiences or treating suicidal people with a lack of empathy or understanding (McGorry 2012). Hesitancy to discuss suicide also filters into research and education. For example, at the turn of the century, Tatz called suicide "the taboo, the secret, the hush- hush and the no-no topic" of the Australian school system, resulting in a culture where neither the media nor the education system are able to inform people on techniques for handling suicide in the community or alternative actions for those who feel suicidal (2005, p. xii). Academic research into suicide clusters has arguably been held back due to concerns that discussions could become inappropriate and lead to self-injurious behaviour (Boyce 2011, p. 1452). In reality, with more education, caregivers and community members more broadly can have a better approach to understanding self-harmful behaviours, interpreting cries for help, and redirecting destructive impulses into healthier forms of emotional expression.

Fostering Pro-Recovery Ideologies

As noted, the pro-recovery movement has been a long-term facet of pro-ana and pro-self-harm communities. From the early days of the pro-ana movement, the term 'recovery' has evolved. Giles traces it back to the late 1990s where it was a term strongly tied to the professional clinical world. A person would speak of recovery as part of a medical treatment agenda. Recovery as determined by one's peers or self only emerged in the reformation phase of pro-ana in response to media demonisation. Terms like 'recovery site' or 'pro-recovery' emerged to distance users from a perceived culture of eating disorder promotion (Giles 2016, p. 322). From the reformation phase onwards, most pro-ana communities have accepted the fact that many members will seek to recover to some degree. Polak believes this fact has often been overlooked by critics who miss some salient features of recovery acceptance in this community. The close friendships that tend to emerge in these spaces lead to people being accepted and supported at any stage of their journey. Most sites have detailed recovery resources on par with material pertaining to other aspects of eating disorders (Polak 2007, p. 93). While some efforts to this end have been a little misguided or lacking in detail, this is a natural consequence of a peer-led movement run by people who are often struggling with their own disordered behaviour. By paying attention to what people have gained from pro-recovery and why it resonates with them, these ideologies can be fostered and encouraged, ideally with some open-minded professional assistance.

Professional services have already tapped into the language and content of pro-recovery. For example, in 2013, NEDA started a campaign targeting sufferers of eating disorders and their allies, inviting them to "join the pro-recovery movement!". This involves sharing positive images and stories of "hope, health and healing" to counter negative influences on the same social media spaces and to make sufferers feel less isolated or misunderstood. They encourage the use of the #prorecovery hashtag to link together this material and make it easier for others to locate (NEDA Blog 2013). This movement was supported by a similar initiative launched by the Eating Disorder Hope website in the same year, reacting against the infectious "black shadow" of thinspiration online. This site invited allies to "be a light of inspiration in the darkness of the Pro-Ana/Pro-Mia online community" in order to counterbalance this negative energy. They were instrumental in advocating the #prorecovery hashtag on social media platforms (Eating Disorder Hope Blog 2013). These professional campaigns did have some success. #prorecovery remains a popular and important hashtag but is not as popular or as global as #proana. Data taken from *hashtagify.me* in 2018[1] gives #proana a popularity score of 45.3 and shows usage in North America, South and Central America, Australia, and Western Europe. In comparison, #prorecovery has a popularity score of 22.4, is limited to use in North America, and is most commonly used by professional organisations including NEDA and the Eating Disorder Center.

Some of the most popular recovery websites have been those run by people who have had eating disorders in the past like *Anorexic Web. Something Fishy*, still active in the 2020s, was very popular at the turn of the century due to its chat rooms and forums with over 15,000 members. This site was established by Amy Medina who identifies as a recovered anorexic and saw an importance in creating a recovery site to explicitly counter and challenge the pro-ana movement (Druley 2002). Peer-facilitated sites of this kind tend to have rigorous moderation and rules to retain their integrity as safe spaces. These often include a ban on: specific numbers to do with weight or body and clothing size,[2] links to material that could trigger disordered eating behaviour, discussion of calories, discussion of celebrities who may have eating disorders, or any serious medical questions that need to be addressed to a doctor (Riley *et al.* 2009, pp. 349, 351). Similar pro-recovery content can be found on other social media sites where there is expression of varied perspectives on the topic. In their study, Branley and Covey found a variety of social media postings where people in recovery sought reassurance from each other about changes to their bodies, gave each other advice about combatting disordered eating habits, and provided empathy in the daily struggle to embrace a healthy lifestyle. Aesthetically, this content tends to be colourful and positive to inspire a sense of optimism. There is also a general emphasis on challenging cultural norms of thinness as beauty (Branley and Covey 2017, p. 1356). There also tends to be similar bans on, or warning about, content that could trigger those trying to recover.

Individual recovery blogs have also been around since the peak of pro-self-harmful content. For example, the *Geocities* page 'Rag Doll's Candlelit Tunnel' was started in 2001 by an anonymous woman in her early twenties who had recovered from a five-year struggle with self-harm. She started her page to make other self-harmers feel less alone and realise that they are not crazy or the only ones to process their pain in this manner. When she self-harmed, she used to scroll through websites on this topic and only very occasionally found sites with recovery content. Even before she started to recover, she found this content encouraging and hopeful. By creating her page, she hoped to reach out to her younger and more depressed self, or anyone else in the same mindset to show that real change is possible (Rag Doll 2001a). In this site, she uses very positive language and cute graphics such as teddy bears, stars, hearts, and flowers. This is in contrast to the typical aesthetic of this era (see Alderton 2018). Pages indexed on her site include tips for alternatives when tempted to self-harm, lists of professional organisations offering crisis support, and a list of steps for beginning the recovery journey. She also shares pages written by her husband who offers an outsider's perspective on understanding self-harm and supporting someone in a recovery journey.

Rag Doll identifies as a 'typical' self-harmer in line with the criteria outlined by Conterio and Lader (1998). She is White, was a high-achieving student, but also suffered from depression and low-self-esteem. She explains how much trouble she had articulating her true feelings and her ongoing struggles with self-care. An early catalyst for her struggles was her father's ill health following a car accident prior to her birth. His traumatic brain injuries caused him to be violent and led to patterns of repeated verbal abuse in her household growing up (Rag Doll 2001b). Because of her personal experiences with trauma and self-harm, Rag Doll is able to offer sincere tips for recovery such as learning to find an identity outside of self-harm, the importance of seeking out help from professionals, and the value that comes from appreciating one's emotions and giving validity to one's needs (Rag Doll 2002a). For those who are unsure where to start, she has a list of ways to seek help and communicate with others who might be supportive – such as providing written lists of facts or to have clear intentions for desired outcomes. She also gives practical ways of challenging negative thoughts and purging them in a healthy way through writing a diary or other creative pursuits (Rag Doll 2002b). Because she is not a doctor, Rag Doll comes across as a supportive friend and mentor whose recommendations are from her own recovery journey rather than simply clinical research.

These recommendations feel genuine, as they are backed up by personal experience and empathy. For example, she encourages readers to stick with therapy and communicate during sessions by describing times when she felt overwhelmed and frustrated during this kind of treatment. She also emphasises the need to pick appropriate people to discuss struggles with and not to burden people who are unwilling or unable to provide the depth of help needed; advice based on her own experience with overwhelming people who could not give her the time and constructive advice she needed (Rag Doll 2002c). Based on her own struggles with communicating to others, and the struggles of her friends and family to support her constructively, Rag Doll has created a series of tools to facilitate better understanding. These include her 'safe coupons', which are designed to be 'cashed in' when needed or act as promissory note for sensible future behaviours. Her coupons include "I promise to tell you when I'm feeling suicidal. Signed: _____" and "I feel unsafe & don't want to be alone right now". Each is decorated with a cute motif like a doll, bear, or honeybee (Rag Doll 2003). For some people, this is a meaningful way of communicating difficult topics and establishing healthy relationships.

In addition to these creators who feel strongly about their stance in the recovery movement, a core of the peer-led pro-recovery movement is acceptance of ambivalence towards illness or recovery. Feeling forced to immediately commit fully to recovery can be a very confronting idea and makes many people feel unready to leave the security of their self-harmful behaviour behind. It is also hard to define exactly what recovery is and what it might look or feel like for any individual person. Having a strict or purist definition of recovery conflicts with the reality of many people who have chosen to move on from behaviours like starvation but who still 'hear' an internal anorexic voice or who feel residual guilt or shame over healthy weight gain. While recovery can ultimately be read as a positive and desirable experience, this does not mean that people never vacillate between health and disease or miss feelings from their disease like control (Jenkins and Ogden 2012, pp. e28–e29). An ambivalent stance is quite common in edtwt. Many accounts have warnings or declarations of their personal status such as "❥ ⋯ pro recovery, but not in recovery ৎ ❥ ⋯ pro harm reduction ৎ" (Madeline ♡ edtwt 2020) or "dont follow if uncomfy! recovery moots dni ~ [mutual friends/ followers who are in recovery, do not interact with this blog]" (𝒞(´｡• ༝ •｡`)ঔ bubba 2021). These warnings make it clear that recovery is accepted as valid, perhaps even encouraged. Yet, 'harm reduction' seems to feel more comfortable than total rejection of harmful actions.

It is also typical for people to feel pulled between different factions of the movement. As one participant explains, it can be hard to relate fully to either extreme pro-disease or pro-recovery groups as "One strikes me as silly and somewhat triggering, the other often upsets me and makes me ashamed to be anorexic" (falls2climb 2003). Another agrees that it can be hard to find much-needed support "without all the propaganda, finger-pointing, holier-than-thou's and mixed messages [sic]" (Pro Reality 2003). Pro-recovery sites, especially of this era, were seen by many as lacking in support when compared to pro-ana. One person who attempted to engage explains, "I WASN'T ACCEPTED – at pro-recovery communities because i couldn't identify with people's motivations for recovering [sic]" (Persepine in Why a pro-ana listing? 2003). This is obviously an area that needs consideration, as Persepine abandoned her search for recovery due to a narrow range of options and returned to traditional pro-ana where she felt accepted. Faux agrees that "pro-recovery sites make you feel like trash for having an eating disorder". She found these spaces just as competitive as facets of pro-ana with participants "preaching the gospel of recovery and making you feel even worse" (Faux 2007).

Pro-recovery sites like *Something Fishy* were excellent resources for people fully committed to recovery but proved difficult for those who remained ambivalent. User 'control_and_chaos' describes how hampered her expression was in this space because she needed to use significant trigger warnings and avoid expressing any thoughts of relapse. She saw this as a space only for "those who have already made the decision to get better and never look back", not for people experiencing uncertainty. This is a valid reaction, as Medina sees recovering people on pro-ana sites as equivalent to drug addicts who still spend time with their dealers. In this era, she carefully monitored the *Something Fishy* boards to prevent any content that might be interpreted as in any way supportive of an anorexic lifestyle (Medina in Druley 2002). To find space for her complex feelings, control_and_chaos turned instead to the *Sinned Boards* – a pro-ana forum where those attempting recovery were welcome to talk freely about struggles such as therapy failing (control_and_chaos in Why a pro-ana listing? 2003). A space for discussing the downsides and struggles of recovery proved important to many.

This much-needed liminal space between pro-ana and pro-recovery has been carved out through groups like *Pro Reality*, hosted as a stand-alone website and a LiveJournal community. This group appeals to people who feel that there are plenty of sites for or against disordered eating "but nothing in between" (studenten in Meg 2003). This community bills itself as a place without "destructive support" like advice to stomach punch or eat toilet paper common in pro-ana spaces. At the same time, it also functions a safe place for people who "aren't ready for gung-ho recovery" and still wish to maintain elements of pro-ana in their life (Pro Reality 2003). Reflecting the flexibility of this space, the *Pro Reality* LiveJournal community includes a variety of content, ranging from people who wish to recover to a call for competitive weight loss buddies who want to lose forty pounds in a month through a juice fast (Mindy 2003). The creator started this community because she was "sick of the holier-than-thous... who speak of those with ED's as if they're the scum of the earth [sic]" (kpachble_makn in Poppy__seed 2005).

Pro Reality functioned as a space where a person could "speak your mind without a fifty-page list of rules" or ask for help without recovery being the default answer (Pro Reality 2005a). Indeed, it is common for members to make claims like "I'm not sure if i want help or not. I'm not sure if i want to stop or not [*sic*]" (Meg 2003) and have this be an acceptable stance. *Pro Reality* is opposed to "glorification of eating disorders" in any form (Pro Reality 2005b) and seeks to point out damaging trends like the use of image manipulation in popular thinspiration media. Instead, the site's focus was bridging insider discourse to the outside world, teaching them about the lived experience of disordered eating through personal stories and opinions (Pro Reality 2005a). As with many sites of this kind, the creator emphasises that disordered eating quickly "becomes devistation and hell [sic]", stressing that no one is aiming to "'recruit' people into this lifestyle". Rather, the aim is providing support to those who have nowhere else to turn (lanthanum in studenten 2003) – certainly a common sentiment in this milieu.

To be successfully persuasive, recovery needs to be framed as something valuable and desirable and space needs to be kept open for those who hesitate. As discussed further, many people fear recovery because their illness gives them a sense of identity, purpose, and belonging that is absent in other areas of their lives. It is no good to attack the illness without modelling how recovery can lead to new meaning and connections that are of equal or greater value. This cannot be achieved through platitudes or the celebration of health alone. For engaging with those who do not wish to recover, one participant has some meaningful advice. She notes,

> You cannot push a person into recovery. They have to want it otherwise it is more likely than not pointless. Some people don't choose recovery. That is their personal choice, and although you may not agree with that, you should try to respect that persons feelings, and maybe find out why it is that they prefer to hang on to their disorder.
>
> (Lou 2003)

While this is perhaps a little too fatalistic, the important point is the value of a dialogue where a person is given an opportunity to explain why recovery does not appeal or why their disordered behaviour feels more desirable. This is the best way for recovery movements to make room for the hesitant and give them a space to honestly reflect on what might seem more appealing about continuing to hurt themselves so that it can be addressed in good faith.

Guided Peer Support

Something integral to the pro-recovery movement is the presence of sincere and impactful peer support. This is often a precursor to a full commitment to recovery, as many participants in movements like pro-ana need to discuss their feelings free of stigma and harsh judgement before being ready to transition to healthier eating practices (Mulveen and Hepworth 2006, p. 292). The internet is a unique place where people can feel freer to discuss sensitive and taboo topics than they would in face-to-face interactions. Personal and intimate information can be shared with trusted strangers who are often more supportive and empathetic than offline connections (Bell and Bailey 2017, p. 82). The vast networks of self-harming people means there is a free exchange of emotional energy and always someone available for friendly remarks or advice (Adler and Adler 2008, p. 45). AnaGirlEmpath notes that eating disorders are, by their nature, isolating conditions that cause people to stop socialising. She calls the internet a 'serendipitous blessing' that helped many people find support – especially those who are physically isolated or mentally disconnected from their surroundings. As people shared information online about their treatments, symptoms, and physicians, this naïve and reformation phase participant feels as though they developed a better quality of life overall (AnaGirlEmpath 2012). There is real potential for this kind of peer support to be used as part of a professional mental health intervention.

For example, Rice *et al.* believe that social media-based interventions could be a good way of both addressing a natural human need to belong and re-ducing the feeling of burdensomeness common in people who are suicidal (Rice *et al.* 2016, p. 82). Younger adults at risk of suicide seem to especially prefer this kind of support (Seward and Harris 2016, p. 617) as it allows for a "person avoidant method of solving problems" (Harris *et al.* 2009, p. 274). Tools like suicide prevention blogs are also very wide-reaching while being low-cost, making them an accessible tool for outreach programs with smaller budgets (Niederkrotenthaler and Stack 2017, p. 2). They are also flexible and asynchronous sources of care and encouragement (Kendal *et al.* 2017, p. 104). Anything that could appeal to a group deemed "among the most reluctant help-seekers" with limited "opportunities for treating and preventing un-necessary suffering and self-inflicted deaths" (Seward and Harris 2016, p. 606) is certainly worthy of exploration. There are also arguments for the relative safety of this material, as participants do not tend to use current suicide support forums to learn suicide techniques (Robinson *et al.* 2016, p. 117). With professional guidance, these kinds of forums could be expanded to include immediate chat services or other communication options, perhaps pushing for active online friendship development if this shows signs of success (Harris *et al.* 2014, p. 392).

It is common for people who share suicidal feelings to support each other and share words of empathy or advice. This behaviour is consistent with data showing that the higher a person's suicide risk is, the more likely they are to say that they have nobody in their lives to seek help from. This disinterest or refusal towards help-seeking *does not* seem to apply to online relationships. Rather, online spaces seem to appeal to those in acute need – especially younger people (Seward and Harris 2016, pp. 611, 615). Qualitative evidence appears to show a similar trend when looking at other self-harmful behaviours. When asked in a non-academic questionnaire what made them feel better and less like self-harming, those aiming to recover outlined a variety of situations – many to do with feeling connected to and supported by others. Responses include "people being nice", "using the internet to talk to people in similar situations", "knowing that someone cares about you", "people understanding, who don't judge you", and "knowing that you are not alone and there are other people with similar problems" (Some Questionnaire Results 2000). Similar findings are echoed in academic studies with Harris *et al.* noting that people with depression and suicidal thoughts feel less ostracised or stigmatised when they can connect with those in a similar headspace, and have been moved towards recovery when people have read and connected with their blog entries (2009, p. 272).

Interventions relying on peer support also seem to help with some of the major barriers towards seeking help felt by those who are suicidal or otherwise engaged in self-harmful actions. Research shows that people in this group are very reluctant to seek help from typical sources such as friends or religious leaders. At the same time, they score significantly higher than average for help-seeking online. It is typical for people in this category to prefer to deal with their struggles alone, be unsure if their needs are serious enough to warrant help, feeling unable to express themselves, or worrying what people around them would think (Mok *et al.* 2016, pp. 117–118). By connecting with peers online, there is far less risk of being judged by those in their offline environment or feeling as though they are wasting anyone's time. Rather, such forums are proven to be spaces of "mutual support and acceptance" where users can practice ways of discussing difficult concepts such as why they feel they have an eating disorder or unexpected situations in which they feel severe anxiety. Peers who can empathise tend to be read as caring and constructive (Kendal *et al.* 2017, p. 103) as opposed to family members or professionals who need to be "managed".

Peers are generally seen to offer a more neutral and more widely accepted source of support than family members. Studies show that positive, open interpersonal relationships limit the use of self-harm as a coping mechanism. For example, people who communicate well with their parents and have a positive best friend relationship are at lower risk of self-harm. This seems especially relevant in the case of depressed girls (Latina *et al.* 2015, p. 120). This is complicated by the fact that self-harmful behaviour tends to lead to conflict with people such as parents. It is typical for conflict to arise, for example, when a child starts to skip meals and show noticeable weight loss (Castro and Osório 2013, p. 326). Parents tend to be seen as force-feeders who fixate on this dimension of the problem rather than adequately addressing underlying psychological struggles (Brotsky and Giles 2007, p. 104). For example,

> They always say they're concerned about me, about my health, when all they want to do is control me. They want to pin me down and force-feed me with lies, with what they call love. Like prisoners everywhere, all I have left is the power to refuse.
>
> (Ash and Heather 2002)

While parents and caregivers can be a very important part of the prevention or recovery journey, this relationship is often strained by the symptomology of self-harmful behaviour. This can reach a point where family members are seen as the enemy and their assistance is read as an attack. Relationships with peers may be more short-term and casual but are far less emotionally fraught as a consequence meaning that constructive messages and advice will not be immediately rejected.

It is common, and not invalid, for people to feel that only those who have behaved in a similar manner can really understand where they are coming from. For example, one self-harmer explains about her behaviour that, "I hate it and I love it. I need it in a way that only a fellow cutter can understand"

(SarahDarkBlue 2001). Another commentator explains the difference between talking to a "therapist who has NO idea how you really feel" versus reaching out to other people with eating disorders who can give true empathy (Lisa 2005). Even those who are known to be generally depressive characters seem to appeal in this space. Melissa Broder of *So Sad Today* (see Alderton 2018, p. 97) has asked why so many people email her, "someone who doesn't have all her shit together" for advice. She concludes, "Maybe it's because a person who doesn't have all her shit together seems safer than a perfect person (whoever that is). Maybe it's because a person who is honest about her shortcomings is more likely to give honest advice" (Broder 2015). This attitude has already been noted in studies of credibility, which show that people who have overcome an addiction or illness are the most trusted to speak to those on this same pathway. This means, for example, the best spokesperson for eating disorder recovery is someone who has been through this process themselves (Perloff 2014, pp. 372–373). Indeed, it is common for those who have struggled with issues like self-harm to use their experiences to discourage others and show firsthand "how gross it is" or "the ugliness of this destructive behaviour" (Rodham *et al.* 2016, p. 1114) in a way that only someone who has been through it can share.

Peers seem to offer the most believable dissuasion overall. Arndt and her *Anorexic Web* site are a prime example of this. She makes it clear that she once dreamed of being thin and having positive experiences as a result. However, once she lost weight, the "fun" she was expecting was not present. Instead, "There was just nothing... just an emptiness and haze and constant thoughts about food and weight and numbers... my soul was depleted of energy and I don't want to waste time like that ever again" (Arndt 2000a). This vision of anorexia is quite impactful as she communicates real wisdom gained from suffering. Arndt identifies as someone whose had an 'insider study' of disordered eating, making her and others in this same position "the most qualified to help anorexics". She calls on all others like her to "turn all this frantic, anorexic energy into something else, something positive" by gathering together and helping each other to heal (Arndt 2000b).

Peers can also be the most empathetic as to what people with a similar mental illness need. To meet needs that are often unanticipated or misread by professionals, tools like comfort Twitter accounts are currently very popular within self-harmful communities. These accounts tend to post content like cute pictures of pets, positive statements and loving support, encouragement to drink water and look after personal hygiene. This is all delivered with a sense of empathic non-judgement. For example,

> if u binged (like me) today, i understand the shame, guilt, anger, and regret u may feel </3 but pls note that u r still beautiful, inside and out. tmr is another day, and u still deserve to eat well tmr. rmb to drink water to keep urself hydrated ok? i believe in u and ily.
>
> (rae *૭* comfort 2021)

#edtwt #shtwt remember to drink water and (try to) eat well today!! Also know that i love youu!! And i'm proud of you today and always <33. shtwt remember to treat ur wounds properly, and edtwt you can do it! You are beautiful/handsome/stunning!

(bl00dy_k1tty 2021)

Zones like edtwt can also provide a place to ask questions that participants are unwilling or unable to ask a medical professional. For example,

ED twitter: Do you believe you can lose weight while being in recovery? If weight loss is achieved in a healthy manner, would you consider that recovery or would you consider that disordered still?

(Disordered Diaries 2020)

A question like this may alarm a health professional as it indicates ongoing disordered ideas in an adult who is supposedly recovering and who was, at that time, in the advanced stages of pregnancy. While answers varied, all respondents paid careful attention to her question, gave her sincere responses, and had no power over her medical care. This discussion was also free and easily accessible. For nearly 20 years, pro-ana spaces have been celebrated because "no one will judge you for not wanting recovery but still wanting help with certain health issues, emotional problems, etc" (Why a pro-ana listing? 2003). Even though many people struggle to care for themselves, they can be extremely caring to friends and strangers with similar problems. As one member of edtwt asks, "Okay fr tho [for real though], i find it kinda in a fucked up ironic way that i care about my other friends' health with eds/mental illness in general more than my own does anyone feel like this??? [sic]" (미소 2020). This depth of care has even extended to people on self-harm boards commonly aspiring to be professional counsellors for this condition in the future (Adler and Adler 2008, p. 48).

There are, of course, some limits to peer support programs. In some jurisdictions, interactions between medical professionals and people seeking help are not allowed. This means there would be difficulties even in terms of mediating or guiding peer discussions. If permitted to engage with people seeking advice online, clinicians would need to adhere to social media policies outlined by their employer or professional organisation at all times, assuming that communications are public and unsecured (Grajales *et al.* 2014, p. e13). Use of these services is also organically limited as the majority of people engaged in self-harmful behaviours prefer open discussion forums with peers to commercial or professional help sites staffed by clinicians. These sites are often considered judgemental, out of touch, or patronising (Harris *et al.* 2009, pp. 270, 272). This means that a successful site would need to operate in an appropriate jurisdiction and would need to be presented in a manner that is palatable to desired users – not seeming out of touch or unduly governed by professionals and not peers.

Such groups would also need to have an ongoing commitment to moderation and guidance as peers can often be inappropriately accepting to the point of causing harm. As they stand, one of the dangers with unmoderated support groups is that they tend to be very supportive of whatever decision members make, even if that decision may be an objectively unhealthy one (Layton 2016a). This can provide deep solace to troubled people, but can also mean that unhealthy choices are uplifted and downward spirals are taken to be a kind of valid emotional expression (Layton 2016b). Advice often includes more problematic topics like diet guidance, tips for deflecting the suspicions of people outside the community, and pushing away close family members who demand they eat more (Haas *et al.* 2011, p. 49). There is also the ongoing possibility of contagion and the chance that a forum ethos may lead to self-harmful behaviour seeming like a valid response to one's problems (Robinson *et al.* 2016, p. 117). Rice *et al.* (2016) provide some in-depth suggestions about moderation practices for safe spaces, which can help to overcome some of these problem areas. While these are limitations to facilitating guided peer support, this project is still a very worthy one.

Safe Spaces for Emotional Expression

An important element of this peer engagement is the willingness that fellow sufferers have in engaging with depressing, negative, or otherwise troubling content. This space for the expression of distress has been seen as a positive function of pro-self-harmful communities (see, for example, Biddle *et al.* 2008, p. 802). In many cases, pro-harm communities are the only space in which users can feel as though their suffering is properly witnessed and their identity is validated as a result. Typical users of pro-self-harm boards have poor self-image and seek validation from others. These users tend to feel upset and invalidated by failure, rejection, blame, or having to present a fake persona to the world. Their validation tends to come from their diagnosis and biography as self-harmers, other people who listen to stories of their 'true self', and the message boards where they can share their ideas and experiences. Aside from such message boards, these vulnerable people tend to isolate themselves or sacrifice their own needs so as to avoid any further sense of invalidation (Adams *et al.* 2005, p. 1301). Rather than taking away such spaces, it would be more constructive to increase opportunities for the expression of distress.

Some people use their self-harmful behaviour to avoid or subvert negative emotions – especially those they receive no support for. For example, the character of ana is presented as someone who can "make it possible for you to stop thinking of motions that cause you stress. Thoughts of anger, sadness, desperation, and loneliness can cease because I take them away and fill your head with the methodic calorie counting [sic]" (Joe 2005). Another agrees, "ED is an emotional issue- it just happens to be expressed through bad eating habits ... counter-productive attempts to cope with bigger issues" (Miarexia 2002). This is supported by academic research that shows how anorexia nervosa is a vehicle for coping with life stress or developmental trauma. The body becomes a way of communicating distress, unhappiness, or a lack of control (Jenkins and Ogden 2012, pp. e26–e27). If these frustrations can be expressed more directly through words in a supportive environment, more damaging coping mechanisms will have diminished importance.

A problem with many forms of suffering is that there are no physical scars to demonstrate the depth of injury. As one self-harmer explains, "Because I have no physical scars from my abuse I cut to show myself I suffered so I have proof of it" (Aurora Jess 1999). Another started cutting because "I was in too much pain, and I didn't know what to do about it. So I cut. To see blood was reassuring, to think I was getting what I deserved" (Kathy 2004). Similarly, Hutchings sees harming one's body as a way of expressing anger and tormenting pain. Learning from a recovery journey, she recommends talking to other people as a way of metaphorically purging it instead (2003a). This kind of purge is modelled in the poetry and creative writing that is common in mid-2000s pro-self-harmful spaces. Through writing poems about their pain and frustrations, community members have been able to express themselves, disclose complex life problems, and connect with each other in sympathetic or empathetic ways. For example, poetry can disclose troubled family relationships:

A simple teenager, Whose heart is easily broke,
I am a daughter, To emotionally absent parents,
A never seen father, and a never caring mother (Chelsea 2005)

I feel like an outcast in my own home,
Crying up in my room I feel so all alone …
I wanted to talk I was ready to share,
I wanted you to hold me and tell me you cared (Rich 2003)

'cause don't you see that I'm dying each day a little more?
My parents are blind, my parents don't care.
Nobody can rescue me from this hell (Gueble 2005)

A very common, and connected, theme is the experience of being ignored while in distress:

You
Weren't
Watching
You didn't see the life fade from my eyes
You didn't see the hope abandon my face
You didn't see the dangers growing
When all the signs were there to read (Free Butterfly 2008)

Reaching out for guidance,
no-one seems to have the time.
I only wish someone would see,
the pain within my eyes!
Can everyone be so blind?
Can everyone not care?
I guess they can when it's only,
ME who's in despair! (anon. in Arndt 2000c)

I'm fucking dying inside
and nobody cares
Eveyones oblivious to my silent screams
No one notices my tear-streaked cheeks [sic] (Cecilia Marie 2005)

Do not assist me
In getting rid of my Demon,
Although she can be fierce-
She watches over me
She keeps me company.
Not a Guardian Angel
But she has been there for me
She has done more for me
Than you ever intended
Or intend to (v_falling_to_pieces 2003)

Also very common in poetry is the idea that self-harm wounds are a kind of
'red tears' to signify pain in those who are unable to cry or do not have anyone
to witness their grief:

This blade to the skin
Makes me real,
Gives a voice to the pain within (Erin 2008)

my soul is weeping
tears my eyes dare not shed
emotion is mine to control
through those
red tears ...
that trickle down my arm instead of my face (Silent Red Tears 2002)

There are tears that I can't cry,
except in this redder hue. (Anon. in Other People's Poetry 2004)

Poetry of this kind is an excellent way of channelling painful experiences and
emotions into a form that can be shared with others, and which can hopefully

diminish some of the pain associated with difficult interpersonal experiences. Arndt would often binge or purge to show anger at a life event. This process lacked lasting efficacy as it did not resolve her underlying issues and would often feed her sense of alienation (2000d). She also attempted to starve herself into a body that could express the pain and anger she could not verbally communicate, but struggled to ever get skinny enough that her severe distress was noticeable (Arndt 2000e). A far more effective process for her was poetic expression. She believes this is a great way to gain insight about one's own feelings and help to communicate emotional needs to others (Arndt 2000d). As such, she used *Anorexic Web* as a place to encourage the process of purging on paper. Arndt sees this kind of purging as "therapeutic, not destructive" and as a way to gain better self-awareness (2001).

She is not alone in finding this useful with others expressing sentiments like, "Writing is my one true love – it has literally saved my life on many different occasions" (Delicate Sylph 2009). Academic studies have demonstrated that writing or reading illness and recovery narratives are a great path for self-improvement and giving vulnerable young women a sense of power and agency (Hipple Walters *et al.* 2016, pp. 225–226). Emotional expression can also be found in other forms of expression, both creative and interpersonal. For example, Troscianko recommends turning to artistic expression in recovery, finding solace or inspiration in music, painting, literature, and sculpture or simply appreciating natural beauty (2017). These could similarly be ways to shift people from destructive expression to something more therapeutic and creative.

Playing out imagined interactions in a creative and embracing space also seem to have potential to help. Useful research to this end is provided by Sheldon *et al.* who explored 'imagined interactions' in pro-ana blogs. Imagined interactions are much as the name suggests: exchanges with other people conducted hypothetically in the pro-ana space rather than directly with the person concerned. Subjects of imagined interactions commonly include family members, peers and friends, romantic partners, children, co-workers, strangers, and ana herself (2015, pp. 166–167). While the content of these interactions can seem negative or focussed on pain, they bring numerous positive outcomes. Emotional release and catharsis are common, relieving tension. Imagined interactions are also of value to those who have become isolated and have limited contact outside of the pro-ana world, allowing them a better chance of clarifying their thoughts and relationships with others (2015, p. 169). They can help to work through suppressed conflict in cases where it is not or cannot be discussed openly (2015, p. 179). There is real value in expressing emotions though poetry and other creative pursuits, including simply having an imagined conversation with another party. These activities can help people achieve emotional catharsis or practice expression of needs, which could be applied to real interpersonal interactions.

Identity Reconstruction

> This is the only way I know
> I would not be anything
> This friend, this enemy is who I am
> Makes me unique, different
> This is part of me, my life
> Starving for attention needing to feel
> Success, approval, acceptance
> What would I be without this? (Jennifer S in Arndt 2000f)

Many people express fears of recovery because their illness has been their primary source of identity for a significant period – often during formative eras of their life such as the teenage years. The most effective way of encouraging recovery is to have participants enthusiastically connecting with this mindset as a sense of meaningful personal identity rather than forcing them into reluctant recovery by removing all other content relating to their illness. It is important to respect how powerful identity as an anorexic is. Many people with this condition report how strongly it defines them as a person and how difficult it can be to leave behind this identity in order to recover due to fears they cannot be anything else (Jenkins and Ogden 2012, pp. e28–e29). For some, disordered eating is the only identity they live for themselves rather than for the sake of others. As one participant notes, "I was always trying so hard to please others, that I felt all i had left for me and me only, was my eating [sic]" (Anon. in Hutchings 2003b). As outlined in the previous chapter, disordered eating can provide a sense of meaning, purpose, and companionship in an otherwise stressful or emotionally impoverished life.

Extreme behaviours like starvation also provide a sense of distinction and elitism. Recovery can lead to a loss of this identity. As one person in recovery explains, getting better means she won't be "special anymore" (Christina in Arndt 2000g). Another expresses the tension between desired health and meaning-laden illness:

> I can feel things changing for the better. My body looks healthier now. Yet sometimes if feels as though I have lost all my willpower. I'm becoming like everyone else, with the same eating habits. This is when winning is loosing. Once I prided myself on my extreme willpower. For this same reason I received praise from those around me. Now that's all gone, and it's hard to keep from feeling like I'm loosing [sic].
>
> (Casey in Arndt 2000h)

Many people in the pro-ana community feel that anorexia is the only thing they are "good at" (Lavis 2016, p. 18), thus leaving it behind is a stressful choice that leaves them vulnerable to being good at nothing. It is common to hear sentiments like "When I starve myself I'm somebody" (Jensen 2005) or "ana is my lifestyle and my saviour because without this illness i am nothing" (anarxia 2016). Pro-ana retains ongoing appeal because it validates the belief that anorexia has more significance than health and a normative life (Ward 2007, p. 9). It can be frightening to leave one's main personality feature of daily practices behind.

It may also leave people feeling voiceless. An important part of the recovery journey is helping people to describe their emotions and needs without re-sorting to harmful behaviour to do so. Just because a person is recovering and gaining weight does not mean they are immune from returning to elements of disordered eating that better expressed their feelings. As one person in re-covery confesses, "I miss being skinny, i miss feeling like i'm about to faint, i miss lying to people, i miss feeling too weak to climb up some stairs, i miss not being able to stay focused... i KNOW it's fucked up but i can't help it, now that my body is 'healthy' i hate it" (^sad ana 2019). Levenkron believes that statements commonly made by anorexics like "I feel fat" are reflective of "identity impoverishment". A reductive statement like this is often used when a person feels anxiety, fear, or other challenging emotions and does not know how to convey these complex states with nuance. Alternatively, they may feel unwilling to be vulnerable so rely instead on coded messages (Levenkron in Sheffer 1999). Some of these issues could be addressed by modelling other ways of describing one's fear and feelings and encouraging others to support them in finding a new kind of voice.

Another area that needs to be considered in identity reconstruction is that using self-harmful practices to gain attention often *works*. An anonymous person who has struggled with anorexia explains how she loses large quantities of weight when she is suffering in order to communicate "LISTEN! I'M FALLING APART!". She finds this tactic successful as it encourages her mother to call her more often and for friends to genuinely ask her own she is feeling and to care about the response (anon. in Arndt 2000i). Similarly, Hutchings feels that "when I was healthy I was ignored by all". When she became severely emaciated her family "doted on" her and men lusted after her body. Despite being a creative person and an academic high achiever, only starvation led to "that kind of love or respect" from those around her (Hutchings 2003c). While this kind of reaction may be unintentional, it does show that harmful behaviour as a cry for attention has the potential to be effective. Again, encouraging a person to have a greater array of commu-nication tools – and listening sincerely when they express themselves – is vital in supporting a recovery journey.

As to what replacement identities might look like, this is very much an individual project. In my previous work on this topic, I introduced the idea of "healing through aesthetics" (Alderton 2018, p. 163ff), which is highly relevant in this context. Because of the strong aesthetic and ri-tualistic dimensions of self-harmful behaviour, new treatment, lifestyle, and identity recommendations must be able to compete with these compelling features. As an example of possibilities, I have explored the aesthetics of Straight Edge, Fitblr, and Radical Softness. More than just a visual language, these aesthetics carry with them a strong community core that values health, wellbeing, fitness, healing, or self-care. They are also tied into communities that provide sophisticated support networks that are equal to those of pro-self-harm spaces, allowing for the expression of negative affect but also for loving guidance towards recovery – often delivered by peers who have been through similar journeys themselves. More work in this area would be a very practical way of delivering the much-needed outcomes written of above.

Conclusion

The typical response to self-harmful behaviour expressed online is censorship. This seems at first glance to be a reasonable approach. Harming oneself is a confronting and sometimes deadly way of dealing with problems and pain. It can also be infectious and cause echoing contagion of destructive behaviours. Nevertheless, while the intention to remove harmful content may be a good one, the outcomes of this action tend to be negative and counterproductive. They can easily radicalise self-harmful groups against mainstream cultures of wellness and recovery, educating them on how to hide their destructive behaviours from caregivers and medical professionals who are seen as the enemy. It is important to understand the many consequences of censorship and the technical difficulties that render current approaches inconsistent and unpredictable. Ultimately, self-harmful spaces have proven extremely resilient to the censorship process. Their ability to resist and subvert attacks against them shows their inherent fluidity (Dias 2003, p. 36). In the process of this resistance, networks have become more secluded, inwards-oriented, and harder for health professionals to engage with (Casilli *et al.* 2013, p. 95). Evasion of censorship has also created very unanticipated problems such as slippage of the term 'healthy', which has been appropriated in some alarming ways by those seeking to validate practices like emaciation (Cobb 2020, p. 27). Negative consequences of censorship outweigh potential benefits by a considerable margin.

There are many solutions that can allow us to move past the ineffective road of censorship and towards sustained cultures of healing. Journalists can be educated in best practice for discussing self-harmful actions in order to prevent not just contagion but also harmful stigma and radicalisation. While medical professionals will always be core to outlining healthy recovery, room needs to be made for the very valuable and meaningful support that peers can provide and how supportive they may be of the recovery process. For example, it is common for eating disorder recovery to be supported when users reach dangerously low weights or take on extreme starvation behaviours (Mulveen and Hepworth 2006, p. 291). While many forum users are of the opinion that recovery is not for them, they tend to treat those seeking this pathway with warmth and respect, validating it as an acceptable personal choice (Brotsky and Giles 2007, p. 106). This can give real encouragement to their peers who see them as sources of genuine advice and opinions untempered by stigma.

Even if a person has an attitude towards self-harmful behaviours that is not ideal, they are still deserving of a safe space to express their emotional turmoil. Pro-self-harmful communities offer desired information about mental illness and its physical consequences, allow global communication without temporal constraints, and act as a safe space where people can find the understanding and support that is often missing in their offline realities (Castro and Osório 2012, p. 171). While there are clear dangers in the graphic discussion of contagious ideas like starvation, Polak rightly argues that these need to be weighed against positive elements that these spaces may provide. For example, they give people a space to wrangle with controversial issues and speak their poignant realities rather than remaining silent and feeling unheard due to stigma and censorship. The discussions that take place are not all destructive with many leading to personal growth and even recovery (Polak 2007, pp. 92, 94). Research suggests that interventions aiming to reduce self-harm should consider targets including emotional regulation strategies, more effective interpersonal communication, and better skills for emotional clarity and expression (Turner *et al.* 2012, p. 16). These are skills that are already being practiced in many of these spaces.

Rather than rejecting self-harmful communities and censoring their content, we should instead learn from what that content offers and what needs are being expressed by those within. Users are not naïve to the bodily damage they are causing themselves, with many seeming resigned to an early death or severe chronic complaints. They are also far more likely to reject rather than embrace anyone who wishes to learn their crafts of bodily destruction. Participants want to help rather than hinder their peers. This drive to assist others can be woven into tools like social media-based interventions that bond together people at risk. There is strong evidence that this can be safely conducted if appropriate protocol is followed (Rice *et al.* 2016, p. 80). Peer connectedness can also foster a sense of identity and life purpose. New avenues for identity and community are indeed required as part of the recovery process. Work needs to be put into the creation of meaningful identities that can supersede self-destruction. This will be of far more lasting benefit than continued attempts to censor and regulate the ultimately uncontrollable space of the internet.

Notes

1 Accessed on 11 September 2018.
2 Despite this being a firm and common rule in these spaces, there is evidence that it was also commonly violated. Riley *et al.* note that many participants still aimed to somehow make real their bodies and the physical legacy of their eating disorder to justify a place on recovery sites. For example, they might note low muscle mass or detail struggles with known anorexia symptoms like orthostatic hypotension – even though specific weight and measurements were not noted (Riley *et al.* 2009, p. 353).

References

Adams, J., Rodham, K., and Gavin, J., 2005. Investigating the "self" in deliberate self-harm. *Qualitative Health Research*, 15 (10), 1293–1309.

Adler, P.A. and Adler, P., 2008. The cyber worlds of self-injurers: Deviant communities, relationships, and selves. *Symbolic Interaction*, 31 (1), 33–56.

Alderton, Z., 2018. *The Aesthetics of Self-Harm: The Visual Rhetoric of Online Communities*. Abingdon: Routledge.

AnaGirlEmpath, 2012. Understanding the ProAna Movement I: Background & precipitating factors [online]. *YouTube*. Available from: https://www.youtube.com/watch?v=GYy1_zNvkHA [Accessed 29 Aug 2018].

anarxia, 2016. introduction and motivation [online]. *in ana's embrace*. Available from: https://web.archive.org/web/20161110051836if_/http://inanasembrace.blogg.se/2016/june/introduction-and-motivation.html [Accessed 23 Apr 2021].

Arndt, L., 2000a. Photo diary [online]. *Anorexic Web*. Available from: https://web.archive.org/web/20000928233914/http://www.anorexicweb.com:80/Taste/photodiary.html [Accessed 7 Mar 2018].

Arndt, L., 2000b. Restricted Access: Page 1 [online]. *Anorexic Web*. Available from: https://web.archive.org/web/20000823224156fw_/http://www.anorexicweb.com:80/InsidetheFridge/restrictedaccess.html [Accessed 28 Mar 2018].

Arndt, L., 2000c. Food For Thought: Page 2 [online]. *Anorexic Web*. Available from: https://web.archive.org/web/20001219092500/http://www.anorexicweb.com:80/FoodForThought/foodforthoughtpag.html [Accessed 13 Mar 2018].

Arndt, L., 2000d. Tongue Tied [online]. *Anorexic Web*. Available from: https://web.archive.org/web/20000823224059/http://www.anorexicweb.com:80/TongueTied/tonguetied.html [Accessed 8 Mar 2018].

Arndt, L., 2000e. The Camera Adds Ten Pounds [online]. *Anorexic Web*. Available from: https://web.archive.org/web/20000823224446/http://www.anorexicweb.com:80/CameraAdds/thecameraaddstenp.html [Accessed 15 Mar 2018].

Arndt, L., 2000f. Food For Thought: Page 7 [online]. *Anorexic Web*. Available from: https://web.archive.org/web/20001219125700/http://www.anorexicweb.com:80/FoodForThought/foodforthoughtpd.html [Accessed 13 Mar 2018].

Arndt, L., 2000g. Food For Thought: Page 5 [online]. *Anorexic Web*. Available from: https://web.archive.org/web/20001219114100/http://www.anorexicweb.com:80/FoodForThought/foodforthoughtpc.html [Accessed 13 Mar 2018].

Arndt, L., 2000h. Food For Thought: Page 4 [online]. *Anorexic Web*. Available from: https://web.archive.org/web/20001219103700/http://www.anorexicweb.com:80/FoodForThought/foodforthoughtpb.html [Accessed 13 Mar 2018].

Arndt, L., 2000i. Food For Thought: Page 3 [online]. *Anorexic Web*. Available from: https://web.archive.org/web/20001219082200/http://www.anorexicweb.com:80/FoodForThought/foodforthoughtpa.html [Accessed 13 Mar 2018].

Arndt, L., 2001. Binge and Purge [online]. *Anorexic Web*. Available from: https://web.archive.org/web/20010107002900/http://www.anorexicweb.com:80/BingeandPurge/bingeandpurge.html [Accessed 21 Mar 2018].

Ash and Heather, 2002. Quotes [online]. *Nothing Tastes As Good As Thin Feels*. Available from: https://web.archive.org/web/20030621230024fw_/http://myweb.ecomplanet.com/FUMB1613/mycustompage0010.htm [Accessed 12 Aug 2020].

Aurora Jess, 1999. My Cutting Page [online]. *Lost Childhood*. Available from: https://web.archive.org/web/20000410080358/http://www.angelfire.com/hi/LostChildHood/cutting.html [Accessed 12 Apr 2021].

Bell, J. and Bailey, L., 2017. The use of social media in the aftermath of a suicide: Findings from a qualitative study in England. *In*: T. Niederkrotenthaler and S. Stack, eds. *Media and Suicide: International Perspectives on Research, Theory, and Policy*. New Brunswick, USA: Transaction Publishers, 75–86.

Biddle, L., Donovan, J., Hawton, K., Kapur, N., and Gunnell, D., 2008. Suicide and the internet. *BMJ*, 336 (7648), 800–802.

bl00dy_k1tty, 2021. wahh!! Gmm #edtwt #shtwt [online]. *@HShuzuki*. Available from: https://twitter.com/HShuzuki/status/1384130515008061440 [Accessed 22 Apr 2021].

Boyce, N., 2011. Suicide clusters: The undiscovered country. *The Lancet*, 378, 1452.

Branley, D.B. and Covey, J., 2017. Pro-ana versus pro-recovery: A content analytic comparison of social media users' communication about eating disorders on Twitter and Tumblr. *Frontiers in Psychology*, 8, 1356.

Broder, M., 2015. I'm not glamorizing depression, I'm staying alive: Advice from so sad today [online]. *Vice*. Available from: https://www.vice.com/en/article/exq4xn/im-not-glamorizing-depression-im-staying-alive-advice-from-so-sad-today-193 [Accessed 10 May 2021].

Brotsky, S.R. and Giles, D., 2007. Inside the "Pro-ana" community: A covert online participant observation. *Eating Disorders*, 15 (2), 93–109.

ᘈ(ᵔ₀ • - •₀ ')ᙏ bubba, 2021. tw!! i interact with 'pro content' [online]. *Twitter*. Available from: https://twitter.com/bruised__ribs [Accessed 21 Apr 2021].

Canetto, S.S., Tatum, P.T., and Slater, M.D., 2017. Suicide stories in the US Media: Rare and focused on the young. *In*: T. Niederkrotenthaler and S. Stack, eds. *Media and Suicide: International Perspectives on Research, Theory, and Policy*. New Brunswick, USA: Transaction Publishers, 27–40.

Casilli, A.A., Pailler, F., and Tubaro, P., 2013. Online networks of eating-disorder websites: why censoring pro-ana might be a bad idea. *Perspectives in Public Health*, 133 (2), 94–95.

Castro, T.S. and Osório, A.J., 2012. Online violence: Not beautiful enough... not thin enough. Anorectic testimonials in the web. *PsychNology Journal*, 10 (3), 169–186.

Castro, T.S. and Osório, A.J., 2013. "I love my bones!": self-harm and dangerous eating youth behaviours in Portuguese written blogs. *Young Consumers*, 14 (4), 321–330.

Cecilia Marie, 2005. 1987–2003 [online]. *Fragile Innocence*. Available from: https://web.archive.org/web/20041216112714if_/http://winkin.phpwebhosting.com:80/~joeic/privet/thin/art/poem015.html [Accessed 14 Nov 2018].

Chelsea, 2005. I Am [online]. *Fragile Innocence*. Available from: https://web.archive.org/web/20041216114933if_/http://winkin.phpwebhosting.com:80/~joeic/privet/thin/art/poem030.html [Accessed 14 Nov 2018].

Cobb, G., 2020. *Negotiating Thinness Online: The Cultural Politics of Pro-anorexia*. 1st ed. Abingdon, Oxon; New York, NY: Routledge.

Conterio, K. and Lader, W., 1998. *Bodily Harm: The Breakthrough Treatment Program for Self-injurers*. 1st ed. New York: Hyperion.

Delicate Sylph, 2009. Summoning My Creative Muse....To Put A Face and Voice To the Eating Disordered [online]. *Haven of the Delicate Sylph*. Available from: http://www.geocities.ws/haven_of_the_delicate_sylph/ [Accessed 5 May 2021].

Dias, K., 2003. The Ana sanctuary: Women's pro-anorexia narratives in cyberspace. *Journal of International Women's Studies*, 4 (2), 31–45.

Disordered Diaries, 2020. ED twitter: Do you believe you can lose weight while being in recovery? [online]. *Twitter*. Available from: https://twitter.com/Thintoxicating/status/1278580976042549253 [Accessed 8 Jul 2020].

Druley, L., 2002. Starving for perfection [online]. *Minnesota Public Radio*. Available from: http://news.minnesota.publicradio.org/features/200205/08_druleyl_lifestyle-m/index.shtml [Accessed 6 Dec 2018].

Eating Disorder Hope Blog, 2013. Anorexia and bulimia promoted by social media [online]. *Eating Disorder Hope*. Available from: https://www.eatingdisorderhope.com/blog/social-media-anorexia-bulimia [Accessed 11 Sep 2018].

Erin, 2008. What life is this? [online]. *Secret Cutting and the Pain Behind Self Injury*. Available from: http://www.angelfire.com/bc3/secondchance/whatlifeisthis.htm [Accessed 25 Aug 2020].

falls2climb, 2003. *Pro Reality*. Available from: https://pro-reality.livejournal.com/1760.html [Accessed 19 Nov 2018].

Faux, M., 2007. House of Thin Mission [online]. *House of Thin*. Available from: https://web.archive.org/web/20070702075910/http://www.houseofthin.com/entrance/mission.php [Accessed 6 May 2021].

Free Butterfly, 2008. Ana Writtings [online]. *~ Free the butterfly within ~: the haven of an ana butterfly*. Available from: https://web.archive.org/web/20080218052720/http://www.freewebs.com:80/free-the-bfly/anawrittings.htm [Accessed 7 Mar 2018].

Giles, D.C., 2016. Does ana=Anorexia? Online interaction and the construction of new discursive objects. *In*: M. O'Reilly and J.N. Lester, eds. *The Palgrave Handbook of Adult Mental Health: Discourse and Conversation Studies*. Houndmills, Basingstoke, Hampshire; New York: Palgrave Macmillan, 308–326.

Grajales, F.J.I., Sheps, S., Ho, K., Novak-Lauscher, H., and Eysenbach, G., 2014. Social media: A review and tutorial of applications in medicine and health care. *Journal of Medical Internet Research*, 16 (2), e13.

Gueble, M.E., 2005. Bubble [online]. *Fragile Innocence*. Available from: https://web.archive.org/web/20041217220319if_/http://winkin.phpwebhosting.com:80/~joeic/privet/thin/art/poem049.html [Accessed 13 Nov 2018].

Haas, S.M., Irr, M.E., Jennings, N.A., and Wagner, L.M., 2011. Communicating thin: A grounded model of Online Negative Enabling Support Groups in the pro-anorexia movement. *New Media & Society*, 13 (1), 40–57.

Harris, K., McLean, J., and Sheffield, J., 2009. Examining suicide-risk individuals who go online for suicide-related purposes. *Archives of Suicide Research*, 13 (3), 264–276.

Harris, K.M., McLean, J.P., and Sheffield, J., 2014. Suicidal and online: How do online behaviors inform us of this high-risk population? *Death Studies*, 38 (6), 387–394.

Hipple Walters, B., Adams, S., Broer, T., and Bal, R., 2016. Proud2Bme: Exploratory research on care and control in young women's online eating disorder narratives. *Health: An Interdisciplinary Journal for the Social Study of Health, Illness and Medicine*, 20 (3), 220–241.

Hutchings, M., 2003a. The Tricks and THE TRUTH [online]. *Body Cage*. Available from: https://web.archive.org/web/20030207085147/http://www.bodycage.com/tricks.html [Accessed 8 Apr 2021].

Hutchings, M., 2003b. Recovery Stories [online]. *Body Cage*. Available from: https://web.archive.org/web/20030207085328/http://www.bodycage.com/recovery.html [Accessed 8 Apr 2021].

Hutchings, M., 2003c. Your Emails and Insights 5 [online]. *Body Cage*. Available from: https://web.archive.org/web/20030207083126/http://www.bodycage.com/yourinsights5.html [Accessed 8 Apr 2021].

Jenkins, J. and Ogden, J., 2012. Becoming 'whole' again: A qualitative study of women's views of recovering from anorexia nervosa. *European Eating Disorders Review*, 20 (1), e23–e31.

Jensen, R., 2005. My Religion [online]. *Fragile Innocence*. Available from: https://web.archive.org/web/20041216113740if_/http://winkin.phpwebhosting.com:80/~joeic/privet/thin/art/poem045.html [Accessed 14 Nov 2018].

Joe, 2005. [l]etter from ana [online]. *Fragile Innocence*. Available from: https://web.archive.org/web/20040821113126if_/http://winkin.phpwebhosting.com:80/~joeic/privet/thin/religion/letterfromana.html [Accessed 13 Nov 2018].

Kathy, 2004. si [online]. *Self-Injury*. Available from: https://web.archive.org/web/20041012043054/http://members.tripod.com/%7Efuschia9/si.htm [Accessed 12 Apr 2021].

Kendal, S., Kirk, S., Elvey, R., Catchpole, R., and Pryjmachuk, S., 2017. How a moderated online discussion forum facilitates support for young people with eating disorders. *Health Expectations*, 20 (1), 98–111.

Latina, D., Giannotta, F., and Rabaglietti, E., 2015. Do friends' co-rumination and communication with parents prevent depressed adolescents from self-harm? *Journal of Applied Developmental Psychology*, 41, 120–128.

Lavis, A., 2016. Alarming engagements? Exploring pro-anorexia websites in/and the media. *In*: K. Eli and S.J. Ulijaszek, eds. *Obesity, Eating Disorders and the Media*. London: Routledge, 11–35.

Layton, A., 2016a. An unexpected language [online]. *A Culture Starved for Love*. Available from: http://starvedlove.blogspot.com/2016/04/language-and-rhetoric.html [Accessed 21 Nov 2018].

Layton, A., 2016b. Author and Friend [online]. *A Culture Starved for Love*. Available from: http://starvedlove.blogspot.com/2016/04/who-am-i.html [Accessed 21 Nov 2018].

Lisa, 2005. Pro Ana Campaign [online]. *Petition Spot*. Available from: https://web.archive.org/web/20060207094330/http://www.petitionspot.com:80/petitions/proanacampaign [Accessed 6 Mar 2018].

Lou, 2003. family & friends; if you want to help [online]. Available from: https://web.archive.org/web/20030428155342/http://silent-screams.org/friendsandfamily.shtml [Accessed 7 Apr 2021].

Madeline ♡ edtwt, 2020. § — ∵ ∴ tw: ED vent account [online]. *@madeline_xs*. Available from: https://twitter.com/madeline_xs/status/1339793889893310465 [Accessed 20 Apr 2021].

McGorry, P., 2012. A deadly silence that has to end. *Sydney Morning Herald*, 10 Sep. http://www.smh.com.au/it-pro/a-deadly-silence-that-has-to-end-20120909-25m58.html

Meg, 2003. *Pro Reality*. Available from: https://pro-reality.livejournal.com/5110.html [Accessed 15 Nov 2018].

Miarexia, 2002. Mission Statement [online]. Available from: https://www.oocities.org/miarexia/mission.html [Accessed 19 Aug 2020].

Mindy, 2003. *Pro Reality*. Available from: https://pro-reality.livejournal.com/6274.html [Accessed 15 Nov 2018].

Mok, K., Jorm, A.F., and Pirkis, J., 2016. Who goes online for suicide-related reasons?: A comparison of suicidal people who use the internet for suicide-related reasons and those who do not. *Crisis*, 37 (2), 112–120.

Mulveen, R. and Hepworth, J., 2006. An interpretative phenomenological analysis of participation in a pro-anorexia internet site and its relationship with disordered eating. *Journal of Health Psychology*, 11 (2), 283–296.

NEDA Blog, 2013. Join the pro-recovery movement! [online]. *National Eating Disorders Association*. Available from: https://www.nationaleatingdisorders.org/blog/join-pro-recovery-movement [Accessed 10 Sep 2018].

Niederkrotenthaler, T. and Stack, S., 2017. Introduction. *In*: T. Niederkrotenthaler and S. Stack, eds. *Media and Suicide: International Perspectives on Research, Theory, and Policy*. New Brunswick, USA: Transaction Publishers, 1–13.

Other People's Poetry [online], 2004. *Red Tears*. Available from: https://web.archive.org/web/20040304105829/http://www.angelfire.com/yt/redtears/otherspoetry.html [Accessed 12 Apr 2021].

Perloff, R.M., 2014. Social media effects on young women's body image concerns: Theoretical perspectives and an agenda for research. *Sex Roles*, 71 (11–12), 363–377.

Pirkis, J.E. and Blood, R.W., 2010. *Suicide and the News and Information Media: A Critical Review*. Australian Capital Territory: Mindframe.

Polak, M., 2007. 'I Think We Must be Normal… There are Too Many of Us for This to be Abnormal!!!': Girls Creating Identity and Forming Community in Pro-Ana/Mia Websites. *In*: S. Weber and S. Dixon, eds. *Growing Up Online: Young People and Digital Technologies*. New York, NY: Palgrave Macmillan, 83–96.

Poppy__seed, 2005. Hi! [online]. *Pro Reality*. Available from: https://pro-reality.livejournal.com/12596.html [Accessed 16 Nov 2018].

Pro Reality, 2003. Profile [online]. *Pro Reality*. Available from: https://www.livejournal.com/userinfo.bml?user=pro_reality [Accessed 16 Nov 2018].

Pro Reality, 2005a. About [online]. *Pro Reality*. Available from: https://web.archive.org/web/20050211214254/http://www.brokensanity.org:80/pro-reality/about.php [Accessed 15 Nov 2018].

Pro Reality, 2005b. Rules [online]. *Pro Reality*. Available from: https://web.archive.org/web/20050211215141/http://www.brokensanity.org:80/pro-reality/rules.php [Accessed 15 Nov 2018].

rae ∅ comfort, 2021. if u binged (like me) today. *@crunchykimchis*. https://twitter.com/crunchykimchis/status/1386303116350427136

Rag Doll, 2001a. Introduction [online]. *Rag Doll's Candlelit Tunnel*. Available from: https://www.oocities.org/self_harm/basics/ [Accessed 12 Aug 2020].

Rag Doll, 2001b. Who Self Harms? [online]. *Rag Doll's Candlelit Tunnel*. Available from: https://www.oocities.org/self_harm/basics/profile.html [Accessed 12 Aug 2020].

Rag Doll, 2002a. Things to Know [online]. *Rag Doll's Candlelit Tunnel*. Available from: https://www.oocities.org/self_harm/know.html [Accessed 13 Aug 2020].

Rag Doll, 2002b. For Self Harmers: Things to Know [online]. *Rag Doll's Candlelit Tunnel*. Available from: https://www.oocities.org/self_harm/todo.html [Accessed 13 Aug 2020].

Rag Doll, 2002c. Things NOT to Do [online]. *Rag Doll's Candlelit Tunnel*. Available from: https://www.oocities.org/self_harm/nottodo.html [Accessed 13 Aug 2020].

Rag Doll, 2003. Safe Coupons [online]. *Rag Doll's Candlelit Tunnel.* Available from: https://www.oocities.org/self_harm/coupons/index.html [Accessed 13 Aug 2020].

Rice, S., Robinson, J., Bendall, S., Hetrick, S., Cox, G., Bailey, E., Gleeson, J., and Alvarez-Jimenez, M., 2016. Online and social media suicide prevention interventions for young people: A focus on implementation and moderation. *Journal of the Canadian Academy of Child and Adolescent Psychiatry = Journal De l'Academie Canadienne De Psychiatrie De L'enfant Et De L'adolescent,* 25 (2), 80–86.

Rich, G., 2003. My Poetry [online]. *genevieve5566.* Available from: http://www.geocities.ws/genevieve5566/proanapoetry.html [Accessed 26 Aug 2020].

Riley, S., Rodham, K., and Gavin, J., 2009. Doing weight: Pro-ana and recovery identities in cyberspace. *Journal of Community & Applied Social Psychology,* 19 (5), 348–359.

Robinson, J., Cox, G., Bailey, E., Hetrick, S., Rodrigues, M., Fisher, S., and Herrman, H., 2016. Social media and suicide prevention: A systematic review: Suicide prevention and social media. *Early Intervention in Psychiatry,* 10 (2), 103–121.

Rodham, K., Gavin, J., Lewis, S., Bandalli, P., and St. Denis, J., 2016. The NSSI Paradox: discussing and displaying NSSI in an online environment. *Deviant Behavior,* 37 (10), 1110–1117.

sad ana, 2019. i miss being skinny [online]. *@silverweak.* Available from: https://twitter.com/silverweak/status/1083240875537383424 [Accessed 16 Jan 2019].

SarahDarkBlue, 2001. Welcome [online]. *Bleeding on the Couch.* Available from: https://web.archive.org/web/20021206202903/http://www.geocities.com/sarahdarkblue/ [Accessed 9 Apr 2021].

Seward, A.-L. and Harris, K.M., 2016. Offline versus online suicide-related help seeking: Changing domains, changing paradigms: Offline versus online. *Journal of Clinical Psychology,* 72 (6), 606–620.

Sheffer, S., 1999. Eating disorders: Cracking the code - An interview with Steven Levenkron [online]. *New Moon Network.* Available from: https://www.susannahsheffer.com/uploads/1/1/6/7/11672632/levenkroninterview.pdf [Accessed 21 Jul 2020].

Sheldon, P., Grey, S.H., Vickery, A.J., and Honeycutt, J.M., 2015. An analysis of imagined interactions with pro-Ana (Anorexia): Implications for mental and physical health. *Imagination, Cognition and Personality,* 35 (2), 166–189.

Silent Red Tears, 2002. poems [online]. *Red Tears.* Available from: https://web.archive.org/web/20021011232447/http://www.angelfire.com/yt/redtears/poems.html [Accessed 12 Apr 2021].

Some Questionnaire Results [online], 2000. *Stories of Hope.* Available from: https://web.archive.org/web/20050114210402fw_/http://members.tripod.com/helen-scott/some%20results.htm [Accessed 12 Apr 2021].

studenten, 2003. *Pro Reality.* Available from: https://pro-reality.livejournal.com/2477.html [Accessed 16 Nov 2018].

Tatz, C.M., 2005. *Aboriginal Suicide Is Different: A Portrait of Life and Self-Destruction.* 2nd ed. Canberra: Aboriginal Studies Press.

Troscianko, E., 2017. How much does a blog title matter? [online] *Psychology Today.* Available from: https://www.psychologytoday.com/blog/hunger-artist/201704/how-much-does-blog-title-matter [Accessed 28 Jan 2021].

Turner, B.J., Chapman, A.L., and Layden, B.K., 2012. Intrapersonal and interpersonal functions of non suicidal self-injury: Associations with emotional and social functioning: Functions of NSSI, emotional and social functioning. *Suicide and Life-Threatening Behavior,* 42 (1), 36–55.

v_falling_to_pieces, 2003. Verses [online]. *Falling_To_Pieces*. Available from: https://www.oocities.org/v_falling_to_pieces/verses.html [Accessed 26 Aug 2020].

Ward, K.J., 2007. 'I Love you to the Bones': Constructing the anorexic body in 'Pro-Ana' message boards. *Sociological Research Online*, 12 (2), 1–14.

Why a pro-ana listing? [online], 2003. *The Thin Files*. Available from: https://web.archive.org/web/20030101191629/http://www.gloomsday.net:80/thinfiles/about.cfm [Accessed 9 Oct 2018].

미소, 2020. okay fr tho [online]. *Twitter*. Available from: https://twitter.com/bullymemia2/status/1269546390713257985 [Accessed 9 Jul 2020].

Index

Printed in the United States
by Baker & Taylor Publisher Services